CENSORSHIP

The Threat to Silence Talk Radio

BRIAN JENNINGS

THRESHOLD EDITIONS

NEW YORK   LONDON   TORONTO   SYDNEY

Threshold Editions
A Division of Simon & Schuster, Inc.
1230 Avenue of the Americas
New York, NY 10020

First Threshold Editions trade paperback edition June 2010

THRESHOLD EDITIONS and colophon are trademarks
of Simon & Schuster, Inc.

For information about special discounts for bulk purchases,
please contact Simon & Schuster Special Sales at 1-866-506-1949
or business@simonandschuster.com.

The Simon & Schuster Speakers Bureau can bring authors to your live event.
For more information or to book an event
contact the Simon & Schuster Speakers Bureau at
1-866-248-3049 or visit our website at www.simonspeakers.com.

Designed by Joy O'Meara

Manufactured in the United States of America

1   3   5   7   9   10   8   6   4   2

ISBN 978-1-4391-5442-7
ISBN 978-1-4391-7289-6 (pbk)
ISBN 978-1-4391-6816-5 (ebook)

I dedicate this work to my wife, Karen, who is a big believer in conservative principles and a fan of conservative talk radio. Her love, support, and input are monumental to me. I also dedicate this book to the hundreds of colleagues in radio who have enriched my life over the years, and I encourage them to speak freely and from the heart. I also want to thank our grown children and their mates, Katie, Mark, Liz, Ariel, Adam, and Ruth, who through their enthusiasm and interest in my career gave me great reason and confidence to excel in radio and ultimately write this book.

Acknowledgments

Thank you to this great nation's Founding Fathers, who had the foresight to guarantee our freedoms in the United States Constitution and the Bill of Rights. Know that we are fighting to preserve the vision you held for this country.

Special thanks to the many voices of talk radio who participated in the "collective voice" that is this book.

I want to express my gratitude to Edward T. Hardy, my friend and mentor throughout much of my radio career, for his unconditional support.

Lars Larson, whose conservative voice is heard locally on KXL in Portland, Oregon, and nationally on Compass Media Networks, was invaluable as a researcher and contributor.

Michael Patrick Shiels, Michigan radio host and accomplished author, encouraged me to write this book and provided collaborative insight.

I want to thank Rush Limbaugh, Sean Hannity, and Mark Levin—three of the great conservative political commentators in America—for their personal contributions to this book . . . and for starting and growing the conservative talk format!

Appreciation to Kraig Kitchin, former head of Premiere Radio Networks and Limbaugh confidant.

To the talented conservative hosts whose experiences and

insights are shared in these pages, thank you for allowing me to share your stories in pursuit of the defense of free speech.

Alan Colmes, our liberal friend, deserves much appreciation for his defense of free speech on the airwaves. And congratulations to Ed Schultz, who is blazing the trail for progressive talk show hosts.

To Mark Masters of Talk Radio Network, a great talk radio visionary, special thanks for use of the quotes of his network's hosts. I support Michael Savage's freedom of expression!

Much respect and appreciation goes to Michael Reagan—son of the President who unleashed free speech on the airwaves—for his participation in this project.

Special thanks to Shannon Sweatte, former general manager at KVI Seattle, who put his faith and trust in me to help develop the all-conservative talk format.

To Congressman Greg Walden of Oregon I say, "Thank you, and please continue to fight the good fight on our behalf!"

Respect and appreciation to Milt McConnell, one of the great talk radio general managers in the nation . . . and to Dan Mason, Pat Frisch, and the hundreds of general managers, radio programmers, talk show hosts, and producers with whom I have had the privilege of working as a national radio program manager over the past years.

My friends Michael Harrison of *Talkers* magazine and Al Peterson of NTS MediaOnline have contributed great material and insights for this story . . . Thank you!

Thanks to Citadel Communications Corporation, where I had fifteen great years in the radio industry, free of the constraints of the Fairness Doctrine.

I could not have had this wonderful forty-year radio career

without the support of my early employers . . . people like actor Danny Kaye, the singing cowboy Gene Autry, owners Les Smith and Larry Wilson—the finest radio owners and operators in the business.

Appreciation to my wife, Karen, who corrected my "radio syntax" throughout this manuscript and helped me think of better ways to communicate this important message . . . and to my friend and neighbor David Dressler, who shared his knowledge of word processing.

Thank you to Kathy Sagan from Simon & Schuster and Frank Breeden of Premiere Authors for taking my hand and walking me through this important process.

To everyone whose experiences are shared in this book—and all who have contributed to the preservation of our liberties— please accept my respect, admiration, and appreciation.

Contents

Foreword

by Sean Hannity

Censorship: The Threat to Silence Talk Radio by Brian Jennings is the collective voice of talk radio fighting against the Fairness Doctrine, which would be the death of conservative free speech on the airwaves.

Censorship details the many assaults on our First Amendment rights by powerful elected members of the United States Congress who not only would silence conservative talk radio, but silence you as well. Freedom of speech is our most cherished right as Americans, and as Brian Jennings notes, without it we have no other rights.

As one of conservative talk radio's best-known programmers, Brian has many associations with those in talk radio nationally and tells a story that will be an important chapter in our nation's continuing struggle to protect and defend our collective rights for free speech. Enjoy the read.

Preface

by Congressman Greg Walden,
cosponsor of the Broadcaster Freedom Act

If Gutenberg had invented the radio rather than the printing press, broadcasters would have free speech rights today. He didn't and they don't, and many want to trample what rights broadcasters do have by censoring what's said in the name of "fairness" or "localism." Proponents of the "Fairness Doctrine" want government bureaucrats in Washington, D.C., to decide if broadcasters need to present appropriate opposing viewpoints. If not, they'll use fines and license revocation to punish those broadcasters who don't follow their dictates. This could surely spell the end for talk radio, whether it's liberal, conservative, or religious. All are threatened.

Don't think it's possible?

This Big Brother interference in programming content has happened before.

The so-called Fairness Doctrine ruled the airwaves from its inception in 1949 until its repeal by the Reagan administration in 1987. Established to encourage political debate, it had the opposite effect and was used by presidents and politicians of both major parties to silence and intimidate those who dared to speak out against them.

In today's world of text messages, Twitter, cable shows, blogs, and more, it's hard to imagine that we could actually revert to government control of broadcast speech. Yet it's indeed on some politicians' to-do list and could happen soon, unless Americans realize what's coming and speak out.

Thankfully, broadcasters and journalists such as Brian Jennings care enough about the right of free speech in America to speak out before it's too late. *Censorship* details the history of the "Fairness Doctrine" and the fate that awaits us if the political leaders get their way.

Congressman Greg Walden has a degree in journalism from the University of Oregon. He and his wife owned and operated radio stations in Oregon for more than twenty-one years.

Introduction

Us vs. Them

This book is written for all who value the rights guaranteed to them by the First Amendment to our great nation's Constitution. It is for those of you who value freedom of speech and open expression of ideas. This book is for those who want to be able to choose what they hear on the radio.

Throughout this book you will read the terms *conservative* and *liberal*. I thought it important to share with you my viewpoint on the differences. Some of you won't agree with my definitions—and others may be offended by certain characterizations, although that is not my intent. But at the time of publication of this book, I am still free to express my opinions under my First Amendment rights. That may change—stay tuned.

This quote from my favorite president pretty much sums up what I feel:

> *Republicans believe every day is the Fourth of July,*
> *but the Democrats believe every day is April 15th.*
> —Ronald Reagan

As I see it, the key issues dividing the left and the right are their views about the size of government, taxation, and personal responsibility vs. entitlement. Oh . . . and freedom of speech.

Conservatives feel that government should impose itself only into areas where we cannot easily provide for ourselves, such as police and fire departments, highway construction, and, importantly, national defense. Liberals would like to have government provide for almost everything, up to and including free health care. Let me think . . . who is it that pays for those "free" goods and services?

Conservatives favor keeping more of their hard-earned money to put it to work in a free-market economy. Liberals favor "income redistribution" through heavy taxation of our nation's producers. We die-hard conservatives call this socialism. After a time, when each has donated to the pot according to his ability, and each has taken from the pot according to his needs—when the balance has finally shifted to the point where the takers are getting more out of the pot than the producers are able to put in—the system collapses. Look at what happened in Russia.

The example I will use for personal responsibility vs. entitlement has to do with what has happened over the past few decades in youth sports programs. When I was playing baseball and football in the 1960s and '70s, we were each encouraged to train diligently and perform to the best of our ability on the field. When the game was over, there was a winning team and a losing team. The winner took home the trophy. In today's youth sports programs, every team member must have equal playing time, regardless of his or her ability . . . and both the winning and the losing teams get trophies. After all, we don't want to hurt anyone's feelings. (It's gotten so far out of hand that recently a nine-year-old Connecticut boy was judged to be too good as a pitcher. His baseball coach was told that the boy would no longer be allowed to pitch. Other teams refused to play his team, and there was talk of "redistributing" the players from his team to others.) What kind of lesson is this about the realities of life? Being a conservative means accepting that there are winners and losers in all endeavors, and that not everyone gets a trophy.

An attitude of "entitlement" is also affecting our education system. Competition for scholastic excellence is on the wane in favor of making sure no one is "left behind." I heard a recent proposal that the 50th percentile should be set as the lowest grade that can be given to any student! As a result our great nation is falling further behind the academic performance curve of other developed countries, with potentially negative consequences for progress in all aspects of our economy.

It also appears that conservatives, in general, are more charitable than liberals. We tend to come personally to the aid of a neighbor in need, whereas a liberal might tend to feel that the government should come and take care of that neighbor. As a talk radio programmer, I have seen conservatives step up to the plate repeatedly to help those in need. Following 9/11 and Hurricane Katrina, I helped spearhead national relief efforts in which conservative talk radio stations successfully collected and donated more than $12 million to victims of those events. Certain voices on the left shouted that the federal government should take full responsibility. Syracuse University scholar Arthur Brooks, who published *Who Really Cares: The Surprising Truth About Compassionate Conservatism*, supports, through his research, the notion that those of us who reject government handouts give more to charitable causes than our liberal friends. In the recent presidential campaign it came to light—because candidates are required to release their tax returns—that the Republican candidates were considerably more generous than their Democrat counterparts.

Liberals certainly don't extend "charity" toward conservative talk radio. They would prefer that you not be allowed access to opinions and information that conflict with their own views. Many of us in radio are worried about the future of our careers and the future of free speech in America. There are sinister forces at work that would shut down conservative political commentary using government regulations disguised under the banner of *fairness*. While elected Democrats tell you that we're being paranoid . . . that they do not have plans to restore the Fairness Doctrine . . . what they *aren't* telling you is that they have plans to come in "through the back door" with regulations that will accomplish the intent of the Fairness Doctrine—to control the content of your radio programs—with dire consequences for your personal liberties and for conservative talk radio.

In the first month of the Obama administration, the Fairness Doctrine rhetoric began boiling over. President Obama fired a warning shot at conservative talk radio when he told Republican leaders, "You can't just listen to Rush Limbaugh and get things done."[1] Clearly, the president was revealing his fear that conservative talk radio represents a strong roadblock to his agenda. Conservatives, including Limbaugh, were quick to respond. Limbaugh stated, "If I can be made to serve as a distraction, then there is that much less time debating the merits of the trillion-dollar debacle,"[2] referring to Obama's controversial economic stimulus plan, which conservatives pointed out was full of wasteful pork barrel spending.

Brent Bozell, who heads the Media Research Center, a large conservative media watchdog group, summarized the fight in these words: "Now we know what Barack Obama means about unity and a nation working as one. It means it's his far left way and no other way. If he had his way, the President would have us all reading the *New York Times* and listening to left-wing *Air America*. He knows his only opposition to enacting a radical left-wing agenda is conservative talk radio. There's something eerie, big-brother-like in Obama's actions. He will deny it, of course, but this is an attack on Limbaugh's and all conservatives' right to free speech. He wants to set the stage for the principles of the Fairness Doctrine, and he's doing it through character assassination. I said the day after the election that Rush Limbaugh would become public enemy number one if the Obama administration had its way. The attack on him personally and on all of conservative talk radio generally has officially begun."[3]

On the heels of the president's statement about Limbaugh, another Democratic Senator talked about returning the Fairness Doctrine. Senator Debbie Stabenow of Michigan was appearing on the *Bill Press Show* when she stated, "I think it's absolutely time to pass a standard. Now, whether it's called the Fairness Standard, whether it's called something else—I absolutely think it's time to be bringing accountability to the airwaves."[4]

Following Stabenow's comments, Senator Tom Harkin of Iowa, another Democrat, also called for a return of the Fairness Doctrine.[5] And so did former president Bill Clinton, who told progressive host Mario Solis Marich, "Well, you either ought to have the Fairness Doctrine or we ought to have more balance on the other side because essentially there's always been a lot of big money to support the right-wing talk shows, and let's face it, you know, Rush Limbaugh is fairly entertaining even when he is saying things that I think are ridiculous."[6]

Shortly after former president Clinton and others weighed in on the Fairness Doctrine, former California governor and current state attorney general Jerry Brown was telling Michael Savage that he also favors the Fairness Doctrine, or a new version of it. And he issued this chilling statement to those of us who cherish free speech: "A little state control wouldn't hurt anybody."[7]

Is it coincidence that so many Democrats spoke out for the return of the Fairness Doctrine in the early days of February? I don't think so. Democrats will point out that President Obama is opposed to reviving the old Fairness Doctrine as he stated on the campaign trail and again on February 18, 2009. They know there are better ways to muzzle conservative talk radio which are discussed in the pages ahead. It's stealth regulation of content through a new Fairness Doctrine. They won't call it a new Fairness Doctrine, but their plans would achieve the same results—censorship of conservative talk radio.

Without the flow of information available through conservative political commentary, we would not have access to certain facts and opinions necessary to make informed decisions in many aspects of our lives, including business, finance, and politics.

Without conservative talk radio . . .

- The positive aspects of the Iraq war would not have been told.
- The other side of the Immigration Bill would not have been explained.
- The flaws in the national health care plan would not have been exposed.

- The theory that global warming is not entirely man-made would not be debated.
- Liberal mainstream media—which dominates the information landscape in America—would not have a counterbalance.

In late February, the U.S. Senate passed an amendment banning the old Fairness Doctrine regulation. But Senate Democrats also passed an amendment leaving the path open for further regulation of the nation's airwaves. Their agenda is to muzzle conservative talk radio and force more liberalism into our programming. House Democrats may follow the Senate lead. They deny it, but it is censorship.

This book is the collective voice of many of America's radio talk show hosts, as well as the managers of talk radio today, who want to make sure you are free to hear what you want, when you want. Talk radio reaches nearly 50 million Americans every week and it has become a powerful force in shaping American values.

Talk radio is a companion that provides information and insights helpful in everyday life. It can make you laugh or cry. It can make you happy or mad. You can turn it on or off anytime, and you can change the station whenever you want. It's your choice to listen or not. But one thing is certain: government has no business regulating the content of the programs you enjoy on the nation's airwaves. We are fighting back, and we want to tell our story of what is at stake in this fight . . . because if the government is the winner, you are the loser.

I hope you feel as strongly as I do that free expression of viewpoints on your radio should not be censored.

CHAPTER 1

Talk Radio in Jeopardy

At What Price Free Speech?

Freedom of speech comes with a price tag. Throughout our nation's history, thousands of Americans have died to protect our freedoms—paying the ultimate price for what they believe in. For others the price may be less, but it is still a great sacrifice. Several years ago my friend Lars Larson paid a price for his views.[1]

As a conservative radio talk show host on KXL in Portland, Lars was outgoing and available to the public. He had always lived openly, even hosting events for listeners in his home. Lars grew up in a small coastal town in Oregon where everyone knew each other and everyone looked out for their neighbors. There was an innocence about how he lived. When Lars moved to the big city of Portland, he maintained that same openness.

On the evening of October 23, 2003, that all changed. Lars was hosting a listener event for his radio station. A few miles away, at Portland's Memorial Coliseum, left-wing filmmaker Michael Moore was in town to promote his causes, including exposing the "evils" of corporate America. Part of Moore's act was to ask his fans for the name of a local conservative he could call to harass.

Someone in the crowd of 8,500 had Lars Larson's home telephone number. He shouted it out to Moore on the stage, and Larson's phone number immediately became common knowledge. Michael Moore dialed the number and held the telephone's speaker up to the microphone. Mrs. Larson's voice was heard on the recorded voice mail greeting explaining that, if the call was urgent, Lars could be reached at the cell number she provided. Life for the Larson family changed instantly and dramatically.

Before continuing to describe what happened to Lars and his wife, let me offer a little background about the community in which it all took place:

Larson lives in an extremely liberal city in a very liberal state. Conservatives call Portland "Berkeley North." It is the land of high taxes—funding some of the nation's most liberal welfare programs—and Lars rails against those taxes. Those who live in Portland pay layer upon layer of taxes: city taxes, business taxes, metro-area mass transit taxes, high county taxes, high property taxes, and a high state income tax, not to mention numerous service taxes. Periodically the state of Oregon also tries to implement a sales tax. This is a state that recently had a large budget surplus and refused—until forced to comply with a law on the books—to return that money to the taxpayers. Lars Larson wants that money to stay in the pockets of hardworking citizens, not in government pockets.

To further explain how liberal Oregon is—and how our civil liberties are at risk—Lars rages against yet another tax proposal that has conservatives asking, "What has happened to our state?" Citizens were encouraged to cut back on use of fossil fuels by driving less and investing in fuel-efficient vehicles. We did. With the decline in gasoline consumption came a decline in gas tax revenue, and state government began to worry about how to pay for road and bridge maintenance. So bureaucrats are working on hatching a scheme to fit vehicles with GPS-type units so they can track how many miles each citizen drives—and presumably where he drives—then tax him accordingly.

Lars uses his highly rated radio talk show to speak up for conservatives who are in the extreme minority in "Berkeley North." He often takes the newspaper to task for its liberal bias, referring to *The Oregonian* as "the local fish-wrapper." He speaks out against liberal politicians at every level, and he calls our schools into question for their lack of scholastic achievement. Larson carries a gun, he hunts, and he defends our Second Amendment rights. Those on the left despise his attitude, and Lars himself is hated by the liberal establishment in Oregon. This is the backdrop against which Lars Larson's personal drama began to unfold.

Immediately after Michael Moore telephoned the Larson home from the Memorial Coliseum, other harassing phone calls began. Lars turned off his phone, and the voice mail quickly filled up. When the attackers tired of calling his home phone and his cell phone, they discovered where Lars's wife worked. They began harassing Mrs. Larson at her office, even threatening rape. She was forced to close her office and move her business to their home. The problem with that change was that the Larsons' home address had also been publicized all over the city.

Larson was forced to move from a home he loved. The

family moved miles away and changed telephone numbers and other contact information, but the threatening callers continued to find them.

One day when his wife called him in tears, Lars blew his stack on the air: "Let's make this deal. Stop threatening my wife. Come and threaten me, so I can just fill you full of bullets. You come threaten me in person. You bring it on, but leave my wife out of this." Lars described the threats that brought his wife to tears. "They said, 'We're going to come and rape your wife to death—we're going to rape her until she bleeds.' If this is offending anybody—good![2] 'cause I'm mad."

Lars's wife no longer answers the phone if the caller is un-identified. Lars is more aware of his surroundings. When new threats are made, his bosses hire off-duty cops to guard him. And Lars carries a concealed weapon for personal protection. "It seems that the only way to keep your First Amendment rights is to let people know you're willing to exercise your Second Amendment rights, too."[3]

Threats such as those made against Larson and his family are not uncommon for conservative political commentators. Free speech does come at a price, especially in an intolerant liberal society. At about the same time that Lars was facing his enemies in Portland, the enemies of conservative views were mounting a national effort targeting all conservative talk radio. A former conservative-turned-liberal was forming an organization called Media Matters for America. The organization says it's "dedicated to comprehensively monitoring, analyzing, and correcting conservative misinformation in the U.S. media,"[4] but its tactics say otherwise. This group, and others like it, want to eliminate conservative talk radio. With support from Hillary Clinton (and, as is the feeling of many conservative commentators, perhaps from billionaire George Soros), Media Matters began to smear every conservative radio and television talk show host in America.

While Media Matters was attacking conservative talk radio with flanker assaults, liberals in Congress launched a frontal assault. Angered by losing the White House twice to George W. Bush, they perceived that conservative talk radio was responsible for the outcome of those elections. They began calling for a return of the Fairness Doctrine to force "fair-and-balanced" programming so that liberal commentators could infiltrate conservative talk radio stations. The assault was led by powerful, elected Democrats including House Speaker Nancy Pelosi, Senator John Kerry, and others.

The attacks on conservative political commentary grew more intense in the years leading up to the 2008 general election. It became evident that liberals wanted to shut down conservative talk radio. This has become a relentless assault on our freedom of speech. Those on the left don't like what they hear—even claiming that conservative talk is "a waste of the public airwaves"—and they want to silence the opposition.

Talk radio is in jeopardy. There is much at stake, no matter what your politics. Please read on.

> *If we don't believe in freedom of expression for people we despise, we don't believe in it at all.*
> —NOAM CHOMSKY, PROFESSOR, WRITER, LINGUIST

STRAIGHT AHEAD: The censors take aim at conservative talk radio.

CHAPTER 2

The First Amendment

Yesterday and Today

You might be like me. Radio has been my lifelong friend. I grew up with it. As a young boy I built a crystal radio receiver and ran copper antenna wire for hundreds of feet outside my bedroom window so I could hear stations all across the United States and Canada. It was magic.

Living out in the country near Spokane, Washington, I listened to KNEW, which later became 790 KJRB. I was introduced to Jimi Hendrix and Steppenwolf by the likes of Larry Lujack, Pat O'Day, Dick Curtis, Emporer Lee Smith, Lan Roberts, Charlie Brown, Steve West, and some of the great disc jockeys of the era. I listened to the Washington State Cougar football games, hoping they would muster a win over their archrival Huskies from Seattle. Radio woke me in the morning, got me through my chores, got me to school and back, and was the last thing I heard before falling asleep each night.

It was only natural—once I knew I would never master physics classes and become a "rocket scientist"—that fate guided me to KPLU FM Radio 88.5 at Pacific Lutheran University in Tacoma, Washington. So began a long career in radio where the magic on the airwaves—even as the voices and the formats changed—only seemed to amplify over the years.

Fast-forward several years and imagine turning on your radio one day, eager to hear Rush Limbaugh share his humorous insights on Barney Frank and the endless parade of clowns we elect to the Congress and Senate . . . but all you hear is rap music. You turn the dial, seeking Sean Hannity's views—and his callers' opinions—on Washington's latest tax-and-spend proposals . . . but instead you hear a nice lady sharing her prize-winning apple pie recipe. You begin frantically dial surfing for your other favorite hosts, but all you hear is National Public Radio airing a lengthy report on the new sewer system in Akron, Ohio. Or, if you're a Christian radio fan, you switch to your preferred station only to hear someone advocating gay marriage. They demand equal time to express their opposition to your views, and they get it.

This is what could happen if Congress and the Federal Communications Commission (FCC) chooses to reinstate the Fairness Doctrine—a regulation that has existed for a long time on the books though not enforced since 1987—or institute other backdoor controls of program content!

Imagine your radio without Rush Limbaugh, Sean Hannity, Michael Savage, Mark Levin, Neal Boortz, Lars Larson, Mike Gallagher, Michael Medved, Laura Ingraham, Laura Schlessinger, Hugh Hewitt, and the many other popular hosts who speak to and for millions of conservative Americans on talk radio every day. Many liberals dream of that reality, and some liberal voices in positions of great power even advocate that reality. They support the resurrection of the principles of the Fairness Doctrine—an antiquated regulation that is an affront to our most cherished right, freedom of speech.

In 1949, the FCC established this regulation, which required broadcasters to provide fair-and-balanced programming on the public airwaves. When one viewpoint was expressed on the radio, equal airtime had to be offered to those who disagreed. The doctrine was repealed in 1987 on the grounds that it was no longer necessary because of the diversity of voices being heard in the media marketplace . . . and that such a regulation might well be unconstitutional.

Those who support government controls of media content fail to understand the First Amendment to the U.S. Constitution. If asked, they probably couldn't even recite it. But there have never been better words written for American citizens. The intent of this amendment is simple but powerful, and it defends the core values and beliefs upon which our great nation was founded. These words provide for what the fathers of our nation understood to be our God-given rights. Much American blood has been shed defending these words, yet they are taken for granted by many of us. This is the First Amendment:

> *Congress shall make no law respecting an establishment of religion, or prohibiting the free exercise thereof; or abridging the freedom of speech, or of the press; or the right of the people peaceably to assemble, and to petition the Government for a redress of grievances.*

The First Amendment was a collaborative effort by our nation's Founding Fathers, including Thomas Jefferson, James

Madison, and many others who preceded them. These great men met in session during the summer of 1789 to draft these freedoms as the first—and arguably the most important— amendment to our Constitution. Without freedom of thought and expression, no other rights can exist. It is the foundation of all other human rights. English poet and social critic John Milton, whose writings were consulted during the drafting of the U.S. Constitution, noted:

> *Give me the liberty to know, to utter, and to argue freely according to conscience, above all liberties.*

We live in an extraordinary country. Ideas and opinions can be expressed freely thanks to the wisdom of our Founding Fathers and the courage of Americans throughout our history who have given their lives to protect and defend our freedoms. Liberty comes in many forms, and the form that Americans cherish most is freedom of speech and press. Without free speech and a free press, we become an uninformed people— a controlled electorate. Few people would disagree with that notion. So why then are some of the most powerful elected officials in the United States bent on controlling what you can hear on our nation's radio airwaves?

Why? Could it be because people now have a media platform to be heard more loudly and clearly than at any time in history? Is it because ordinary citizens have been given a voice through the medium of conservative talk radio? Could it be because talk radio airs important questions that force transparency on our elected leaders, some of whom feel threatened by that? The answers are clearly "yes" to all!

One example of the power of conservative talk radio

occurred when the controversial Senate Immigration Bill[1]—which would have given automatic U.S. citizenship to millions of illegal immigrants—was defeated on June 28, 2007. Millions of talk radio listeners were livid that some of their conservative senators favored passage of the bill. At the recommendation of their favorite conservative talk show hosts, these listeners contacted their elected leaders and shared their disapproval through a collective voice that reverberated loudly in Washington, D.C. Republican Senator Trent Lott of Mississippi raised the ire of fellow conservatives when he stated, "Talk radio is running America. We have to deal with it."[2]

Lott would later say that he did not favor a return of the Fairness Doctrine, but his widely used statement showed his frustration and the frustration of many politicians over the influence of talk radio. On June 24, 2007, he seemed to retreat from his widely quoted statement and told Fox's Chris Wallace, "I've been defended by talk radio many times, and I will support their right to tell their side of the story—right, left, or the middle, forever."[3]

Democrats were livid about the defeat of the Immigration Bill. Lott's statement got my attention and the attention of my radio colleagues nationwide, and it galvanized key Democrats who indeed want to restore regulation of radio program content. The left wants to make it difficult for you to hear on the radio a discussion of any viewpoint contrary to its own.

Immediately after Lott's statement, Rush Limbaugh—the conservative icon of talk radio—said on his program, "Talk radio *is* the American voter. That's what bothers Trent Lott."[4] And Michael Savage stated on his Talk Radio Network program, "Trent Lott saying today that talk radio is running America and we have to deal with that problem is gangsterism."[5]

The ability to speak freely without government control of information and opinions broadcast over our airwaves has changed the landscape of America. Locally, it has helped defeat wasteful tax measures and elect or defrock many politicians. Nationally, it helped usher in a Republican Revolution in the early 1990s.[6] It's helped galvanize Americans in times of national disaster, as we witnessed after 9/11 and Hurricane Katrina. And it has raised countless millions of dollars for relief efforts and charities.

But there is increasing discussion about the need to "deal with" talk radio, and one can only guess that America's forefathers would have harsh words for those who advocate government control over information to which you have access. You heard right! Many elected officials in both the Senate and the House of Representatives want to return to government regulation of what is said over the airwaves . . . control over the content of what you hear on your local radio station.

Since 1987, there have been numerous attempts to restore the Fairness Doctrine, conservative talk radio's worst nightmare. The Fairness Doctrine required a balance of views on controversial topics on both radio and television programs. The authors of this regulatory doctrine felt that since there were so few media outlets in the United States at the time — and the airwaves had a limited spectrum — balance needed to be mandated in broadcast programming to properly serve the public interest. The FCC was charged with enforcing this regulation, and if an offended party complained about fairness, renewal of a station's license could be in jeopardy.

But the result of the Fairness Doctrine was the opposite of what its authors intended. Rather than airing thought-provoking discussion, radio stations purposely shied away from controversial topics for fear of being reported to the FCC. In newsrooms, we were constantly reminded to seek out "the other side of a story" just to be safe. There were no controversial opinions expressed on talk shows. It just simply wasn't allowed. The Fairness Doctrine dampened controversy and prevented the development of conservative political commentators such as Rush Limbaugh, Sean Hannity, Mark Levin, and other popular talk show personalities whose programs you enjoy today. Ironically, proponents of the Fairness Doctrine avoided suggesting that the same controls should apply to the print medium. They argued that the limited airwave spectrum is "public domain" and therefore subject to government control . . . even while newspapers could print anything they chose.

I was privileged to hire talk radio's Lars Larson at KXL Radio in Portland, Oregon, when he was only nineteen years old. This young man displayed a keen intellect even then and has since developed a rich background in investigative reporting in both radio and television. Lars is a highly respected conservative talk show host heard locally on KXL and nationwide on Compass Media Networks.

Lars has shared with me his recollections of life under the Fairness Doctrine: "I began working in radio in the mid seventies when the Fairness Doctrine was the law of the land. Very few radio stations did editorials, and I have a very specific recollection as a young reporter of talking with KXL General Manager Ray Watson. I asked Ray why he didn't do station editorials. (There were a couple of radio stations and one television station that still did them at that time in Portland.) He told me that if he were to offer up two minutes of even the most commonsense, down-the-middle editorial, he would be besieged by demands from every extremist group (left *and* right) that they be allowed an equal amount of time at the same time of day to present an alternate point of view. Realizing that the resulting freak show would not represent the community, nor present a good public face for the radio station, he simply didn't do editorials.[7]

All that changed in 1987 when President Reagan's FCC voted to suspend enforcement of the Fairness Doctrine. Modern talk radio was born. The popularity of this medium reaches far and wide, and those in positions of influence in our government have experienced the power of talk radio and its potential to inform and incite their constituents. As Rush Limbaugh so aptly put it, "Talk radio *is* the American voter."

As the sun rises over the United States each day, millions of Americans turn to the airwaves to get the latest news. Millions more tune in to talk shows, which have grown in stature and popularity over the past two decades, to hear exciting discussions about current issues. Talk radio *is* the American voice. As the sun rises over Russia, China, Iran, Syria, Venezuela, and other totalitarian regimes, the content of their radio broadcasts is tightly controlled. American talk radio is an extremely unique media platform that would not be allowed in dictatorships. In our country, the average citizen can take to task elected officials—even the president—on the pubic airwaves without fear of reprisal.

It's time that we stop taking our freedom of expression for granted. A movement is under way that could change American talk radio through the return of government control of information and opinions broadcast over the airwaves. A return of content regulations would take away your right to hear what you want when you turn on your favorite radio station. Those of us who toil in the radio business and defend the right of free speech feel that the government has no right to control the content of our programs. But the battle over free speech on our airwaves is under way. Conservatives are outwardly alarmed—with good reason—over Democrat congressional efforts to restore censorship controls. They are lining up to pitch their battle cry.

In a widely publicized Rasmussen Reports national survey of one thousand likely voters, conducted just before the 2008 presidential election, Democrats favored government involvement in the airwaves more than Republicans. Fifty-four percent of Democrats said they supported it, while only 26 percent were opposed. Republicans were fairly evenly divided on the subject.[8] Key Democrats have been promoting the Fairness Doctrine because they think conservatives dominate talk radio. They are right, yet there is a reason. To date, liberal talk radio has failed to resonate with listeners. For the most part, it is poorly rated. Conservatives are warning loudly that if liberal talk won't work in the marketplace on its own merit, Democrats—now firmly in control of Congress—are ready to change the balance by forcing radio programmers to add liberal hosts to their talk lineups. To many of us in talk radio, the term "Fairness Doctrine" is an embedded code phrase for *censorship*.

> *The only valid censorship is the right*
> *of the people not to listen.*
> —TOMMY SMOTHERS, AMERICAN COMEDIAN

STRAIGHT AHEAD: The Fairness Doctrine. How unfair!

CHAPTER 3

The Fairness Doctrine

What It Means for You

When you Google "Fairness Doctrine," you'll get about eight hundred thousand responses. Established in 1949 and enforced by the FCC, this regulation required fair-and-balanced public-affairs-related programming on radio and television. Station license holders were in fear of losing their permits or being fined if they were found in noncompliance. The result was that broadcasters avoided controversial programming like the plague. Complaints about fairness were taken seriously, and in some cases broadcast licenses were revoked because of it. When the FCC voted to repeal the doctrine during the Reagan administration in 1987, there were immediate attempts by liberals in Congress to restore it. They failed when President Reagan exercised his veto power.

Before the repeal of the Fairness Doctrine, fewer than one hundred talk radio stations existed in the United States. Two decades later, there are more than two thousand stations offering talk programs in one form or another. The repeal of this doctrine opened the floodgates of both expression and discussion on radio and television stations nationwide. But powerful forces are gathering to try to again close the gate on free speech on the public airwaves.

The debate over regulating the nation's airwaves to force more-balanced programming has been heating up, with a new liberal president and a Democrat majority in Congress. Discussion about the possibility of censorship has been dominating the talk radio landscape as one of the hottest current topics, because every such host has a personal stake in this issue. Free speech is in jeopardy.

Let's look more closely at the Fairness Doctrine and what its return would mean for Americans who value their personal liberties. Fairness sounds like a positive thing, right? According to the Rasmussen poll cited earlier, nearly half of respondents said they would favor the regulation's restoration. After all, wouldn't most people want life to be fair? But is it possible that those responding to that poll did not understand the far-reaching consequences of such regulation? Would they really vote in favor of a form of censorship?

The Fairness Doctrine is blatantly unfair. In the words of former president and general manager Chris Berry at WMAL Radio in Washington, D.C., "We have to quit referring to it as fair."[1] Because under its influence broadcasters avoided controversy for fear of reprisal by our government, we were forced to air less-than-exciting programs that were often poorly rated and failed to generate revenue. When radio operators received countless requests for balanced access, they were often compelled to broadcast segments that were boring and sounded unprofessional—not to mention a pain to deal with. (Rush Limbaugh shares a personal story about this in an

upcoming chapter.) Out of fear, radio owners and programmers alike avoided the talk format and chose instead to air
other, more lucrative and less labor-intensive programs such
as seventies music, personal advice, gardening, and car repair
shows. Some stations even broadcast the classified sections of
newspapers. Now *that* was interesting radio!

The Fairness Doctrine has been shown to be one of the
worst regulations ever imposed on this country. In many ways,
it is un-American. Many of those in radio today feel that the
liberal left's push to restore this regulation will result in the
death of talk radio as we know it.

Consider California Democrat Dianne Feinstein's statements to Fox News, widely quoted in all media, that she is
looking to restore the Fairness Doctrine: "I am looking at
it. Talk radio is one way. It tends to be one-sided. Talk radio
dwells on hyperbole. It pushes people to extreme views without a lot of information."[2] Let's translate that: what Senator
Feinstein means is that talk radio is dominated by highly rated
conservative personalities, while liberals have met with much
less success on the radio. She wants to change that, and she is
willing to consider having government intervene once again.
In an upcoming chapter, we'll address some reasons why
liberal talk radio personalities don't command high ratings
and . . . advertising rates. Stay tuned.

Let me share with you an example of the Fairness Doctrine in action: In 1964 a pastor broadcast a fifteen-minute
Christian program on WGCB Radio in Pennysylvania. The
reverend, in discussing a book with which he disagreed, criticized the author's political beliefs and his background. When
the author heard this broadcast, he demanded that WGCB
give him free airtime to respond to what he considered a per-

sonal attack. The station refused, and the matter was referred to the FCC. The FCC ruled that the reverend's program did indeed qualify as a personal attack; that the radio station had not met its obligation as a licensed broadcaster to offer a fair-and-balanced viewpoint in all its programming; and that WGCB must provide the author with free airtime. In this case, the U.S. Supreme Court upheld the FCC's right to enforce the Fairness Doctrine. However, the court did warn that if the doctrine ever restrained speech, then its constitutionality should be considered and brought into question.[3]

The FCC is composed of five members appointed by the president and will have a Democrat majority in the current administration. The commission regulates traditional free over-the-air radio and television stations nationwide and can fine them all for off-color words and language. But those same regulations don't apply to cable television or to satellite radio where Howard Stern doesn't have to worry about what he says, because viewers pay to view or listen to these channels. Most cable channels self-regulate, but some don't and they aren't held to the same standards.

Under the leadership of then FCC chairman Mark Fowler, the commission began to repeal parts of the Fairness Doctrine in 1985, stating that the regulation hurt public interest and violated the First Amendment. Then, in 1987, the FCC voted to stop enforcing the doctrine 4–0. At the time the FCC stated, "The Fairness Doctrine, on its face, violates the First Amendment and contravenes the public interest."[4]

Congress then attempted to overturn the FCC decision, but that attempt was vetoed by President Ronald Reagan. Another attempt to revive the doctrine later in 1991 failed when

President George H. W. Bush threatened to exercise his veto power. Talk radio and its millions of fans should be grateful for the actions of Presidents Reagan and Bush.

Fast-forward from 1987 to the present and remember that since repeal of the Fairness Doctrine more than twenty years ago, the number of radio stations programming talk has increased dramatically. It would seem to those who support freedom of speech that the repeal of the regulation had a positive result. After all, hundreds more stations offer the free-speech format, making certain information more accessible to all Americans.

But apparently House Speaker Nancy Pelosi doesn't agree. She told reporters in 2007 that the Democrat caucus was interested in once again restoring the Fairness Doctrine. Asked by HumanEvents.com if she favored the Fairness Doctrine, she responded "Yes."[5] Senator Richard Durbin followed suit, stating in a publication by TheHill.com that "it's time to reinstitute the Fairness Doctrine."[6] He has been joined by Senate Majority Leader Harry Reid of Nevada. Former Democrat presidential candidate John Kerry of Massachusetts also weighed in saying that the Fairness Doctrine should be restored. Senators Jeff Bingaman of New Mexico and Charles Schumer of New York—both Democrats—have also expressed support of the Fairness Doctrine.

When the August 2008 national survey by highly respected pollster Scott Rasmussen found that nearly half of the thousand poll participants favored the return of the Fairness Doctrine, the survey also found that 57 percent were opposed to requiring presentation of opposing viewpoints for Internet websites and bloggers who offer political commentary.[7]

Isn't it interesting that these likely voters cited by Rasmussen are willing to keep the Internet free of government controls, but when it comes to the spoken word over the radio airwaves, it's a different story? Are words read on paper or on a computer screen less shocking than words heard over the air? Talk radio executives and hosts nationwide think that is absurd. And, as noted, cable television and satellite radio are exempt from regulation because they are not considered "over-the-air" broadcasts. Perhaps even more telling in the Rasmussen poll is that 71 percent of those surveyed say it is possible to hear just about any political view in today's media, leaving many wondering why anyone would feel a need to regulate radio programming.

Doug McIntyre, morning host at KABC in Los Angeles, shares his thoughts on the topic: "The public-owns-the-airwaves argument was valid for eighty years, but technology has rendered this a moot point. Between satellite radio and podcasts, the delivery system has become an irrelevancy. How long before cars have browsers built in? Consumers will then have millions, literally millions, of audio choices. The only true regulator of content is the marketplace. If a show is lousy, it's gone. Period."[8]

Efforts to revive this censorship doctrine—which are backed primarily by Democrats—demonstrate nothing short of contempt for conservative talk radio. It is time to tell the full story through the voices of those who have toiled to make conservative radio the great service to Americans that it is today. It is a great story, a significant part of American broadcast history, and an important chapter in our continuing quest for free speech. The outcome of this epic argument will impact the preservation of some of our most cherished freedoms and beliefs for generations.

*What is freedom of expression? Without the
freedom to offend, it ceases to exist.*

—SALMAN RUSHDIE, INDIAN-BORN BRITISH NOVELIST

STRAIGHT AHEAD: Senator Jeff Bingaman drops a bombshell
or lays an egg.

CHAPTER 4

The Bingaman Bombshell

A Call for Censorship

Jeff Bingaman is a Democrat senator from New Mexico. He is a fairly unassuming individual who created quite a stir in a studio interview on Albuquerque's KKOB radio. Like many career politicians, he's been doing the bidding of his party elders in Washington, D.C., for years. Their agenda includes restoring regulations to censor the content of conservative talk radio. Bingaman revealed a glimpse of his intentions when, on a trip to our nation's capital in early 2007, he told KKOB general manager Milt McConnell that his station should think about balancing its talk show lineup. According to McConnell, Bingaman "hinted strongly" that Democrats wanted to restore the controversial regulations.

Bingaman made his feelings crystal clear later on October 22, 2008, when he appeared on KKOB's top-rated Jim Villanucci program.[1] Bingaman's interview immediately reverberated across the country, and it has been widely quoted in local and national media since then. Here is the newsworthy conversation on what is billed as "New Mexico's Talk Monster," 770 KKOB:

Villanucci: You would want this radio station to have to change?

Bingaman: I would. I would want this station and all stations to have to present a balanced perspective and different points of view instead of hammering away at one side. . . .

Villanucci: I mean in this market, for instance, you've got KKOB. If you want liberal talk, you've got Air America in this market, you've got NPR [National Public Radio], you've got satellite radio—there's a lefty talk station and a rightie talk station. You think there are people who aren't able to find a viewpoint that is in sync with what they believe?

Bingaman: Well, I guess my thought is that talk radio and media generally should have a higher calling than reflect a particular point of view. I think they should use their authority to try to [use] their broadcast power to present an informed discussion of public issues. KKOB used to be a . . . used to live under the Fairness Doctrine, and . . .

Villanucci: Yeah, we played music, I believe.

Bingaman: But there was a lot of talk also, at least it seemed to me, and there were a lot of talk stations that seemed to do fine. The airwaves are owned by private companies at this point. There's a license to private companies to operate broadcast stations, and that's the way it should be. All I'm saying is that for many, many years we operated under a Fairness Doctrine in this country, and I think the country was well-served. I think public discussion was at a higher level and more intelligent in those days than it has become since.

Democrats aren't even blushing at this frontal assault. After the interview aired, the phone lines at KKOB melted down . . . furious listeners calling in who couldn't believe their U.S. senator would change the format of New Mexico's most successful radio station!

The station has been top rated for more than eight straight years and has won most of radio's top awards including the prestigious Marconi Award from the National Association of Broadcasters. But Bingaman apparently thinks a programming lineup change at the station to present both conservative *and* liberal talk show hosts wouldn't have a negative impact on ratings.

Senator Bingaman isn't an expert on radio programming, but KKOB Program Director Pat Frisch is, and he says Bingaman is in left field, no pun intended. Frisch said, "Bingaman needs to be put out to pasture in the next election. He would be putting many hardworking people out of work. Obviously, it would substantially hurt our ratings and our profits would suffer. If liberal talk worked, we would do it . . . but it isn't [working] and there's no profit in it."[2] Jim Villanucci, the radio personality who interviewed Bingaman, quickly weighed in with this reaction: "It caught my attention because the senator could potentially put me out of work!"[3]

House Republican Leader John Boehner of Ohio heard Bingaman's remarks and issued a statement from his office one day after the surprise call to restore the Fairness Doctrine rocked the talk world. "I am very troubled by Senator Bingaman's comments supporting the revival of outdated government broadcast regulations that would return America to the days when Washington bureaucrats literally rationed free speech rights. Support for this disturbing idea is becoming more and more commonplace in a Congress that is controlled by the Democratic Party and increasingly determined to clamp down on the free expression of conservative viewpoints."[4]

Boehner also accused Democrats of censorship: "The Senator [Bingaman] joins a growing list of liberal Democratic leaders, including House Speaker Nancy Pelosi, Senate Majority Whip Dick Durbin, and Senator John Kerry, who have indicated their strong support for the so-called Fairness Doctrine, a policy that would curtail the constitutional rights the Founding Fathers put in place at the beginning of the Republic. What Senator Bingaman refers to as a 'higher calling' for radio is, in reality, a thinly veiled attempt to silence opinions and views with which he and other powerful Democrats disagree."

Bingaman's bombshell suggestion to restore the Fairness Doctrine was not a major surprise to KKOB General Manager Milt McConnell. McConnell has said: "We take pride at KKOB in providing access to our entire congressional delegation, regardless of party affiliation. As a testament to that fact, Senator Bingaman's office called last Friday to set up something for this week, and we set it up right away. We have always given him access to this station to state his views. Clearly, in these days and times there are so many outlets for any point of view that it really renders the need for any discussion of a return of the Fairness Doctrine moot."[5]

Bingaman's comments quickly hit the Washington, D.C., airwaves, too, and grabbed the attention of former ABC News Radio general manager—and later general manager of WMAL Radio—Chris Berry, who is outspoken against the Fairness Doctrine. Berry predicted that if Democrats try to invoke the doctrine to force "balanced" content, listeners nationwide would respond in a "massive way" to oppose it.[6]

National radio talk show personalities were quick to grab Bingaman's statement. The senator's comments were played back on the air by Rush Limbaugh, Sean Hannity, Mark Levin, Michael Savage, Glenn Beck, and others, followed by extensive commentary. Hannity's producer, Eric Stanger, e-mailed me when he heard the Bingaman comments: "Hearing this on El Rushbo . . . scary stuff." And Sean e-mailed me, saying, "This is a top priority for them. We have a huge battle ahead."

Sean Hannity is a longtime friend and one of the greatest broadcasters I know, and I helped place his radio show on many stations around the country. On his nationally syndicated radio program, Sean quickly labeled Bingaman "Senator Censorship." I talked with Sean afterward, and he subsequently issued this statement:

> *Senator Bingaman has become "Senator Censorship" with his statement to restore the Fairness Doctrine. This isn't just about silencing me or my other friends in talk radio such as Rush Limbaugh or the great one Mark Levin, or my friend Neal Boortz. The real danger here is if they silence talk radio, they silence our listeners. They would be silencing a huge segment of the American electorate. You find one or two and maybe three conservative talk stations in a market where there are more than 40 stations and they want to silence the one station they don't agree with. Do you notice they never talk about censoring liberal media? They never talk about censoring the* New York Times *or the* Washington Post. *They never talk about fairness with NPR.*

Sean continued: "When Senator Bingaman made his comments, I invited him to come on my show by simply picking up the telephone. I offered him access to my radio show out of fairness. He didn't take the offer. With House Speaker Nancy Pelosi, Senator Harry Reid, Obama and Biden, we have the most liberal leaders in our nation's history and you can bet they will continue an assault to shut down conservative talk radio and the voices of millions of Americans who enjoy the format."[7]

Following Senator Bingaman's controversial remarks, the *Albuquerque Journal* carried some immediate feedback from irate constituents, who stated their right to choose what they want to hear, when they want to hear it, and for how long they want to listen. Their message was clear—that government has no business trying to regulate the free marketplace of ideas— and they expressed their shock and anger at the senator.

There were two headlines in the letters to the editor that especially jumped out:

"Let Sen. Bingaman Pick His Own Stations"
"Did He Miss the Fairness Doctrine Class?"[8]

One constituent e-mailed the Senator and received this response:

Dear Mr. Stascina:

Thank you for contacting me regarding the discussion of the Fairness Doctrine on the Jim Villanucci show on KKOB radio. I appreciate your taking the time to write. As you may know, the Fairness Doctrine required that broadcasters present opposing viewpoints on controversial issues to the public. This was in place until 1985

*when the Federal Communications Commission (FCC)
determined that, due to the number and diversity of
voices available through media, such a doctrine was not
required. That said, the media should present balanced
viewpoints on issues of public importance. I also believe
it is important that a few large media companies do not
control most means of news dissemination in many areas
of the country, which can lead to less informed debate. I
am sorry that we disagree on this issue. Again, thank you
for writing. Please continue to inform me of issues important to you and your community.*

> *Sincerely,*
> *Jeff Bingaman*
> *United States Senator*[9]

Despite taking severe heat from constituents and from
members of the media, it doesn't sound like Bingaman is
backing off his statements, and he shows no embarrassment
about his lack of understanding of the First Amendment. But
pay particular attention to Senator Bingaman's statement that
"I also believe it is important that a few large media companies do not control most means of news dissemination in
many areas of the country, which can lead to less informed
debate." That is an important part of our unfolding story of
Censorship!

On any given day on the nation's airwaves, as well as other
media platforms, all views are heard. As the sun rises over
America tomorrow morning, we can get any viewpoint we
want, anywhere we want, and anytime we want. Liberal views

can be accessed on National Public Radio (NPR), the major networks, CNN, niche television programs, the Internet and Internet radio, satellite radio, the liberal radio network Air America, most newspapers, and more. If the Fairness Doctrine or new Democratic versions of it are enforced, it would return radio to its status in the 1950s and 1960s. Message to Senator Bingaman: This is 2009. As Supreme Court Justice William O. Douglas stated, "Fear of ideas makes us impotent and ineffective."

> *Talk radio is taking Joe Six-Pack and*
> *giving him collective voice.*
> —MILT MCCONNELL, GENERAL MANAGER,
> KKOB RADIO, ALBUQUERQUE

STRAIGHT AHEAD: El Rushbo checks in on what he calls the "Hush Rush" bill and says this will be an "epic battle."

CHAPTER 5

Hush Rush

Limbaugh Sounds Off

Okay, I have to admit it . . . I'm a big Ditto Head. I've been a Ditto Head since August 1988. When I first heard Rush Limbaugh on the radio, I felt the same excitement and gratitude as many of his other fans. . . . Finally I heard someone expressing the thoughts about political issues that I was afraid to voice for fear of reprisal, especially in the liberal environment where I worked at that time, programming Seattle's KING 1090.

I left KXL radio in Portland—which was owned for many years by the actor Danny Kaye and his business partner Lester M. Smith—after seventeen years as news anchor, news director, and operations manager. Kaye/Smith Radio was a great operation whose owners cared deeply about serving their broadcast communities.

When I arrived at KING radio, I began to look for new programming that would make a difference for the station. It was severely underperforming in the Seattle market and getting killed in the ratings war by longtime market leader KIRO radio, an excellent station.

When I accepted the job at KING, owned by the prominent Bullitt family, little did I know that they really didn't care if the station was profitable. The family had so much money that ratings didn't matter. They would only allow the station to offer programming that matched their ideological preferences. And they were liberal—very liberal. I quickly became the politically incorrect figure in the KING building.

So, what did I do to improve programming on KING? I put Rush Limbaugh on the air about two weeks after he began syndication in August 1988. But I only aired the program on weekends. Of course Rush was controversial. Some of his most memorable topics from those early days included discussions of environmentalist "wackos" and talking about abortion with the sound of a vacuum cleaner running in the background. It was wonderful entertainment and social commentary.

Well, about four months after Rush's program began airing, I received a visit from the vice president of the company, who told me to take it off the air because it wasn't in line with the Bullitt family philosophy. With a wife and two young children to support, I didn't have a choice in the matter if I wanted to keep my job, so I reluctantly cancelled Rush's program despite the fact that there had been a major surge in the station's ratings. Years later, Rush joked with me that he got "the Bullitt" in Seattle.

My supervisors would also visit my office later, during the first Persian Gulf War when scud missiles were bombarding Tel Aviv, to strongly urge me to tone down one of our talk show hosts—who was staunchly pro-Israel. I came away from that meeting with the firm impression that KING ownership had sentiments against certain U.S. Middle Eastern policies. I knew my days at KING 1090 were numbered anyway, so I never had that conversation with my friend and colleague

Mike Siegel, who later developed into a Seattle talk legend. To me the command was not only unpatriotic, it was also an assault on our valued freedom of expression. It was censorship.

Fast-forward two years. Another Seattle station—570 KVI, owned by the great cowboy Gene Autry—put Rush on the air and hired me to program the station after I was fired from KING 1090 because of my conservative views. Thus began a ride that earned me hundreds of hate letters from the left. But my station's ratings soared from number 23 to number 1 in the market.

KVI became one of the first all-conservative stations in America, if not *the* first as documented in *Talkers* magazine.[1] With now-retired general manager Shannon Sweatte, we've been given a great deal of industry credit for establishing the all-conservative news/talk format that swept the nation. The KVI format never would have come into existence if the Fairness Doctrine hadn't been repealed in 1987.

Rush Limbaugh became the poster boy for conservative talk radio. His huge ratings demonstrated a pent-up frustration in America that was finally finding a voice. Rush and I had sweet revenge when we connected at KVI with one thing in mind—destroy KING 1090, where we both got "the Bullitt."

We were successful! No one wanted to listen to a station that said the first Persian Gulf War was wrong, and that our troops would be slaughtered by the Iraqi Republican Guard as we were defending Kuwait. No one wanted to listen to a station that thought the protection of the spotted owl's habitat was more important than jobs that housed, fed, and clothed families. And, as the ratings indicated, few people did listen. The Bullitt family finally gave up and sold KING 1090. Today, many years later, the frequency is billed as "progressive talk."

The station has respectable ratings, and I applaud that. Even as a conservative, I root for progressive talk's success on the radio . . . because if it succeeds, it will do so without the return of a new censorship doctrine and government intervention in programming content. That's the way the free-market system should work.

I also have to admit that I alerted Rush Limbaugh to Bingaman's Fairness Doctrine statements, and I knew he would have a field day with it on the air. His immediate return e-mail stated, "We're on it." On October 23, 2008, all hell broke loose on his Excellence in Broadcasting (EIB)/Premiere Radio Show. Rush prominently featured the senator's statement that he hoped the Fairness Doctrine would be restored in the United States. Following is a full transcript[2] of Rush's on-air excursion into excellence heard on approximately six hundred stations nationwide:

Limbaugh:	Let me show you what the Democrats are planning. This actually gives voice to it. Jeff Bingaman of New Mexico on our affiliate, the EIB affiliate KKOB, during the *Jim Villanucci Show* was asked if he thinks there will be a push to re-instate the Fairness Doctrine.
Bingaman audio:	I don't know. I certainly hope so. I would hope this station and all stations have to present a balanced perspective and balanced points of view instead of hammering away at one side.
Limbaugh:	Stop the tape.

Essentially Rush presented the Bingaman statement to restore the Fairness Doctrine as it was heard the previous day on

770 KKOB and documented in the previous chapter. Then Rush made the same point I have made, telling his audience of 20 million that before the Fairness Doctrine was repealed there were only about one hundred talk radio stations nationwide. According to Rush and others, there are now approximately two thousand stations if you include the NPR stations.

Limbaugh described those earlier times, saying, "You know what was on those stations? Most of the time it was the correct carrot cake recipe for the holidays, where the next traffic problem was going to be in town. Then you had a little segment that if your dog was lost, you could call the station. They did lost animal reports—all this wonderful stuff nobody wanted to listen to, Senator! Senator Bingaman, do you know how many talk radio stations there are in America today? Try over two thousand since the Fairness Doctrine was lifted.

"And, on those two thousand radio stations are countless points of view, from the extreme communist left to the wacko out-on-the-fringe right. What Bingaman is saying is he wants every station to be balanced. What he wants is for this kind of programming to be stopped, because the way the Fairness Doctrine worked and will work is within five minutes of my show open, fifteen extremist groups in every city hearing this program will call the station carrying this show demanding a response to the outrageous thing that I just said."

Rush continued, "And then after the next ten minutes they would call again. After an hour, the management of the local station would probably have received over one hundred and fifty phone calls demanding a chance and an opportunity to reply, at which point the manager would say 'I can't keep up with this. In order to maintain my license I'm going to have to grant all these people access? I'm going to have to put amateurs on the radio? I have to put talentless complaining whiners on the radio? I'm not gonna mess with it.' That's how it works. It's not that the Fairness Doctrine is passed and all of us go away, it's that the stations will not put up with the grief they are going to get—and that's what Senator Bingaman and that's what the Democrats are doing. They don't want balanced programming on a radio station. They want no conservative programming on a radio station."

Limbaugh continued with his monologue:

"Hell, I'll tell you a little story. I got to Sacramento in 1984 and the Fairness Doctrine was in force. It's October 1984, maybe three weeks from the Reagan reelection. So I get into town early, driving around and listening to the other talk stations, and nobody was talking about the election. Nobody was talking about it! Honest to God folks, it was carrot cake recipes, the latest fashion show going on at Neiman Marcus or what have you. I said to myself, 'This is going to be a gold mine!'

"So I got out there and started talking about this stuff. One day I said something about some issue, and some community Black leader called and demanded to come in and respond to what I had said. Management bent over and grabbed the ankles and said 'Sure, come on in.' He came in, and I had to give up an hour of my show to this guy, and I did my best to make it entertaining, but I had to let him speak in order to let him have his access to the Fairness Doctrine, and it was the most boring damned hour of radio I've ever done! Bingaman doesn't know what the hell he's talking about. Well, maybe he does know what he's talking about because he wants all this kind of conservative talk—because it's effective—shut down."

Dittos, Rush! As a longtime radio programmer, I also believe that many talk stations will throw in the towel because they don't want to put up with the frivolous and meaningless demands for "balanced" access and the cost and headache that would result. As one who worked in radio both before and after the Fairness Doctrine, I remember that the intimidation, fear, and paperwork the doctrine created were monstrous. If censorship regulations are restored, the number of talk stations will decline. First free speech will be controlled, then it will diminish.

Following Rush's program, I e-mailed him with my compliments on the passionate and accurate way he described the reality of the Fairness Doctrine. Always the gentleman, Rush responded appreciatively, "Thanks, Brian. Very much."

Rush Limbaugh summarized the bias perfectly: "And by the way . . . even with the Fairness Doctrine, NPR is going to be there all day, all the time, and all liberal."

It is well-known that NPR broadcasts primarily liberal programs. But not many people think about the fact that tax dollars help support NPR, whether you listen or not. Commercial stations must pay their overhead and earn their profits through advertising sales, but public stations are funded in part by your money. So conservative talk stations must broadcast what their listeners want to hear if they want to stay in business. Public radio isn't bound by that requirement.

Speaking of NPR, its audience is reaching all-time highs among American radio listeners. According to the ratings research, stations supported by the Corporation for Public Broadcasting are heard by more people than ever before, reaching more than 28 million listeners each week. In fact, listener growth for public radio has grown faster than the population. As with conservative talk radio, public radio ratings improve in times of great national interest or crisis, and national elections certainly help. So why do we need new regulations to force balanced programming? We don't. Conservative talk radio is the only present balance.

> *The problem of freedom in America is that of maintaining a competition of ideas, and you do not achieve that by silencing one brand of idea.*
>
> Max Lerner, American journalist and columnist

STRAIGHT AHEAD: A national talk radio firestorm!

CHAPTER 6

Radio Hosts Tee Off

The Perfect Firestorm

Having been in the radio business for nearly forty-one years, I've learned that stations routinely share breaking news items with their network partners. It's expected. The news of Senator Bingaman's declaration was so major that KKOB asked me to offer the audio to most of the major national talk show hosts. I knew that when commentators such as Rush Limbaugh, Sean Hannity, and Mark Levin got their hands on the interview, it would create the perfect storm. It created the perfect firestorm!

Soon after Bingaman's recommendation to restore the Fairness Doctrine hit the airwaves at KKOB, I saw it in countless blogs and newspaper reports and heard it discussed on numerous national talk shows and cable television. My phone was ringing for days with requests for reaction. It seemed that every conservative host in America used the story as show prep to smack the liberal left for not understanding that free speech should remain free. Where did they miss that lesson?

My friend Al Peterson, who writes *NTS MediaOnline*, a

daily industry newsletter targeted to all news, talk, and sports stations in the country, also covered Bingaman's comments. Well, that just fired up the storm even more. Senator Bingaman can thank KKOB for making him a household name, but I'm sure it's not in the light he would prefer. Al Peterson's entire column[1] dealt with the Bingaman statement after it was made on KKOB radio. The article included my reaction, and that of KKOB General Manager Milt McConnell, stating that government has no business regulating the content of radio station programming. Then—in his great wisdom and following his instincts as a longtime journalist—Peterson asked for reader response. And respond they did.

Check out this comment from Mark Davis, the very talented and highly rated talk show host at WBAP in Dallas: "I've never met Jim Villanucci [who interviewed Senator Bingaman], but I would hop a plane to Albuquerque to shake his hand. The vile authoritarianism that Senator Bingaman reveals when telling Jim he would indeed want government to determine KKOB programming should be a wake-up call to anyone doubting the darkest instincts of the fascist political hordes who wish to silence speech they disagree with. When people like this consider government-imposed balance a 'higher calling,' [rather] than letting people hear what they wish, they reveal their genuine contempt for liberty and market choices."[2]

And Ken Charles, a well-known programmer and radio professional for Clear Channel Communications, told Al Peterson: "The problem is we face election every day while politicians run only every two, four, or six years. We do it every day with ratings and in a PPM [ratings measurement] world, it really is every day. Maybe if these politicians had to face their constituents at the ballot box every moment of every day, in a field of not just one opponent but thirty or forty or more depending on the market, they would have more respect for the job we do every day. If we do not give our voters what they want, they leave and we get 'voted out.' What's more fair than that? When these guys screw up our street like they screwed up Wall Street, will they be there to bail us out, too?"[3]

Andrew Deal with CelleCast took his response to Peterson in a different direction but with the same theme: "This issue makes my blood boil! Forcing any speech in a multimedia world can be an infringement on free speech. Forcing equal time in the on-demand world is logically impossible."[4]

Our friends across the border to the North even weighed in with Peterson. Here's what Shawn Smith of Momentum Media Marketing told Al: "From a fairly left-leaning Canadian, government should have no business legislating content on commercial media outlets. It is one thing to make it obligatory to offer an opposing candidate equal time during a national live address in the midst of a national election campaign. It is quite another to get involved in content decisions of media companies on a daily basis. I don't know many liberals outside of government who would disagree. I say let the government take control and fund PBS like the CBC [Canadian Broadcasting Corporation] and institute all the equality measures they like. There is some societal value in having at least one truly fair-and-balanced broadcaster that is legislated to be so. Just don't bring it to the private sector."[5]

Don't bring it anywhere! If it starts somewhere, it will spread everywhere.

Al Peterson has a sense of fairness, and he offered some balance in his newsletter by publishing the comments of twenty-five-year broadcast veteran Roy Fredriks—most recently a host at WCTC/New Brunswick, NJ. Fredriks wrote, "It absolutely should be reinstated. There are very few local stations in this country that give jobs to local talent. With the economy in dire straits, people like me, who would like to get on the air somewhere after twenty years in the medium, are stymied by all the network shows in most markets. Plus there are simply very few local issues being discussed; it's all national and that, frankly, is boring. So, if it takes a Fairness Doctrine to change the landscape and give more broadcasters more opportunities, then it's got my vote."[6]

I agree with Roy on the need for some voluntary localism on talk radio today. But it should be voluntary. We also need ratings to stay in business. Most great radio stations provide a blend of local and nationally syndicated programs in their lineups, and audiences respond positively to that combination of programming. But there is one entertainment law that seems to be true for radio hosts and all other types of talent: If you get big ratings, you'll usually find work. I hope Roy does.

The fallout over the call to restore a new Fairness Doctrine has reached far and wide. It even caught the attention of the playwright David Mamet, who delivered the prestigious Alistair Cooke Memorial Lecture for 2008, honoring the late British commentator. Writing in London's *The Independent* on November 19, 2008,[7] Mamet warned of grievous consequences should the Fairness Doctrine be restored:

The Media Must Not Allow Government to Proscribe Free Speech

The so-called Fairness Doctrine, the enforcement of the doctrine that any broadcast medium, voicing one political opinion must voice another, dissenting opinion will be the beginning of the end of free speech. Here's why: Who is to say what is political opinion? The line between political opinion and reportage is so blurred now as to be almost indistinct. Should such a pernicious doctrine become widespread, energy will be devoted to persuading and inevitably suborning those authorities who seek to rule on any utterance.

Such a doctrine, rather than forcing open discourse, will tend to limit it, for those media organs with a limited budget will shy away from political speech as they may have to present opposing doctrine—offending their listeners and their advertisers. Thus they will be limited to non-political speech. Lastly, such a so-called fairness doctrine will clog the courts. And, what of the off-hand comment, which the individual and his broadcast medium will have to self-censor rather than risk offense or prosecution for lack of fairness? The less we can say, the less we can see.

The great danger here, as in all government, is a default not to the rule of law, but to the administrative committee, acting—whether "good-willed" or not—in reference only to its own wisdom. This is the beginning of the tyranny of the police state. The government is not made of geniuses, it is not made of the wise. It is a natural and necessary adjunct of human life but it is made of politicians and bureaucrats.

The wisdom of the multitudes is the treasure of mankind and our greatest treasure, not only the guardian but the inculcator of wisdom, is our language. The great heroes of the English-speaking people have been poets—Lincoln, Churchill, Dr. King—whom by the freedom and

beauty of their language presented generally unaccept-
able ideas in a new way, thus changing the world. Our
language is our heritage and our plaything, ever evolving
and shaping our world. Through language the unknown
becomes the unthinkable, which becomes merely the im-
possible and then the commonplace, and the nature of
the world, which, finally, exists to us only to the extent
which we can perceive it, changes. But speech must re-
main free. Thank you.

British law is the backbone of the U.S. legal system and
those advocating a return of new regulations to control programming content are wise to heed these profound words that
have captured interest even overseas.

> *Censorship reflects society's lack of confidence in*
> *itself. It is the hallmark of an authoritarian regime.*
> —POTTER STEWART, FORMER U.S. SUPREME COURT JUSTICE

STRAIGHT AHEAD: Nationally syndicated Mark Levin invites
Senator Bingaman to his show; Glenn Beck says to get ready
for socialism, and the outspoken Michael Savage calls Bingaman a little person.

CHAPTER 7

The Lilliputians

Savage Calls Censors Little People

I've known Mark Levin for about three years now, and I love his show. As a national radio programmer, I had the privilege of placing his show on fifteen radio stations. His ratings are terrific, the show has grown dramatically, and listening to Mark is not only informative but entertaining.

Mark Levin has a fascinating background. He is an attorney and a bestselling author, and he has known the inner workings of government firsthand. Mark was an advisor to several cabinet members in the Reagan administration (the administration that dumped the Fairness Doctrine!) and served as chief of staff for Attorney General Ed Meese. He really is, as Sean Hannity calls him, "the Great One."

When Levin heard the Bingaman tape, he was stunned by the senator's remarks and dedicated a large segment of his show[1] in response, calling the senator a "knucklehead from New Mexico." Mark told his national audience, "Tell Senator Jeff Bingaman I would like him to come on the air, in fairness of course, but to be ready for a real debate. Not one of those phony debates in the Senate. I'll be respectful but I'll be tough. Let's see if he comes on and if he does, let's see if he hangs in there because I'm fed up with this." Mark is an impassioned defender of our freedoms, and his new book, *Liberty and Tyranny: A Conservative Manifesto*, is a must-read.

Lars Larson, a Peabody Award–winning broadcaster, also devoted a lot of his program[2] to reacting to Bingaman's attitude: "In his comments, Senator Bingaman says 'there were a lot of talk stations that seemed to do fine' under the Fairness Doctrine. Nothing could be further from the truth. Fact is there were around one hundred talk stations in the whole country compared to more than two thousand now. Just as America confronts some of its biggest challenges (the economy, terrorism, international relations, etc.), it has a huge pool of diversified talk radio ready to allow three hundred million people to have an outlet for their opinions and a supply of information. Contrast that with three TV networks, five major national newspapers, a hundred talk radio stations, and no Internet of the good 'old' days."

Lars also said about Bingaman's call to restore the Doctrine: "What Senator Bingaman disparages as 'hammering away at the same political point of view' is something most of us conservatives call 'values.' Do liberals have values? Sure. A liberal will always give you the shirt right off someone else's back. A liberal has never met a tax increase he doesn't love. He also believes government is the best and sometimes the only solution to every problem. I am not surprised that Senator Jeff Bingaman wants to see the return of the Fairness Doctrine."

The morning host at talk radio KABC in Los Angeles,

Doug McIntyre, says he voted for Barack Obama. But his liberal vote does not extend to restoration of the Fairness Doctrine. "Senator Jeff Bingaman believes Fairness Doctrine era radio was at a 'higher level and more intelligent.' Well, there are millions of us who believe the United States Senate was at a 'higher level and more intelligent' when Henry Clay and Daniel Webster held office. Clay and Webster are long dead, and so is the audience for 1970s-style talk radio."

McIntyre also noted a major conflict in Senator Bingaman's comments: "Apparently, Senator Bingaman does not have enough faith in the American people to choose what they want to hear. Ironic, isn't it? He's pro-choice on abortion but not on Sean Hannity vs. Ed Schultz."[3] Schultz—the poster boy for progressive talk radio—is among the most successful of liberal radio talk show hosts in the country.

Bill Manders is the longtime afternoon conservative host at KKOH radio in Reno, Nevada. He says that if Bingaman truly understood radio, there would be no need for a Fairness Doctrine: "Every day I go on the radio and give the numbers of six telephone lines and solicit callers from all walks of life on hundreds of topics that concern them. That is the Fairness Doctrine in practice."[4]

Glenn Beck is also one of my respected friends. I didn't meet Glenn until he was well on his way to success on his national radio show, but we quickly hit it off. Glenn had spent some time in the Pacific Northwest, where I have lived all my life, so we immediately had something in common. I sat in on one of Glenn's shows at the XM studios in Washington, D.C., and immediately knew I was talking to a gentleman whose conservative convictions and faith run deep. He has very successfully combined humor with conservative political commentary.

Well, Glenn heard the Bingaman tape, too, and offered this commentary[5] to his audience: "Now you don't think freedom of speech is on the run? Let me ask a few questions. Do you think if Air America [the liberal talk radio network] would have been successful they would have been talking about this? No. They would have reclassified right-talk stations as hate speech. But, nobody would have been talking about balancing Air America. They're not interested in free speech. Go back to what Al Gore has been telling us for the last five years; the discussion is over! If you believe that global warming is not happening, then you're a holocaust denier. They don't believe in free speech."

Beck continued, "We used to have the Fairness Doctrine and we lived under that, and there used to be slavery, too. We used to have segregation and we all lived under that. Times change. I'm passionate about this because this is my job. This is my passion."

Glenn Beck is absolutely right about times changing. There are thousands of sources of information and opinion available to each and every one of us. If one source is controlled through censorship regulations, we lose part of our most important freedom. Then the domino effect—destroying other freedoms one by one—will be unstoppable.

On the West Coast, Michael Savage got fired up on his award-winning nationally syndicated radio show, *The Savage Nation.* Here is what he had to say on his Talk Radio Network program about the Bingaman call to restore the Fairness Doctrine:[6]

"You're not hearing this on the man-tan NBC. That's why

they're going out of business. That's why little men and little women like Nancy Pelosi want to put talk radio out of business because we actually raise questions that need to be answered. That's why little men, little tiny men, Lilliputians like Senator Jeff Bingaman, want the Fairness Doctrine to come back. You want all sides, then why don't you start with NPR? And then send the same rules over to ABC, CBS, and NBC, you Lilliputian you."

Michael Savage is a fascinating individual who holds, among other degrees, a Ph.D. in epidemiology and nutrition science from the University of California, Berkeley. For years Savage has challenged authority, and he isn't afraid to tell it like it is. Phrases such as "liberalism is a mental disorder" have earned him the criticism of left-wing groups, but I love his passion and his directness as a populist. I will always appreciate his introduction of me as "the grandfather of conservative talk" when I joined in to congratulate him on one of his milestone anniversary shows. Michael would later win the Freedom of Speech Award, presented by *Talkers* magazine, and I applaud and salute him for that honor.

Laura Ingraham is another well-respected conservative political talk show host. A graduate of Dartmouth, Ingraham clerked for Supreme Court Justice Clarence Thomas during her time at law school at the University of Virginia. She gained considerable political perspective as a speechwriter for the domestic policy advisor during the Reagan administration. Laura summed up her opinion concisely during a news conference to promote the Broadcaster Freedom Act—legislation sponsored by Republican Congressman Mike Pence of Indiana that would ban the Fairness Doctrine forever—when she said, "If we had no audience, they wouldn't shut us down."[7]

*If you don't have this freedom of the press, then all
these little fellows are weaseling around and doing
their monkey business, and they never get caught.*

—Harold R. Medina, federal judge, teacher, lawyer

STRAIGHT AHEAD: The congressman who oversees Domestic
Policy checks in on why he wants the Fairness Doctrine restored.

CHAPTER 8

Silence

Rumor Has It More-Balanced Talk
Could Have Prevented the War

Democrat Congressman Dennis Kucinich of Ohio chairs the House Domestic Policy Subcommittee. As with House Speaker Pelosi, Senate Leader Harry Reid, Senator John Kerry, and other powerful Democrats, one of the policies near and dear to his heart is the Fairness Doctrine. Kucinich argues that this regulation actually promotes free speech in the marketplace and thus supports the First Amendment.

Like many career politicians, Kucinich has very little "real world" experience outside of sitting in his offices in Washington, D.C. So when he makes a broad claim like this, it's obvious he doesn't really know how the Fairness Doctrine impacted radio and television stations and how it affected you, the listener and viewer. Either that or he chooses to ignore the truth about how it intimidated broadcasters and suppressed freedom of expression.

Kucinich also believes changes in media ownership and the consolidation of media into fewer and larger companies over the years have diminished the variety of viewpoints and reduced the choices for dialogue in the marketplace. Apparently Kucinich doesn't notice all the liberal media venues available to him—which far outnumber conservative choices—because he clearly has conservative talk radio in his crosshairs. He doesn't like conservative political commentary and he's in a powerful position to speak out against it and in favor of censorship regulations.

Like many Democrats, Kucinich suggests that increased debate—access to the media by those with diverse viewpoints—leads to a more informed citizenry. I have no problem with that. But during a CNN interview[1] he seemed to suggest that many policy decisions—including the Iraq War and controversial trade issues such as NAFTA—might have been different if there had been broader discussion. To imply that the Iraq War might have been avoided with more discussion in the media leaves room for debate about his common sense.

Many of us remember plenty of debate on the Iraq War, and most of Congress—although not Kucinich—lined up on the issue against Saddam Hussein and in favor of President George W. Bush, based on information available at that time. Had the Fairness Doctrine been in place, it's a far stretch to suggest it would have helped avoid war in Iraq by balancing the dialogue and debate in the media. Understanding the emotion of the day, soon after September 11, 2001, it's doubtful that things would have been different with regulation imposed by the Fairness Doctrine. Frankly, we did hear the opposing argument to the war on all media outlets. With all due respect, the criticism of the war—then and now—has been center stage in mainstream media in the United States of America.

So, another powerful voice—that of Democrat Congressman Dennis Kucinich—lends itself to the effort to hush Rush and other conservative political commentators heard daily on your radio.

There have been numerous threats to conservative talk radio on other fronts, too. In Los Angeles, a suit was filed against KRLA AM claiming that the station misrepresented its broadcast license by serving in the interest of Republicans rather than the public at large. The complaint,[2] filed on August 27, 2008, against seven talk show hosts and station owners, claims that they used the airwaves to push a Republican agenda. The syndicated hosts named were some of our favorites, including Laura Ingraham, Dennis Prager, Michael Medved, Hugh Hewitt, Dennis Miller, Mike Gallagher, and Kevin James. So how many other media outlets does Los Angeles have? Specifically, how many *liberal* sources for information does Los Angeles have? Hundreds? No . . . its residents have access to *thousands* of liberal media outlets!

The complaint read in part that "Salem [owner] entities and Ed Atsinger [CEO] had no intention of serving the public interest, convenience, and necessity. Instead, these defendants always intended to use the public airwaves to serve the interests exclusively of the GOP at the state and national level." The plaintiff also alleged that the station never allowed Democrats to host shows, and that it screens out Democrats who call the talk shows. Translated, the complaint is just another example of intimidation to silence expression of conservative viewpoints.

Where are the lawsuits going to line up next? Should legal action be taken against those stations that have all-liberal programming with hosts from Air America and others? And what about NPR, which is partially funded by our tax dollars, whether or not we choose to listen to its programs? And NPR presents primarily the liberal point of view!

The assault on conservative talk radio takes many forms. Another example involves KVI radio in Seattle, where I helped develop the all-conservative format on that great station. This is a story about standing up for free speech and telling government officials—who would intervene—to go back to school and study the First Amendment.

In 2005, the radio talk show hosts I hired in the early 1990s—John Carlson and Kirby Wilbur—waged an on-air campaign promoting a citizen initiative to overturn a huge increase in the gasoline tax approved earlier that year by the Washington state legislature. The initiative failed, but it sparked a major court battle that got the attention of all talk stations and conservative personalities nationwide. Local governments, including the city of Seattle, which stood to gain millions of dollars in new gas-tax revenues for transportation projects, sued the group backing the measure. They argued that the campaign to overturn the tax should be required to report the on-air efforts by Carlson and Wilbur as "in-kind" campaign contributions. When Thurston County Superior Court Judge Chris Wickham agreed, those who champion free speech—namely talk radio stations nationwide—went into a state of absolute shock. I remember sitting at my desk reading the first news and shaking my head in disbelief. How has the state of politics declined so dramatically in the Evergreen State?

When the case was brought before the Washington State Supreme Court, reason and logic prevailed with a unanimous 9–0 ruling that sharply rebuked the local governments. Justices Jim Johnson and Richard Sanders called it an "abusive" attempt by the municipalities to silence political opponents. When the ruling was announced, the talk radio industry breathed a collective sigh of relief. "It's a great day for freedom of speech in Washington and a great day for freedom of speech in America," said Carlson.[3]

Speaking later with John Carlson—who is now at sister station KOMO—he shared with me that he still can't believe the overt attempt to oppress free speech. At least the good guys won in this case, and the Washington State Supreme Court demonstrated its understanding of the right to freedom of expression. Had the case not been overturned, the shockwaves would still be rippling across the nation. The First Amendment was placed in jeopardy yet again.

Congressman Kucinich and his Fairness Doctrine gang should understand that the gas-tax measure was argued on both sides. The tax increase prevailed even with the on-air campaign to prevent it, but government officials still—after the fact—wanted to curtail free speech on one of the nation's premier radio stations. This case demonstrates that conservatives must be vigilant at all times. There will be other tests.

Let's hope other courts are as enlightened as the Washington State Supreme Court. Following their victory in the lawsuit, Carlson said, "The intent was to take our free speech rights away by pressuring and intimidating Fisher Broadcasting into silencing us. But, to their credit, Fisher stood tall."[4]

John Carlson and Kirby Wilbur are great broadcasters who serve in the public interest. It cost Fisher a ton of money to defend this suit, but freedom of speech—our most important freedom—is worth the price, and they should be congratulated on their courageous fight.

Message to Congress: If you invoke a new Fairness Doctrine, or other censorship controls, you shut down this type of vital dialogue, and you deprive the public of a valuable service.

The test of democracy is freedom of criticism.
—DAVID BEN-GURION, FIRST PRIME MINISTER OF ISRAEL

STRAIGHT AHEAD: An offer of unobstructed access to KKOH, Reno.

CHAPTER 9

Dingy Harry

Reid Gets It Wrong

Bill Manders is a talk radio veteran on the West Coast. Like many of us, he got his start on the airwaves in the early rock n' roll days, which was one of the most creative and energetic times in radio history. Manders is a conservative political commentator who holds forth at Reno's powerful 780 KKOH from three to six in the afternoon. At sunset, you can hear KKOH from Tijuana to Vancouver, British Columbia. With the guidance of Program Director Dan Mason, the station's ratings have led the market for more than eight years.

As a conservative, Manders often challenges the leader of the U.S. Senate, who is also Nevada's own longtime senator, Harry Reid. (Rush Limbaugh's pet name for Reid—who would not block restoration of the Fairness Doctrine—is "Dingy Harry.") Manders has asked Reid's office repeatedly for the senator to appear on the show and talk to his constituents on KKOH's great signal. But he won't. According to Manders, "I've offered Reid my entire three hours to take callers and talk to his constituents without my interference, and he won't do it." This is confirmed by Manders's producer, Sean Patrick, "We have offered Harry Reid three hours, without Bill in the studio, to just talk with his constituents. We say this on the air frequently. He never takes us up on it."

Patrick continues, "Our phone lines are open to everybody. I do not screen out anybody based upon their political beliefs."[1]

What Reid has offered to do is prerecord a program that the station could broadcast in that time slot. Prerecord it? What that means is that Harry Reid doesn't want to have to converse on the air with callers who might ask uncomfortable questions. He wants to control the content of the show with a prepared monologue instead of engaging in conversation and debate with his constituents. Apparently that is Reid's definition of free speech.

As a longtime talk radio programmer, I know that would bore the listener to tears. Ratings would suffer. Reid should be brave . . . he should sit in with Manders on KKOH and engage in lively discussion. As an elected official from the state of Nevada, he owes that to his constituents. They should hold him accountable.

Who can ever forget the famous Harry Reid letter to Clear Channel CEO Mark Mays demanding that Rush Limbaugh apologize to the men and women of the armed forces for his remarks about "phony soldiers"? The comments on Limbaugh's show on September 26, 2007, were brought to Reid's attention by Media Matters, a liberal nonprofit organization that claims to repudiate what it deems as false conservative statements and claims. (We call Media Matters "smear mongers.") The demand letter was signed by forty other senators, including Barack Obama, Joe Biden, Hillary Clinton, and other Democrats favoring restoration of the Fairness Doctrine, or other censorship regulations.

Below is the text of the famous letter sent by the forty-one Democrats to Clear Channel chief executive officer Mark Mays:

Dear Mr. Mays,

At the time we sign this letter, 3,801 American soldiers have been killed in Iraq, and another 27,936 have been wounded. 160,000 others awoke this morning on foreign sand, far from home, to face the danger and uncertainty of another day at war.

Although Americans of goodwill debate the merits of this war, we can all agree that those who serve with such great courage deserve our deepest respect and gratitude. That is why Rush Limbaugh's recent characterization of troops who oppose the war as "phony soldiers" is such an outrage.

Our troops are fighting and dying to bring to others the freedoms that many take for granted. It is unconscionable that Mr. Limbaugh would criticize them for exercising the fundamentally American right to free speech. Mr. Limbaugh has made outrageous remarks before, but this affront to our soldiers is beyond the pale.

The military, like any community within the United States, includes members both for and against the war. Senior generals, such as General John Batiste and Paul Eaton, have come out against the war while others have publicly supported it. A December 2006 poll conducted by the Military Times *found just 35 percent of service members approved of President Bush's handling of the war in Iraq, compared to 42 percent who disapproved. From this figure alone, it is clear that Mr. Limbaugh's insult is directed at thousands of American service members.*

Active and retired members of our armed forces have a unique perspective on the war and offer a valuable contribution to our national debate. In August, seven soldiers wrote an op-ed expressing their concern with the current strategy in Iraq. Tragically, since then, two of those seven soldiers have made the ultimate sacrifice in Iraq.

Thousands of active troops and veterans were subjected to Mr. Limbaugh's unpatriotic and indefensible comments on your broadcast. We trust you will agree that not a single one of our sons, daughters, neighbors and friends serving overseas is a "phony soldier." We call on you to publicly repudiate these comments that call into question their service and sacrifice and to ask Mr. Limbaugh to apologize for his comments.[2]

Mark Mays defended Rush, stating in a letter to Senator Reid on October 2, 2007, "The First Amendment gives every American the right to voice his or her opinion, no matter how unpopular." Mays also stated he would not impose his views on Rush Limbaugh or other Clear Channel hosts: "I hope you understand and support my position that while I certainly do not agree with all views that are voiced on our stations, I will not condemn our talent for exercising their right to voice them."

Mark Mays is a defender of liberty, and his remarks to Senator Reid were welcomed by all of us who fight to protect the First Amendment.

Senator Harry Reid called Limbaugh's comments "unpatriotic." Anyone who listens to Rush knows his unquestioned patriotic feelings about our troops and their mission in Iraq. Limbaugh was livid about being labeled as unpatriotic, and his audience quickly came to his defense. Callers heatedly denounced Reid and his colleagues, labeling their efforts a smear campaign. Here's what Rush had to say:

"The forty-one Democrats who signed the letter wanted Mark Mays, CEO of Clear Channel and my syndication partner, to 'confer' with me about what I had said. When you run a business that's federally regulated and the Senate majority leader tells you that he wants you to confer with me, what he means is you get him to stop criticizing us! You get him to apologize. You make him! There's an implied 'or else' when the Senate majority leader calls a CEO of a broadcast company and says those things. That's the abuse of power. That is the arrogant abuse of power and an attempt to essentially negate what I do, and to render me unable to do it."[3] It's also what the Fairness Doctrine allowed when it was enforced by the FCC.

Limbaugh explained that his comment was taken out of context, that he was referring not to actual Iraq war veterans but to persons falsely claiming to be such veterans. Rush referenced a news story describing Jesse MacBeth, who had joined the army but didn't even complete basic training before being discharged from the military as unfit to serve. Yet MacBeth stated publicly that he was a U.S. Army Ranger who had received the Purple Heart for injuries suffered in combat, and that he and his unit routinely committed war crimes in Iraq. MacBeth pleaded guilty to making false claims to the Department of Veterans Affairs and was sentenced to five months in jail. Jesse MacBeth is a "phony soldier."[4]

Rush then trumped Senator Reid by putting the now-famous original demand letter up for auction on eBay. We had no idea how much money that letter would raise: it sold for $2,100,100—the largest amount ever received on eBay. Limbaugh matched the money with his own, then donated the total amount to the Marine Corps–Law Enforcement Foundation, which provides scholarship assistance to children of Marines and federal law enforcement personnel whose parents have fallen in the line of duty. Limbaugh called on Reid and the other senators to do the same.

Rush then asked, "Where's the apology for calling me 'unpatriotic'? Where's the apology for repeating a smear and a bunch of lies from Media Matters for America?"[5]

Following the sale of the "Dingy Harry Letter," Limbaugh again repeated that the senator's demand letter was an abuse of power against a private citizen. "Harry Reid in a speech on the Senate floor at 12 noon today [Oct. 19, 2007], a little over an hour ago, attempted to horn in on all this and take some credit for it, claiming that he and I had buried the hatchet, or implying that that had been the case, and then kept using the pronoun 'WE' in discussing how good this was, the money going to the Marine Corps–Law Enforcement Foundation. So the Marine Corps–Law Enforcement Foundation, it's now official, is going to get in excess of $4.2 million because I am matching Betty Casey's bid on eBay—$4.2 million. I asked Senator Reid to match and all the other senators who can afford to do so. I haven't heard from them on that. I asked Senator Reid to go on the program and discuss his discussion of me as 'unpatriotic.' He did not accept my offer to do that, and now has the audacity to climb aboard this, praising the effort, saying that 'he' never knew that it would get this kind of money. It got this kind of money because it represents one of the most outrageous abuses of federal power in modern American history, and that is what makes it a collector's item. This letter that Senator Reid wrote will forever memorialize him as a demagogue, and the same for the other 40 who signed it. Senator Reid will be remembered forever, here, as a disgrace."[6]

As an illustration of how Democrats feel about Rush Limbaugh and conservative talk radio, Senator Tom Harkin even used the Senate floor to take a shot at Rush, referencing his battle with painkillers—a battle Rush faced head-on and won. Harkin doesn't like Rush, and he used his Senate power to strike a blow. In discussing the "phony soldier" comment, Harkin stated, "Well, I don't know. Maybe he was just high on his drugs again. I don't know whether he was or not. If so, he ought to let us know. But that shouldn't be an excuse."[7]

Conservatives saw through the cheap shot—understanding Harkin's free speech rights—and chalked it up to a leftist liberal who would love to see Rush leave the airwaves. Harkin himself has been called on the carpet for making false claims about his service as a navy pilot, backing off statements that he was a combat pilot in Vietnam.[8]

On October 15, 2007, the *Las Vegas Review-Journal* newspaper released a poll showing that Rush Limbaugh had a higher approval rating in Nevada than Senate Majority Leader Harry Reid . . . in the senator's home state![9]

Harry Reid and other Democrats underestimate the power of Rush Limbaugh and conservative talk radio . . . and just how willing conservatives are to reach into their own pockets to help others. The Eugene B. Casey Foundation purchased the famous letter, making a significant difference in the lives of the children through the Marine Corps–Law Enforcement Foundation. Yet Reid is one of those Democrats who would like to shut down conservative talk radio.

Harry Reid will always be "dingy" to Limbaugh for his well-publicized statement that the "war has been lost." And KKOH Radio in Reno will continue to offer Reid a three-hour show to talk directly with his constituents. But don't count on that happening. It's a shame that the most powerful member of the U.S. Senate won't even appear on his own state's most powerful radio station. Harry Reid wants free speech, but only on his terms.

Meantime, the assault on freedom of speech and expression continued on other fronts. A poll by ATI-News/Zogby released on October 27, 2008 — just before the presidential election — indicated that, among those who said they would vote for Barack Obama, 53 percent supported reinstating the Fairness Doctrine. ATI News president Brad O'Leary stated that "[Obama's] Presidency, combined with super-majorities for Democrats in Congress, would almost certainly bring back the so-called Fairness Doctrine and allow the Democrats to snuff out any broadcasters with whom they disagree." [10]

Republican Congressman Greg Walden of Oregon issued this warning: "At least we've awakened the public and some in the media to the very real threat of the return of the Fairness Doctrine. It's the liberals' way of silencing conservative and religious voices. My hope is that if the talk show hosts really fire up their listeners (as they certainly better do) they could cause such a firestorm as to slow, or even stop, a legislated Fairness Doctrine. However, an Obama administration will control a majority on the FCC, and they could reinstate it without a vote of Congress." [11] This is chilling news to anyone who truly understands and values our rights granted by the First Amendment.

Speaking of the FCC, it started an investigation of on-air military analysts by sending letters suggesting they may have broken the law when they appeared on television networks to comment on and explain their views on the war on terror. The FCC probe began after complaints in May 2008 by Democrat Representatives Rosa L. DeLauro of Connecticut and John Dingell of Michigan suggested that the arrangement might violate the Communications Act of 1934.

In a letter to then FCC chairman Kevin Martin, DeLauro and Dingell said, "We write to express our deep concern with regard to a troubling story recently reported in the *New York Times* detailing an extensive program within the Department of Defense to recruit ex-military officers to support the Administration's position on the war in Iraq, conditions at Guantanamo Bay, and other activities associated with the efforts to combat terrorism under the guise of objective analysis on major television news programs and 24-hour cable news networks. Many of these military analysts were simultaneously representing more than 150 companies competing for billions of dollars in Pentagon contracts. While we deem the DOD's policy unethical and perhaps illegal, we also question whether the analysts and the networks are potentially equally culpable pursuant to the sponsorship identification requirements in the Communications Act of 1934 and the rules of the Federal Communications Commission." [12]

The Defense Department briefings were placed on hold, shutting down the flow of information. As you would expect, the chill factor among military commentators was sub-freezing.

As documented in *Human Events* by Rowan Scarborough, author of the bestselling book *Rumsfeld's War*, some of the military analysts see the move as one in a series the left is making to intimidate and silence its critics. Retired Air Force Lieutenant General Tom McInerney told *Human Events*, "We are seeing the dawn of a new era of the current Democratic leadership trying to muzzle free speech and the First Amendment."[13] Fox News analyst McInerney continued, "It may be the most invasive intrusion that we have seen in our history. There will be more of these tactics to follow."

Another Fox military analyst, retired Army Major General Paul Vallely, says, "It's an affront to freedom of speech. As retired officers, we're private citizens and can say anything we want under the First Amendment. The whole thing was to explain to the American people what was going on in the war and analyzing it."[14]

Talk to any conservative and they will tell you that all we've heard on mainstream media about the Iraq War is the roadside bombs, the numbers of soldiers killed, and the civilian casualties. Only in the conservative media did we hear about the progress toward democracy in Iraq and the new roads, schools, and hospitals being built. Vallely also discussed radio's fight against the Fairness Doctrine: "They're going to implement the Fairness Doctrine to basically do away with right-wing radio. In their minds, balance means left wing. It's Socialists trying to infringe on our First Amendment Rights," he told *Human Events*.[15]

To some it was a conflict of interest and a violation of law. To the military analysts, and to many others, it was another attempt to muzzle conservative voices in the news media . . . another blow to the First Amendment.

*Free speech, exercised both individually and
through a free press, is a necessity in any country
where people are themselves free.*
—President Theodore Roosevelt

STRAIGHT AHEAD: Democrats propose censorship.

CHAPTER 10

Censorship by Congress

Legislative Efforts Exposed

Congressman Greg Walden, Republican from Oregon, thinks Democrats have one thing in mind regarding conservative talk radio: "I believe restoration of the Fairness Doctrine is a plank in their party platform, and . . . more and more Democrats are openly calling for a crackdown on talk radio."[1] With the strong gains in both the House and Senate, it would appear the Democrat locomotive has left the station and is picking up an unstoppable head of steam. As Obama said during his campaign, just before the election, "We are about to transform America." A return of censorship regulations would certainly result in a monumental transformation of our rights under the First Amendment!

When the Fairness Doctrine was revoked in 1987 by a 4–0 vote in the FCC, there were congressional attempts to restore it. President Reagan vetoed one effort, and a later attempt was dropped when President George H. W. Bush also threatened a veto.

There can be no question that the Fairness Doctrine

chilled free speech and expression of opinion. When the doctrine's restrictions were lifted, the talk format exploded. The vast majority are conservative voices, to be sure, because that's what appeals to listeners who are finally finding a platform to validate their views—views that they perceive they do not find in the liberal mainstream media.

Sensing the power of talk radio, House Democrats drafted legislation in 2005 to bring the Fairness Doctrine back as congressional law rather than an FCC regulation. New York Congresswoman Louise Slaughter authored such legislation and stated that conservative talk radio was a threat to America—"a waste of good broadcast time, and a waste of our airwaves." She was interviewed about her views by PBS's Bill Moyers.[2] She told him "you bet" when asked if she thought the Fairness Doctrine should also apply to cable channels that are not regulated by the Federal Communications Commission—which would, of course, include Fox News.

Defeated Democrat presidential candidate John Kerry sounds a bit like a sore loser when he refers to the repeal of the Fairness Doctrine. He told WNYC's Brian Lehrer on June 27, 2007,[3] that it has resulted in conservative dominance on the radio "to squeeze down and squeeze out opinion of opposing views, and I think it has been a very important transition in the imbalance of our public eye."

More and more Democrats are sharing a common voice, contending that the country would have been on a different course if the regulations of the Fairness Doctrine had continued in force. The left feels that conservative talk radio has led the nation down the wrong path, and they're suggesting that the country would be better off without it. Even the head of the Democrat Party, Howard Dean, lent his voice to the chorus calling for changes in reregulating the media for more points of view—in other words, less conservative talk radio and more progressive talk radio.

Democrats are also aware that no new legislation would be required to accomplish this goal. All that is necessary is to appoint different people—liberals—to the Federal Communications Commission. In October 2008, Congressman Walden, a former radio station owner, confirmed that the only thing necessary to return the Fairness Doctrine is a shift in power at the FCC. Walden told me, "An Obama administration will eventually control a majority on the FCC, and they could reinstate it without a vote of Congress."[4]

On the day of the 2008 presidential election, I awoke to yet another call to restore the Fairness Doctrine when I received an e-mail from my friend, national talk show host Mark Levin, urging me to check out what Democrat Senator Charles Schumer had just told Fox News: "The very same people who don't want the Fairness Doctrine want the FCC to limit pornography on the air."[5] Schumer said it was inconsistent to regulate one and not the other—the "other" being conservative talk radio.

The Schumer comments were swiftly rebuked by most talk show hosts, who were incensed by the not-so-subtle comparison of conservative talk radio to pornography. Lars Larson, who hosts two radio programs featuring conservative political commentary, said, "Schumer compares talk on the issues of the day to pornography? The obscenity lies in suggesting the government should control the content of radio or television programs that the public trusts to inform them on critical issues. I used to associate that kind of thinking with TASS [Soviet Union news agency] or communist China."

Larson said he personally does not want a Fairness Doctrine: "My built-in Fairness Doctrine in seven hours of daily talk radio is having guests and callers who strongly disagree with me and can clearly back up their opinions . . . makes for *great* radio and profits for Westwood One and KXL. Echo chamber radio won't pay the bills and I won't do it. America benefits from the uncensored speech of talk radio free from the so-called Fairness Doctrine."[6]

So, was the bottom line of Senator Schumer's statement that if you regulate pornography, you must also regulate conservative talk radio, because the second is a reflection of the first? Perhaps Schumer does consider conservative political commentary to be pornographic. This suggestion fueled the fire under talk hosts. The senator may have been pointing out an inconsistency, but he also succeeded in slapping the collective face of talk radio. Since he started the fight, conservative talk radio finished it on Election Day 2008, when hosts across the country spent a good part of the day discussing Schumer and his outrageous comments.

With a Democrat in the White House and Democrat gains in Congress, we are hearing more discussion of programming regulations as the new Administration settles in. With the prospect of a Democrat-controlled FCC, FCC Commissioner Michael Copps told WBAL in Baltimore that the Fairness Doctrine would probably not return in its present form. But he left the door open for new ways of controlling radio programming content: "I don't think we need to go back to it exactly as it was constructed years ago, but I think we need to have a debate on how you keep these airwaves serving the public interest and nourishing the civic dialogue that our democracy depends on."[7]

Copps cannot deny that there are powerful Democrats who want to muzzle conservative talk radio and reinstate the Fairness Doctrine or other controls on conservative talk radio. And Copps knows that Democrats have all the power necessary to do that if they so choose. He knows the Federal Communications Commission once again has a liberal majority.

You have not converted a man
because you have silenced him.
—John Morley, British statesman and author

STRAIGHT AHEAD: Obama plays hardball.

CHAPTER 11

Obama Weighs In

Our New President's History of Censorship

"Senator Obama does not support re-imposing the Fairness Doctrine on broadcasters. He considers this debate to be a distraction from the conversation we should be having about opening up the airwaves and modern communications to as many diverse viewpoints as possible. That is why Senator Obama supports media-ownership caps, network neutrality, public broadcasting, as well as increasing minority ownership of broadcasting and print outlets."[1] This statement was issued in June 2008 by the Obama campaign and again in February 2009. It would seem, on the surface, to reassure those concerned about broadcast censorship.

But as conservatives pointed out during the presidential campaign, Obama has voted the Democrat party line 97 percent of the time, earning him the honor of being the most liberal senator in the chamber . . . to the left of even Senator Ted Kennedy. Given Obama's voting record, along with strong efforts by some of the most powerful Democrats to restore the doctrine, can we really trust this statement? Perhaps an analysis of how Obama treats the press can provide some insight into what he might do in the White House, with Democrat control of both the Senate and the House of Representatives.

In late August 2008, Obama supporters unleashed their venom on Chicago's WGN Radio for allowing a critic of Obama to come on the air. The station had scheduled an interview with Stanley Kurtz, author of an article that linked Obama to sixties radical William Ayers.[2] (Ayers, now a professor in the College of Education at the University of Illinois, was cofounder of a radical left-wing organization called the Weather Underground which was responsible for bombings of public buildings in the sixties and seventies, which resulted in injuries to and deaths of several people.)

Obama supporters were incensed that the radio station would interview someone such as Kurtz, whom they accused of being a "hatchet man," spreading what they considered to be lies and distortions about their candidate. Their intent was clear and to the point. They wanted to intimidate WGN and force management to reverse its decision to put Kurtz on the air. They urged their supporters to send intimidating e-mails and make phone calls to WGN radio to complain. The station was deluged with calls and e-mails.

This controversy developed into a major story not only in Chicago, on Obama's home turf, but all across the country. It was yet another frontal assault on free speech. According to my longtime friend, former WGN program director Bob Shomper—who now programs WLS in Chicago—the controversy developed as a result of trying to give Obama's campaign the opportunity to come on the radio show with Kurtz. How ironic! In other words, the station offered to provide balance to the show, but Obama supporters declined that offer and continued their intimidating tactics to try to prevent the interview from being aired. Shomper said, "Instead, they e-blasted their national database to clog our call-in lines." Rather than choosing to debate the issues, the campaign resorted to intimidation.[3]

A few weeks later, David Freddoso, author of the bestselling book *The Case Against Barack Obama*, was likewise asked to appear on WGN. The Obama attack machine again sprang into action with another e-mail blast to supporters, urging them to contact the station to try to prevent the interview from taking place. The intimidation tactics were blatant and, even more alarming, these groups now have a voice in the White House. Even though Obama has stated that he does not favor restoring the Fairness Doctrine, can he be trusted in light of these outward attempts to silence free expression of opinion?

The author of the Broadcaster Freedom Act, Congressman Mike Pence—a Republican from nearby Indiana—sounded the warning bell. In an interview with WBT Radio during the Republican National Convention, Pence stated, "[WGN] is the most powerful talk station in Illinois, if not the Central region of the Midwest, and to suggest that a Presidential campaign should be throwing its weight around and telling a radio station whom they can and cannot interview—to me it's a bit of a precursor to what Democrats want to do with the Fairness Doctrine. I think the only people who should be making decisions about what thrives on the broadcast airwaves are the American people."[4]

There were other reported incidents involving the Obama campaign that leave conservative political commentators wondering how they will be treated by the new White House. Unhappy with the questions posed to him during an interview done by a television station in Florida, vice presidential candidate Joe Biden had his campaign staff cancel a subsequent interview of his wife scheduled by that station.[5] These were questions to which the American public deserved answers. Here, again, is another direct assault on the free press by the elected administration. The American electorate was deprived of access to insights that could help them cast an informed vote on November 4, 2008.

Another shocking case of intimidation occurred in St. Louis when a television station reported that prosecutors and law enforcement officials in Missouri had joined in an effort to act as "truth squads" assigned to target the John McCain presidential campaign and any organization that ran radio and television ads critical of Obama. The report included a short interview with City Prosecutor Jennifer Joyce, who stated, "We don't want people to get distracted, and Missourians don't want to be distracted, by these divisive character attacks. So, we're here to respond to any character attacks, to set the record straight."[6]

When Missouri Governor Matt Blunt heard the report, he issued a scathing statement condemning Obama's campaign: "What Senator Obama and his helpers are doing is scandalous beyond words. The party that claims to be the party of Thomas Jefferson is abusing the justice system and offices of public trust to silence political criticism with threats of prosecution and criminal punishment."[7]

Here are more of the governor's comments: "This abuse of the law for intimidation insults the most sacred principles and ideas of Jefferson. I can think of nothing more offensive to Jefferson's thinking than using the power of the state to deprive Americans of their civil rights. The only conceivable purpose of [the prosecutor], Obama, and the others is to frighten people away from expressing themselves, to chill free and open debate, to suppress support and donations of conservative organizations targeted by this anti–civil rights [action], to strangle criticism of Mr. Obama, to suppress ads about his support of higher taxes, and to choke out criticism on television, radio, the Internet, blogs, e-mail and daily conversation about the election."

Governor Blunt concluded, "Barack Obama needs to grow up. Leftist blogs and others in the press constantly say false things about me and my family. Usually, we ignore false and scurrilous accusations because the purveyors have no credibility. When necessary, we refute them. Enlisting Missouri law enforcement to intimidate people and kill free debate is reminiscent of the Sedition Act, not a free society."

One prosecutor named in the report denied he would use his office to prosecute those who might lie about Obama, calling it "nonsense." And other national reports pointed out that both Senator McCain and running mate Governor Sarah Palin used prosecutors to examine untruthful statements made about them. But the actions of the Obama camp seemed to be intentionally intimidating.

In Tennessee, the state Republican Party encouraged broadcasters to remain strong against intimidation efforts by the Obama campaign to prevent radio and television ads connecting Obama to the radical sixties activist William Ayers.

Then there's poor Joe the Plumber. Samuel Joseph Wurzelbacher, "Joe the Plumber," became a household name when he was filmed asking Obama about his tax proposals during a campaign visit to Joe's neighborhood near Toledo, Ohio.

When we first heard news of this encounter, some in the

liberal media were suggesting that Joe was a "plant" on the rope line at an Obama campaign rally, hired by the McCain campaign to ask an embarrassing question. The reality is that Joe was playing football with his son in the front yard of their home when Obama came down the street with his camera crew. In a conversation captured on video, Wurzelbacher suggested that Obama's tax plan would be at odds with the American dream to work hard and create wealth for one's family. The part of Obama's response remembered most prominently was that "it's good to spread the wealth around."[8]

Because Obama's comment—played over and over on many media outlets across the nation—seemed to contradict his message of "hope" and "change" for the middle class, Barack supporters apparently felt that the best way to save their candidate from embarrassment was to malign the person asking the question.

Because he had asked an "inappropriate" question of the Democrat candidate while standing in his own front yard, Joe became the subject of harassment, unwarranted background checks, and personal attacks by the left in all mainstream media. The message? Be careful of the questions you ask and of whom you ask them! Because Obama's answer to Joe's question sparked emotional debate about a perceived move toward "income redistribution" in this country, and because the exchange was used extensively by McCain's campaign, Joe Wurzelbacher immediately became the target of a serious left-wing smear campaign.

"Joe the Plumber" received more press when a San Francisco radio host was fired after his comments were accidentally picked up by an open microphone. Talking over an ABC News report, the host said, "I want Joe the Plumber dead!"

Fired for hate-mongering, the host made Fox News's host Bill O'Reilly's "Pinhead" list.[9]

The treatment of Joe Wurzelbacher sent a clear message: Exercise your right of free expression at your own risk. If you see Barack Obama walking through your neighborhood, you might want to think twice about talking to him. But if you give up your right of free speech because of intimidation, you risk losing many other freedoms, too.

The intimidation factor was present on Election Day in 2008, when a voter in Philadelphia told Fox News that there was harassment of voters approaching the doors of the precinct polling place where they cast their ballots. He told Fox, "As I walked to the door, two people in Black Panther garb—one of them brandishing a nightstick—were standing immediately in front of the door."[10]

Freedom of speech comes at a price. WGN had to stand up to the Obama intimidation machine. Joe the Plumber stood up for his rights, even though it meant being attacked by left-wing groups. Voters in Philadelphia pushed past intimidating figures positioned near the door to their polling place. These are courageous actions that protect our right to freedom of expression, and we should be grateful to them for standing up against the forces of intimidation that would censor us.

Conservative talk radio fights that same battle every day. The left-wing smear machine went into high gear against the conservative media during the 2008 election campaign. Without conservative political commentators acting as watchdogs, millions of Americans would not have heard many important stories that were ignored, intentionally, by the mainstream news media.

These left-wing smear mongers are among the supporters who elected Barack Obama. Can we trust them to leave conservative talk radio alone and back away from attempts to restore censorship regulations? Will Obama stand in the way of reestablishing regulation of media content? Or will these people who threatened the media and ordinary American citizens continue their intimidation with the approval of those newly elected to serve in our nation's capital? Maybe they will, and maybe they won't. But their actions on the campaign trail speak volumes about their plans for conservative talk radio.

And never underestimate Barack Obama. He knows how to play hardball. In his first run for political office in 1996, Obama used what some refer to as "Chicago rules."[11] As a community organizer he had helped register people to vote. In 1996 he used his skills to invalidate the voting petition signatures of his three challengers—including the incumbent senator, who had been a supporter—so he could run unopposed on the Democrat ticket in his mostly Democrat district. His team is tough, intimidating, and they know how to win.

It should be pointed out that fairness works both ways, and we must be vigilant in defending our political opponents' rights to free speech. Ed Schultz is a leading progressive/liberal talk show host in America, and his voice is heard in most major radio markets on one hundred stations nationwide.

Ed recounts this personal story, which should make every conservative—including me—think twice: "George W. Bush brought the conservative talkers to the Oval Office to talk about Iraq and his economic policy. The meeting made the front cover of *Talkers* magazine. Hannity, Boortz, Medved, Levin, Ingraham, and Gallagher were all on hand and were pictured on the magazine's front cover with Bush in the Oval

Office. I knew the meeting was going to take place, so I called the White House and asked if I could be included. First the Communications Office told me there was not going to be a meeting. After I pressed them, they told me I could not attend the meeting."[12]

Every White House adminstration has the right to invite whom they want to attend functions. Will President Obama invite conservative talk show hosts to personal briefings? Time will tell, but conservative hosts aren't holding their breath for the best of treatment from the Obama administration.

> *I think the Fairness Doctrine debate will energize talk radio as never before, because our literal existence will be at risk. This isn't about my taxes going up; this is about my freedom to speak and the listener's freedom to hear.*
> —JOHN CARLSON, KOMO RADIO, SEATTLE

STRAIGHT AHEAD: Why conservative talk radio is highly rated and liberal talk radio isn't.

CHAPTER 12

That's Entertainment!

Why Conservative Talk Radio Works
(and Liberal Talk Doesn't!)

In radio, we always joke that our jobs beat real work! If we look at it that way, I haven't had "real work" in more than forty years of programming at the local and national level. Thirty-seven of those years have been spent in the news/talk radio format. I've had the pleasure of working with countless personalities, all of whom I admire because they are some of the hardest working and most dedicated people I've ever known. So I am frequently asked why conservative talk radio is so powerful and liberal talk radio so weak. I have pondered that question myself and with my colleagues for many years.

First, let me say that I root for liberal talk radio to be successful. I believe in freedom of expression. But I also want the marketplace—not government—to dictate the content of our broadcasts. Frankly, if liberal talk radio worked, it would give me more choices in programming, and my job would be much easier. So c'mon, you liberal talkers—get ratings!

Ratings are at the heart of the matter. Radio, like all broadcast media except NPR and PBS, is a business. Radio lives and dies by whether or not people listen. Radio's revenue is generated by selling advertising, and businesses choose to advertise on stations where the largest audience will hear about their product or service. So ratings drive revenue. If a merchant carries a product that doesn't sell, he removes it from his shelves and offers a different product. It's no different in radio.

Over the years I've often been asked by listeners, "Why did you get rid of that program—I liked it!" My response is that not enough listeners liked it for me to justify keeping it. When I use the analogy of the merchant, listeners usually understand even though they may be disappointed about losing a favorite radio show.

Radio is show business. The reason the format has grown exponentially since repeal of the Fairness Doctrine in 1987 is that talk radio is popular. When combining news, talk, and sports stations, the ratings are usually the highest of any type of program in that marketplace. And what drives the popularity of talk radio is conservative political commentary. If conservative talk didn't resonate so well with listeners, we would find another product for our shelf! But it does, and it has been immensely popular for more than twenty years.

Why? Much of its popularity has to do with a pent-up desire and frustration that had grown over decades in many Americans. Many people perceived that the media did not reflect their views. A large number of these people were conservatives, and they could not find a radio station with programming that validated their opinions. The reason was simple: the Fairness Doctrine. This regulation discouraged debate on the radio, and owners shied away from political commentary. It was just too much trouble to deal with the countless requests for balanced access. And there were the threats of large fines for not complying with the regulations. As a result, many Americans were underserved by conservative viewpoints on the radio. I was one of them.

Then the Fairness Doctrine was repealed in 1987 during the Reagan administration. It was as if the fog lifted and the sun began to shine. It was so new to us that it took a few years to figure out what to do with this gift of free expression on the radio. We were free at last! It wasn't until the early nineties that some of us figured out there was a huge market for conservative political commentary. A few of us were privileged to pioneer the all-conservative talk radio format, which was my experience at KVI in Seattle, where our ratings skyrocketed from number 23 to number 1 in less than three years. We had figured out the right product for the shelf space!

Suddenly there were conservative political commentators such as Rush Limbaugh saying the kinds of things I had always wanted to say . . . thoughts and opinions I had been afraid to express for fear of reprisal. We were given permission to come out, pound our chests, and be proud of our views instead of cowering in the back of a room. The news/talk format that we developed at KVI spread across the nation like wildfire. I received dozens of calls from around the country asking for advice in duplicating this phenomenon.

When I left KVI Radio in 1994, that experience spawned a very successful business for me as I consulted for sixty-five radio stations and several national talk show hosts across the country for the next ten years. Every day I thank the Reagan administration for allowing that to happen. And so I will do everything I can to protect the right to free expression on the radio without government controls.

During those new and exciting times, I remember taking a phone call from the Associated Press (AP) bureau manager in Seattle, who challenged me for placing talk shows on the air that freely expressed opinion. He was aghast that I would do that, and he contended that it was illegal to do so without airing the opposing viewpoint. He was ill-informed and out of touch.

And I received calls from listeners threatening to report my station to the FCC. I responded by giving them the phone number of the local FCC office. And the ratings soared. Conservative talk radio was off and running, and there was no turning back. Listeners couldn't get enough of it. They demanded political commentary . . . and they wanted conservative voices, not liberal views.

When the regulations of the Fairness Doctrine were first lifted, I still tried to be the "fair-and-balanced" radio broadcaster. I even used that slogan when first programming KVI Radio in 1991. I put Alan Colmes's liberal talk show on the air in the time slot right after Rush Limbaugh. Please know that I like Alan very much, and I owe him a debt of gratitude for endorsing this book. But his shows' ratings on KVI paled compared to Rush's. Colmes is an extremely talented broadcaster . . . but Limbaugh's audience had no taste for liberal political commentary, so they turned the radio dial. Alan's views just weren't a fit at that time on a station where conservative listeners dictated our ratings.

So like a good merchant needing to sell his wares, we sought a new product. When I found that right product—conservative political commentary—the ratings began to climb, and the all-conservative talk radio format was under way. With that ratings success, revenues followed. Station owner Gene Autry and general manager Shannon Sweatte had my bonus checks sitting on my desk the morning after each ratings release. In Autry's honor, I still have the two pairs of cowboy boots that the Cowboy himself gifted me to express his appreciation.

Another reason the conservative talk format is still popular is that it has had twenty years to develop a loyal following. It's hard to change that momentum. The format is rich with seasoned talent . . . individuals who witnessed the creative rock 'n' roll radio era and know what constitutes real entertainment . . . personalities who have honed their skills on the radio for years. Liberal talkers have tried to develop the same following, and I encourage them to keep trying . . . but do it without implementing regulations that *require* us to put them on the air. Liberals should have to stand on their own merit and earn the listening audience that conservatives have developed. So far, that's been a tough road.

There are a few exceptions, such as in Portland, Oregon, and Seattle, Washington, where liberal political commentary works because of the extremely progressive views held by a majority of citizens in those cities. But it's an uphill battle for liberal talk show hosts in most markets. Still, don't get the government involved in content decisions just because liberal talk isn't popular. Radio program content must be free from government regulation, or we are at risk of becoming puppets of the state.

My longtime friend Michael Harrison, publisher of *Talkers*, is a solid champion of free speech. Stressing that his highly respected national industry magazine is nonpartisan, he states, "What I'm in favor of is what should be on every American's agenda regardless of where they stand politically—free speech, the free marketplace of ideas, and the First Amendment."[1]

Michael, I couldn't agree more.

David Limbaugh, Rush's brother, writes with clarity when talking about conservative talk radio: "The reason liberals can't compete in talk radio, besides their hosts being boring, oppressively cynical, and pessimistic, is that their would-be audience is already fed through the mainstream media. Conversely, conservative talk has been successful, not just because it is more entertaining, professional, and optimistic, but because conservative audiences were starved for a like-minded message."[2]

Tony Russell, talk show host at WNBF in Binghamton, New York, had this to say: "Fairness is in the ear of the listener. Our sister station ran Al Franken and other liberals straight up against me and our big three. They all finished last in the market in all slots and demographics. According to Congressman [Maurice] Hinchey and Pelosi and Senator Clinton and the rest, we should run programming that makes no money and has no listeners just to be fair. Brilliant!"[3]

One of my good programming friends, Dan Mason at KKOH in Reno, suggests that liberal hosts are boring because they are pessimistic. He perceives that conservative hosts have been successful because it is their nature to express more positive viewpoints. Since the recent election went to the left, we'll see if liberal talk becomes more popular in this country. This I know: Conservative talk radio will generate high ratings for years to come. It resonates with the fundamental values of a majority of Americans . . . and it's entertaining!

In an interview with industry magazine *Radio Ink*, Bennett Zier, CEO of the liberal radio network Air America, was asked why he thought liberal/progressive talk hasn't been as successful as conservative talk. He answered, "Anything that goes on the radio needs to be entertaining. . . . Air America's opportunity is by being an entertainment company that happens to use politics as its vehicle, like other companies use sports or music."[4]

This is what conservative talk show hosts have known for years. It's what makes Rush Limbaugh successful. Whether you agree with Rush's opinions or not, most listeners agree that he's a great entertainer who happens to be a conservative political commentator. When liberal media first organized their network, Air America, they put forth an agenda that valued political dogma over entertainment value. Time will tell if they can change that perception.

Time wasn't on the side of a radio station that tried to establish liberal talk programming in Washington, D.C. "Obama 1260" was established to counter-program "McCain 570" and provide listeners with a true balance. By the end of January 2009, it was apparent the experiment with progressive talk was a failure once again. According to then Program Director Greg Tantum, "There were issues with the signal, technical plant, and talent, but I have come to strongly believe the big reason [for failure] in Washington, D.C., the critical mass of listeners needed to succeed is already well served by NPR and WAMU."[5] In other words, there was no need for another liberal radio station—those listeners are well served by liberal NPR.

News of the demise of "Obama 1260" quickly caught the attention of another Democratic Senator, Debbie Stabenow of Michigan. Appearing on the Bill Press radio show she quickly verbalized her support to restore the Fairness Doctrine as previously noted. When Press asked if the senator would push for Senate hearings, Stabenow said, "I have already had some discussion with colleagues and, you know, I feel that's gonna happen."[6]

It should be noted that Stabenow's husband, Tom Athans,

has worked for liberal radio producers such as Air America. As for Bill Press, the liberal talker thinks there is a conservative media conspiracy to keep liberal talk show personalities off radio by station owners.[7] Press is just wrong on this issue. Having worked as a national programming executive for one of these companies for nearly fifteen years, I was never pressured to keep liberals off the radio. We only wanted ratings, and when we tried liberal talk radio such as Air America, it failed. Press cites a few examples of success for liberal radio programs, but compared to the overwhelming success of conservative talk radio, that success is minuscule. I wish him well with his show and hope for his success.

Had "Obama 1260" been a ratings success, it would still be on the air—rest assured. When liberal talk fails in the free marketplace, Stabenow and other liberals whine and run to Daddy (government) for help. They fail to admit liberal talk radio has been a ratings failure, and if they can regulate it onto the airwaves, they will. Westwood One's Jim Bohannon sees the irony in this logic when he quipped to NTS Media-Online's Al Peterson, "I can't wait to watch Senator Stabenow enforce structural balance by requiring NPR affiliates to carry Michael Savage."[8]

And to my liberal friends in radio I say: Your message of criticizing America isn't resonating with listeners. You need to be more entertaining. Get top ratings—I mean *top* ratings like Rush, Hannity, Levin, Savage, Beck, Larson, Boortz, and countless other national and local hosts—and the marketplace will open to you. Lighten up and have some fun! In our society, the best talent always rises to the top and will find an audience. But don't legislate your way onto the airwaves because you can't do it on your own merits with ratings. While the feminist Greenstone Media failed, and Air America is working its way back from financial disaster, I say, "Keep up the good fight, and may the best hosts win."

So far, those are the conservatives . . .

> *The right to be heard does not automatically include the right to be taken seriously.*
> —Vice President Hubert H. Humphrey

STRAIGHT AHEAD: A high-profile liberal speaks out against the Fairness Doctrine.

CHAPTER 13

A Liberal Rejects Censorship

Alan Colmes Just Says "No!"

I have great respect for talk show host Alan Colmes despite the chiding of my conservative neighbors. They've always wished that he didn't have to appear on the successful *Hannity & Colmes* television show on Fox. But Alan was there for just that reason—to push their hot buttons, which he does so well, and to present a counter-viewpoint. But they eventually got their wish in January. Colmes stepped away from the highly rated show and now offers special commentary for the popular cable television network. His interaction with Sean on their final program proves once again there can be respect and common ground in spite of differing ideologies.

As mentioned previously, I put Colmes's liberal talk show on KVI Radio in Seattle in the early nineties but was soon forced to take it out of the programming lineup for lack of ratings. That was not Alan's fault. Conservatives would listen to Rush Limbaugh, then leave during Alan's show, suggesting that there is a valid reason why radio stations have separated conservative and liberal program lineups. Liberals prefer to listen to liberal personalities, and conservatives prefer to listen to conservative personalities.

Several years later I had the privilege of consulting Colmes, along with several other radio personalities, at the Major Talk Network in Chicago. Although we share different political points of view, I have always respected Alan's right to express his opinions and his ability to verbalize them. And I like seeing Alan prove that liberals and conservatives can get along! When a prominent liberal speaks out against the Fairness Doctrine, it makes news headlines. Colmes understands what the First Amendment means for the fundamental rights of the American people.

The Fairness Doctrine battle should not be a fight between liberals and conservatives. It should be a fight waged by liberals and conservatives and all of talk radio against government interference in free expression. The Broadcaster Freedom Act, authored by Republican Congressman Mike Pence, would ban the Fairness Doctrine once and for all. It should be passed, because this battle for free speech affects broadcasters and reporters of all political persuasions. As of this writing, House action is unclear and some think doubtful because of powerful Democrats in Congress who are angry at conservative talk radio and believe the medium should be muzzled.

In program after program on Fox News, Alan Colmes has spoken out against the Fairness Doctrine, challenging proponents, including Democrat Congressman Steve Cohen of Tennessee and others, who have appeared on the network. In January 2007, Colmes pointedly told Congressman Cohen, "You want the government to be involved in content and dictate to some extent the content of radio and television and I thought we've gotten away from that. The idea would put a chill down the spine of free speech."[1]

Colmes is quick to remind those who favor regulation that there are thousands of choices for information in the Internet age, and he warns strongly against government intervention in programming.

In 2007, I attended a freedom of speech address given by Alan Colmes at the New Media Seminar in New York, an annual industry convention hosted by *Talkers* magazine's Michael Harrison. Alan was eloquent and steadfast in his defense of free expression, again speaking out against government control of media content. He was there to defend the selection of Michael Savage—despite protests from detractors—as recipient of the annual Freedom of Speech Award. As Alan put it, "I don't like what Savage has to say, but I defend his right to say it."

I caught up with Alan on December 3, 2008, and asked him some pointed questions about the Fairness Doctrine. Here is our conversation:[2]

Jennings: Why do you think key Democrats favor the Fairness Doctrine and have been so vocal about it recently?

Colmes: Democrats are frustrated that they don't have the reins on talk radio and talk television. But it is incorrect that they are actively trying to reinstate it. This is more right-wing paranoia, and it gives conservatives something about which to beat up liberals. Obama supports diversity, not a new Fairness Doctrine.

Jennings: Is the Fairness Doctrine the means to really increase points of view in media, or is there a better way to do it and why?

Colmes: There is a better way than the Fairness Doctrine if increasing viewpoints is the goal. Diversity in ownership. Government should not be involved in programming content. But what government can do is discourage monopolies and make sure that there are limits as to how much of the public airwaves can be controlled by one entity in a given market.

Jennings: Do you think conservative talk radio should be forced to include liberals on the same station?

Colmes: No, there should be no forcing of programming whatsoever. I don't want a job by government mandate. When the tide is turned, liberals won't want government mandating conservatives on the air, either.

Jennings: Former Republican Senator Trent Lott said in June of 2007, after defeat of the Immigration Bill, that "talk radio is running America—we need to deal with that." After this election, is that really true?

Colmes: It was never true. If Rush Limbaugh has a ten percent share, that means ninety percent of people listening to the radio at any given time aren't listening to him. Never mind the rest of the population that isn't even listening to radio. Too many radio hosts are drunk with self-importance and delusional about their impact on the rest of the world.

Jennings: What would you say to fellow liberals who favor the Fairness Doctrine?

Colmes: Be careful what you ask for. If it ever happens, which it won't, you'll be victimized by it one day.

This conservative is in agreement with that liberal.

For years I've had a relationship with a southern talk radio host known to his audience as "Rocky D." Rocky just lets fly with his opinions, and there's nothing subtle about anything he does on the radio at WTMA in Charleston, South Carolina. He agrees with Colmes's assessment that liberals should be careful about asking for a return of a Fairness Doctrine: "If the Censorship Doctrine went into effect, I could grab a lawyer and *demand* to have my views on *every* media outlet everywhere. I'd file for equal time every day at every TV and radio station here in Charleston. Can you imagine me on the local hip-hop station or NPR blasting the NAACP and the ACLU? Hell, I look *forward* to it! The liberals will be sorry they ever mentioned the word *fairness*."[3]

Most liberal talk show hosts avoid advocating a return of the actual Fairness Doctrine. Instead they talk about creating more diversity in media ownership, which they think will result in more diverse talk programming. They seem to understand what is at stake.

As Alan Colmes pointed out, if program balance is restored, liberal stations will be required to air conservative programming! The left would like to see a greater number of station owners and a breakup of the large media companies that own most of the nation's radio stations. Forcing a breakup of large media conglomerates, they hope, will result in a better opportunity for them to find work at radio stations that have previously shut them out. But there is one flaw in this logic. Radio advertising provides the revenue that keeps the station in business. Advertising is driven by ratings. More diverse ownership in media could, in fact, result in more liberal or progressive programming . . . but if nobody listens, the argument becomes moot when these new owners go out of business.

Ed Schultz is a very successful liberal talk radio host in America. During a monologue on his show in June 2007, he stated, "The numbers are undeniable—this industry is owned, operated, and programmed by conservatives." A bit later, he stated, "This is about market opportunities. This is also about ownership. This is also about being given an opportunity to be on an equal signal with equal promotion."[4]

So the argument that more ownership diversity would create more opportunity for liberal radio talk show hosts is partially accurate. They would also have to generate big ratings to remain on these stations, and radio programmers around the country question their ability to do that based on the low ratings of the all-liberal network Air America. Michael Harrison, a prominent spokesman for talk radio in America, states, "The only standard anyone is held to in this business is ratings and revenue. Liberal or progressive hosts face the same challenges that conservatives do because above all else, commercial talk radio is a business."[5]

As a radio programmer, I have reviewed ratings data for years. If you look hard enough at ratings information, you can generally find at least one demographic in which a radio station performs well. Certain programs appeal to men, others to women, yet others to different age groups, for example.

I've kept a close eye on the progressive, all-liberal Air America talk radio stations over the years, and I have to say that the ratings are not good. There isn't an obvious listener demand as of this writing. Of the top radio markets in the country, Seattle and Portland have the best-rated liberal stations in America. But in major markets such as New York, Los Angeles, and Chicago, all-liberal stations are rated so low that it's hard to find any optimistic news. Perhaps that will change with the new Democrat administration, but most radio programmers are skeptical.

There are several schools of thought on why all-liberal talk radio isn't working. Some ratings experts and radio programmers suggest that those on the left don't use the radio as much as conservatives, and so therefore these stations won't attract as large an audience. (After all, liberals have most other mainstream media speaking to and for them.) Some of these liberal stations are low power and have limited geographical reach. But until liberals generate better ratings, larger power stations won't change proven lineups that attract dominant ratings to take a chance on these programs that, so far, aren't rated well. These stations don't want to tamper with success. If it isn't broken, don't fix it.

As I said earlier, the key to success for liberal talkers in radio is very simple—they need to be less dogmatic and more entertaining. Listeners tune in to hear information, and they tune in even more frequently if they are entertained at the same time. There are several liberal hosts who have enjoyed a great deal of ratings success at the local level. As I've mentioned at the national level, Ed Schultz is one of the highest-rated syndicated progressive/liberal host in America. He ranks among the industry's leaders in numbers of listeners. According to *Talkers*, the former college football player/turned play-by-play announcer/turned talk show host ranks among the top twenty most popular hosts in America.

Schultz says liberal talk works: "When I started the *Ed Schultz Show* in January of 2004, before Air America started, I was jammed with the talk of negativity by every conservative in the industry that it would never work. Eleven talkers in the past had tried it and failed and nothing would change. Well, six years later the *Ed Schultz Show* is still on the air in ninety-seven markets, including New York, Chicago, San Francisco, Seattle, Washington, D.C., Denver, and Minneapolis. Our show is profitable with five full-time employees, yet the scum talkers of the industry like to throw out how Air America has trouble."

It should be noted that Schultz is not part of the all-liberal talk network Air America.[6]

If more progressives like Ed Schultz find a way to resonate in an entertaining way on the radio, success will follow. But they shouldn't legislate their way onto the air by hiding behind the skirts of programming regulations. Give listeners what they want and liberal talkers will have success. Doug McIntyre, KABC Radio's morning host in Los Angeles, says, "It's true syndicated radio is a conservative monolith, but the remedy isn't the Fairness Doctrine, it's the FCC and SEC turning down megamergers and massive consolidation in the broadcasting industry."[7]

> *I see 20 million talk radio listeners surrounding the Capitol with pitchforks. I see conservative and liberal hosts standing together to fight this. I hope they try it, it would be the best thing that could happen to us.*
>
> —JIM VILLANUCCI, KKOB RADIO, ALBUQUERQUE

STRAIGHT AHEAD: What a censorship doctrine would do to Christian radio.

CHAPTER 14

The Gospel According to Radio

The Impact on Christian Broadcasting

For many years, hundreds of Christian radio stations have spread the Gospel across the nation. Their programs are a significant part of American radio history, and they have touched the lives of millions of people. Christian programs are very conservative, espousing traditional family values and the right to life.

Christian radio listeners have become concerned about the future of their programs if a new censorship doctrine is restored or if balanced programming on American radio stations becomes a legal requirement. Would Christian radio, advocating for traditional marriage, be required to give up valuable airtime to gay rights activists? Religion is controversial, and assertions of belief—such as that life begins at conception—would result in petitions for equal time from those who hold different views. Without question, the potential for mandated "balanced" access is there, and it sends a chill through religious broadcasters.

Chris Squires programs KERI Faith & Family 1410, a

Christian radio station in Bakersfield, California. He says a return of equal time regulations would cripple Christian radio because it would make the Word of God impossible to hear on the airwaves. "I think this would be grossly unfair. Christians need to be bold about speaking their mind and speaking out against censorship. I think about all the views presented by the media in Hollywood and in the music industry. None of that gets legislated and they are free to speak, but believers wouldn't be able to do the same if speech regulations were restored."[1] He warns that Christians cannot be complacent in fighting a new version of the Fairness Doctrine.

Focus on the Family Action, based in Colorado Springs and led by Dr. James Dobson, is one of the foremost religious and conservative voices in America. They also are not complacent in this fight. The organization mailed thousands of petitions to Democrat members of Congress urging them to drop their support of the Fairness Doctrine and encouraging them to support Congressman Mike Pence's Broadcaster Freedom Act, which would permanently ban the Fairness Doctrine and guarantee free speech rights to radio.[2] Dr. Dobson was quoted as saying, "There is such a danger out there lurking for all of conservative talk radio and Focus on the Family." Religious and conservative voices alike are quick to point out the cozy relationship Obama and congressional liberals have with the mainstream media, but "it's people like us that they want to muzzle," stated Dobson. Religious leaders across the nation are fearful of losing their ability to preach the whole counsel of God if the Fairness Doctrine—or a new version of it—is reinstated.

Many conservatives feel that Democrats signaled their intent to muzzle the opposition in January 2007, when Democrats regained control of Congress. The first bill introduced was Senate Bill 1. In it were onerous fines for organizations that would coordinate large e-mail campaigns to speak against positions taken by our elected representatives on important issues. The intent was clear—they wanted to deny our rights as U.S. citizens to express opposing viewpoints. Fortunately, the provisions were eliminated, but it signaled what Democrats hope to achieve. And, with more control in Washington, this voice is likely to become even stronger.

Filibuster may be the conservative's only hope in the months and years ahead . . . the only thing standing in the way of losing our right to free speech in America.

Focus on the Family commentary with Dr. Dobson can be heard daily on hundreds of commercial news/talk stations as well as Christian stations nationwide. This excellent program would be a target for anyone with opposing values who could demand balanced programming from the radio station on which it was aired. Christian radio broadcasters, like other commercial radio stations, are licensed by the FCC. To be forced to offer equal access for opposing viewpoints would cost them valuable airtime and alienate loyal listeners. Christian radio would be in jeopardy . . . not to mention that Gospel listeners would leave the station in droves because those "balanced" views would violate their belief system and, in fact, be offensive to them.

Focus on the Family Action published a "Letter from 2012 in Obama's America"—a work of speculative fiction—which suggested that voters didn't know that Obama's far-left agenda would take away many freedoms and potentially lead to a decades-long liberal majority in the Supreme Court. In this fictional letter the author states, "I can hardly sing 'The Star-Spangled Banner' anymore. When I hear the words, 'O say, does that star-spangled banner yet wave, O'er the land of the free and the home of the brave,' I get tears in my eyes and a lump in my throat. Now, in October 2012, after seeing what has happened in the last four years, I don't think I can still answer *Yes* to that question. We are not the land of the free and the home of the brave."[3]

The author continues, "The Fairness Doctrine would have been restored and nearly all conservative stations have now gone out of business. Conservative talk radio, for all intents and purposes, was shut down by the end of 2010."

For those who love talk radio and Christian radio, there is real concern. They hope the vision in the letter doesn't become reality.

The Christian Coalition of America is also warning of the dire consequences to free speech should the censorship doctrine or a new version of it be implemented. Like many groups, the coalition feels that conservative talk radio is the only balance preventing liberals from implementing a radical liberal agenda. The president of the coalition, Roberta Combs, says, "Congress should resist the urge to shut down radio talk show hosts around the country, which is what the 'Fairness Doctrine' would effectively do if brought back. Christian Coalition of America has begun an on-line campaign to ensure that the onerous 'Fairness Doctrine' is not reinstituted by Congress or by the Obama administration."[4] The coalition wants free speech rights so radio can preach the gospel and you can hear it freely.

President George W. Bush made it clear that legislation to control free expression by broadcasters would never see the light of day during his administration. In fact, he said he would veto any legislation that would control the content of media broadcasts. Speaking to the National Religious Broadcasters (NRB) 2008 convention in Nashville, President Bush stated it this way: "There's an effort afoot that would jeopardize your right to express your views on public airways. Some members of Congress want to reinstate a regulation that was repealed twenty years ago. It has the Orwellian name called the Fairness Doctrine. Supporters of this regulation say we need to mandate that any discussion of so-called controversial issues on the public airwaves includes equal time for all sides. This means that many programs wanting to stay on the air would have to meet Washington's definition of balance. Of course, for some in Washington, the only opinions that require balancing are the ones they don't like." [5]

The president continued his statement on the Fairness Doctrine, noting, "We know who these advocates of so-called balance really have in their sights: shows hosted by people like Rush Limbaugh or James Dobson, or many of you here today. By insisting on so-called balance, they want to silence those they don't agree with. The truth of the matter is they know they cannot prevail in the public debate of ideas. They don't acknowledge that you are the balance; that you give voice. The country should not be afraid of the diversity of opinion. After all, we're strengthened by diversity of opinions."

President Bush guaranteed that the Fairness Doctrine would not be restored under his administration, but those days are done. Conservatives can only hope that cool heads will also prevail in the Obama administration. Before Obama became president, his office said on June 25, 2008, and again in February 2009, that he had no interest in restoring the Fairness Doctrine. But conservatives take that comment lightly, considering the heavily Democrat-controlled House and Senate and the growing number of liberals who say they want to regulate the radio and television airwaves to provide balanced programs.

And there are other ways to obtain the same results as the Fairness Doctrine without congressional intervention. We'll speak more to those efforts later in this book. President Bush is no longer around, and the Democrats have a near-stranglehold on Washington. Continued vigilance by conservatives is the only proper response to this threat.

Cliff Kincaid is a researcher and writer for Accuracy In Media, a group that fights left-wing bias. Kincaid interviewed Jay Sekulow, chief counsel for the American Center for Law & Justice, who told him, "Christian broadcasters would be put in the uncomfortable position of having to air positions that violate their conscience and sincerely held beliefs. The proclamation of the Gospel, the definition of marriage and the issue of abortion would all be deemed 'controversial topics' that require giving airtime to opposing views."[6]

On February 16, 2007, the NRB passed a resolution noting that the Fairness Doctrine has a "chilling and stifling effect on broadcasters and programmers." The NRB also stated that it "strongly opposes any attempt to reinstate or make the Fairness Doctrine the law of the land and further pledges to vigorously oppose any such action."[7] Hundreds of radio stations spreading the Gospel would be threatened. We pray the Fairness Doctrine or new censorship regulations never come to pass.

*I have wondered at times about what the
Ten Commandments would have looked like if
Moses had run them through the U.S. Congress.*

—President Ronald Reagan

STRAIGHT AHEAD: Media bias and the rise of conservative talk
radio.

CHAPTER 15

Bias!

Talk Radio as a Balance to Mainstream Media

Boston Legal, the television series starring William Shatner, James Spader, Candice Bergen, and many other great stars, was one of my favorite evening TV escapes. My wife and I loved to watch the wacky antics of the characters on this wonderful, insightful show. The continuing adventures of Denny Crane and his "mad cow" disease provided some of the most entertaining television created in years. The plot of the hardcore conservative lawyer vs. the liberal establishment brought not only laughs but also some terrific social commentary.

But, personally, we were disappointed in *Boston Legal* on election eve, 2008. In that episode, Denny Crane and his best friend and legal colleague Alan Shore get into a great debate about who will get their vote in the presidential election. Crane defends McCain; Shore wants Obama to be elected. They were each so adamant about their personal beliefs that they even engaged in a vigorous paintball fight—right in the law offices, of course—because of their differing views.

At the end of the show, when Denny and Alan are out on

the balcony having their scotch and cigars, Denny acknowledges that he has changed his mind and is going to vote for Obama. Translation: Even someone suffering from mad cow (the show's euphemism for Alzheimer's disease) has enough sense not to vote for a Republican. My wife jumped up and shouted, "Media bias!"

I suggested to her that this is why conservative talk radio has gained such a strong foothold in America. This *Boston Legal* episode was an example of why many conservatives perceive widespread bias against them in the mainstream media. We would like to remind those who want to return "balance" and "fairness" to talk radio that no controls are needed . . . because conservative talk radio *is* the balance to most other media.

Two weeks later, after the election, *Boston Legal* was back at it. We lost count of how many times in the script the words *stupid* and *idiot* were used to describe a character in that episode who had voted for McCain. ABC made a strong political statement through a popular sitcom. The network is free to do that. We live in America, and free speech rights are guaranteed to all . . . supposedly. But clearly this is one of many examples that demonstrate a need for conservative talk radio in America, if only to air the other side of the story.

There were numerous examples of liberal news bias leading up to the 2008 presidential election that also illustrate the need for balance provided by conservative talk radio. Coverage of the war in Iraq is one of the key examples.

The Iraq War was not going well. The news from the front was bad—U.S. and Allied soldiers were being killed by pockets of insurgents backed by terrorist organizations. We were losing the war. The country of Iraq had been destroyed. That's all the major networks seemed to cover. There was never any good news to report about any progress being made in Iraq . . . until "the Surge" sent more American troops into the battle, and the tide began to turn in our favor. Even then, network television news and the major newspapers continued to report only the negative aspects of the war.

Conservatives' desires to hear about the positive strides being made in Iraq were ignored by the mainstream media. With all the liberal antiwar sentiment, liberal media outlets certainly wouldn't want it to appear that we might, in fact, be winning the war.

Suddenly British media were announcing that the war in Iraq had been won . . . but nobody in the United States knew it! Just ahead of the U.S. political conventions on July 6, 2008, London *Sunday Times* reporter Marie Colvin stated, "American and Iraq forces are driving Al-Qaeda in Iraq out of its last redoubt in the north of the country in the culmination of one of the most spectacular victories of the war on terror."[1]

Only conservative talk radio reported any good news from Iraq—progress toward democratic elections, new schools and hospitals—while mainstream media conveniently ignored it.

Discussion about a timetable for the withdrawal of American troops was another indicator of U.S. victory in the Iraq War, but the mainstream press didn't report much of that story, either. Liberals were looking forward to giving Barack Obama credit for ending the war, and it certainly wouldn't do to have liberal media sources letting the public know that the Iraq War was already winding down even before Obama took office.

Bias against conservatives in the mainstream media is a reality. Even some major metropolitan newspapers admitted to readers that their coverage of Barack Obama during the presidential campaign was more favorable than that of John McCain. A study released by Pew Research Center's Project for Excellence in Journalism, just ahead of the 2008 election, documented that in the six-week period following the conventions through the final debate, "unfavorable stories about McCain outweighed favorable ones by a factor of more than three to one—the most unfavorable of all four candidates."

The Pew Research Center tracks media coverage on a continual basis. In the report, titled "Winning the Media Campaign: How the Press Reported the 2008 General Election,"[2] Pew's Project for Excellence in Journalism stated that a majority of the print and broadcast stories about John McCain during this time period of the presidential campaign were negative. Their research showed that reporting on Obama was more balanced: "Just over a third of the stories were clearly positive in tone (36%), while a similar number (35%) were neutral or mixed. A smaller number (29%) were negative.

For McCain, by comparison, nearly six in ten of the stories studied were decidedly negative in nature (57%) while fewer than two in ten (14%) were positive."

The report was released October 22, 2008, and measured the tone of coverage from September 8 to October 16 following the national political conventions. Conservatives heard and saw the bias . . . and the Pew Research Center confirmed it for them. The need for conservative political commentary to be the counterbalance is even more apparent in the face of such liberal bias in mainstream media.

The Pew Research Center for the People & the Press also polled voters for their perception of coverage and found that "by a margin of seventy percent to nine percent, Americans said most journalists wanted to see Barack Obama and not

John McCain win the election." Guess who won. The report also stated, "In recent presidential campaigns, voters repeatedly have said they thought journalists favored the Democratic candidate over the Republican. But this year's margin is particularly wide."[3]

Media Matters, the left-leaning, Web-based organization that claims it is dedicated to "comprehensively monitoring, analyzing, and correcting conservative misinformation in the U.S. Media"[4] criticized the Pew research, saying that it left conservative talk radio listeners out of its poll. Media Matters and its many battles with conservative talk radio are the subject of an upcoming chapter.

When the 2008 Democratic National Convention was due to be broadcast on TV, I asked one of my Republican friends if he planned to watch it. He responded, "Why would I want to watch Democrats covering Democrats?" On the other hand he predicted, at the moment Sarah Palin stepped on stage at the Republican National Convention, that mainstream media would set out to destroy her. They did.

Conservatives appreciate small-town values, but the all-American image just doesn't play well with the big-media types on the East Coast. We appreciate Sarah's Alaskan roots, her real-world experience, and even her non–Ivy League educational background. Liberals hate her because she knows how to catch and clean a fish and how to shoot and field dress a moose. Ironically, liberal women criticized her because she balanced the responsibilities of being both a governor and a mother. The instant she stepped on that stage at the Republican convention, liberal media wanted to prove that Sarah Palin wasn't worthy—and that the values many conservatives believe in are wrong.

My friend John Ziegler, who produced the documentary

Media Malpractice: How Obama Got Elected,[5] was able to get Sarah Palin to talk about how the media had covered her campaign. Many of her comments supported the conservative perception of bias in mainstream media today. Ziegler himself said, "I think this woman was assassinated by the media." In this exclusive interview, Palin described the media reporting of her family as "very scary."

When CBS's Katie Couric asked Palin what publications she reads, the governor interpreted Couric's question, she later told Ziegler, as "Do you read, what do you guys do up there?" She was offended. She also took a swipe at Couric stating, "Katie, you're not the center of everyone's universe." The governor said her press office is still getting questions asking if she is really the mother of her infant son Trig and she said it was "absurd and frustrating" that she isn't believed.

Palin was also critical of Internet bloggers who often claim to be credible news sources. "When did we start accepting as hard-news sources, bloggers, anonymous bloggers especially? It's a sad state of affairs in the world of the media today, mainstream media especially, that they're going to rely on bloggers, anonymous bloggers, for their hard-news information." Sarah knows something about reporting from her days in television.

Palin also bristles at news media accounts suggesting her daughter Bristol and Bristol's fiancé are "high school dropouts and they're going to just look for government handouts to raise their child and stuff; nothing could be further from the truth. And I've asked some in the media to correct that, and they haven't corrected it, and that gets frustrating."

The governor was also critical of actress Tina Fey. When Ziegler showed a clip of Fey saying, "I believe marriage is meant to be a sacred institution between two unwilling teenagers," Palin responded, "Cool, fine, come attack me, but when you make a suggestion like that—that attacks a kid, that kills me."

Left-wing media bias against conservatives is rampant. Liberals are frustrated that they haven't yet shut down conservative talk, Sarah Palin's only media friend in 2008.

The Center for Media and Public Affairs at George Mason University also found liberal bias in the 2008 presidential campaign. In a press release issued October 30, 2008, CMPA stated the following:

> *Coverage of the presidential election on CBS and NBC strongly favors the Democratic presidential ticket, while the coverage on ABC and FOX is more balanced, according to a new study by the Center for Media and Public Affairs (CMPA). The study finds that the three broadcast networks combined have given twice as much good press to the Democratic presidential and vice-presidential candidates as they have to the Republicans, and only FOX has given better press to the GOP ticket than to the Democrats.*[6]

The Center for Media and Public Affairs examined nearly a thousand news stories broadcast from August 23 to October 24, 2008.

Former NBC anchor Tom Brokaw is one of the media elite and is highly critical of conservative talk radio. He issued these fighting words at the National Press Club in 2003: "Radio stations have become instantly jingoistic and savagely critical of any questions raised about any decisions leading up to, for example, the war in Iraq, motivated not by ideological or intellectual passions, but by the raw commercial possibilities of creating a mob mentality."[7]

On Laura Ingraham's highly respected Talk Radio Network show on November 26, 2007, Brokaw was promoting his sixties book *Boom* when he showed typical mainstream news anchor dismay about conservative talk radio. Here is a partial transcript:[8]

Ingraham: I just resent the whole, you mention Rush Limbaugh in the book, you [have] kind of a throw-away line about Limbaugh and it's in the Drug section, and without a doubt, Rush Limbaugh is the most influential boomer, I think, in the media today. There is no person who has had more of a profound impact on the way people think about politics than Limbaugh, and he gets a line in kind of the Drug thing. And I just, don't think that's right.

Brokaw: My problem with the whole spectrum [of talk radio] is that there is not, you know what Rush's, what his whole drill is. He doesn't want to hear another point of view. Except his. That's my issue.

Ingraham: Oh, I disagree. He talks to all sorts of people. Well, he doesn't interview people like I do, I mean, I have guests on.

Brokaw: He doesn't interview people, and he mocks people on . . .

Ingraham: But he's not an objective person. He doesn't say he is. That's the difference between him and anchors on some of our networks who have a political agenda, but then pretend that they're objective.

Later in the interview, Brokaw stated, "My problem with talk radio is they only want to hear one note. . . . My problem with talk radio is they mock anyone else's point of view, and they do it often in a mindless fashion. You know that—as well as I do. Because it's a hot button for the choir that's listening to them, and it works for them commercially."

But hooray for Laura for pointing out that conservative talk show hosts don't pretend to be objective, unlike the many news anchors on network television today.

And, a week after the election, a Zogby poll conducted for Ziegler[9] found evidence that suggested overt media bias in the election. It found those voters easily remembered negative coverage of McCain/Palin but struggled to correctly answer questions about coverage associated with Obama/Biden. The poll questioned 512 Obama voters. Here are the results:

- 57.4% could NOT correctly say which party controls Congress.
- 71.8% could NOT correctly say Joe Biden quit a previous campaign because of plagiarism.
- 82.6% could NOT correctly say that Barack Obama won his first election by getting opponents kicked off the ballot.
- 88.4% could NOT correctly say that Obama said his policies would likely bankrupt the coal industry and make energy rates skyrocket.
- 56.1% could NOT correctly say Obama started his political career at the home of two former members of the Weather Underground.

On the other hand, these Obama voters could remember a lot about McCain/Palin:

- Only 13.7% FAILED to identify Sarah Palin as the person on which their party spent $150,000 in clothes.

- Only 6.2% FAILED to identify Palin as the one with the pregnant teenage daughter.
- And 86.9% thought that Palin said that she could see Russia from her house, even though it was Tina Fey who said that on the television show *Saturday Night Live*.

As you would guess, Ziegler was instantly taken to the woodshed by the left, who suggested he should have done the same quick poll of McCain voters. John released this reply:

> *Many critics who are obsessed with this issue are totally missing the point of the entire project. I was not trying to prove that Obama voters are dumber or less informed than those who voted for McCain. I only polled Obama voters because I was trying to test the media's impact on the election. Since Obama won, it would be pointless (not to mention twice as expensive) to poll McCain voters.*[10]

And why were there no real conservatives serving as moderators in the presidential debates? It will be a cold day in hell when the likes of Bill O'Reilly, Sean Hannity, or Rush Limbaugh are selected to moderate a presidential debate, but it's okay for CBS, NBC, and PBS to have their personalities chosen to moderate—and choose the questions for—these critical events. Again, conservatives are shut out, providing yet another reason why there is no need to restrict the reach of conservative media.

With bias against conservatives becoming more pronounced, Fox News Channel—universally hated by liberals—has won many ratings battles. And it all started with conservative talk radio paving the way for much of the success of Fox News by building an audience that was eager for a conservative television news source. Liberal Democrats know that conservative talk radio has changed the media landscape, and they would be happy to shut it down with new censorship regulations. Now some Democrats are also targeting cable television.

Democrat Congresswoman Anna Eshoo of California is widely quoted as saying she would restore the Fairness Doctrine, and even take it one step further. She would apply regulations to cable and satellite programming, not just over-the-air radio and television. This is upsetting news to those who think government should have no role in deciding program content for the media. Such a move would set freedom of speech back dramatically, and it would eventually eliminate conservative political commentary from the media.

Left-wing pundits continually try to make talk radio seem bigger than it is. Talk radio comprises only one-sixth of the radio stations in America, and a significant number of those stations are liberal NPR affiliates. Considering that there are thousands of sources of information available, talk radio is small by comparison. Its power stems from the fact that it is the most important medium conservatives have available to provide them with a voice.

As Doug McIntyre, morning host at KABC Radio in Los Angeles, observes:

"The pro–Fairness Doctrine crowd has turned conservative talk radio into a hydra-headed monster of remarkable power. The reality is very different. If we're so powerful, how did Bill Clinton win two terms? How did the Democrats take the House and the Senate in 2006? How did Barack Obama beat John McCain in 2008? The reality is talk radio is just one component of an enormously diverse national discussion. It's not nearly as powerful as its enemies or some of its biggest stars think." [11]

> *I know a lot of you believe that most people in the news business are liberal. Let me tell you, I know a lot of them, and they were almost evenly divided this time. Half of them liked Senator Kerry; the other half hated President Bush.*
> —ANDY ROONEY, *60 MINUTES,* NOVEMBER 7, 2004

STRAIGHT AHEAD: Historic media bias and the rise of conservative talk radio.

CHAPTER 16

The Birth of Talk Radio

The Origins of Conservative Talk

If you want to be a good journalist, you don't need to gradu-ate from journalism school. In fact, if you want to be a great journalist, don't even consider going to a journalism school. Consider getting a degree in life experience. Consider get-ting a degree in the workings of government. Consider law school, but forget journalism school. Good journalism is common sense. What journalists need is a general knowl-edge of where to go for information and how to get it, and a desire to share critical information with the American public.

Lars Larson, who hosts a nationally syndicated radio show heard on 150 stations, was an investigative reporter before turning talk show host. He never went to journalism school; in fact, he doesn't mind sharing that he's a college dropout. But he's won numerous Emmy Awards and the prestigious Peabody Award for his journalistic excellence.

Lars shares his thoughts on why there seems to be increas-ing left-leaning bias in mainstream media:

*Journalists for the most part get their training in uni-
versities populated with liberal professors. That doesn't
guarantee liberalism in the freshly minted reporter, but it
augurs in that direction. Add to that the fact that when
you are a student doing a lot of writing for your professor
and are dependent on his good grades and favorable en-
dorsement for your career, and you can see how it influ-
ences those that come out of J-schools.*

Larson continues,

*Then add in the fact that journalism, which for hundreds
of years was a trade, is now a highly paid profession. That
high pay means you will likely find your friends and asso-
ciates outside of journalism in other university-educated,
well-compensated professions. Writing stories about the
debilitating effect of government social programs, the
importance of individual gun rights, or the desirability
of capitalism isn't likely to impress your journalist colleagues, your professors, or your friends. It's one reason
that when surveys are done, no one is surprised that some
surveys show more than ninety percent of journalists are
registered Democrats.*[1]

I never went to a journalism school, either, but I had
the privilege of leading one of the Pacific Northwest's leading radio news departments and—alongside my late friend
and colleague Jeff Grimes—anchored a morning news show
for more than fifteen years. With the help of many great
radio journalists, the station was honored with more than
two hundred local, regional, and national journalism awards,
including the DuPont Award—radio's version of the Pulitzer
Prize—from Columbia University. But working in a journalis-

tic environment during the era of the Fairness Doctrine, I still felt that my right to express myself was constrained.

When I had the opportunity to move from the news studio to the talk studio and programming chair, I did. Talk radio eventually allowed me to come out of the journalistic closet and speak freely, openly, and with opinion. For years as a news reporter and radio anchor, I felt there was so much more to the story that I wasn't allowed to tell. I wanted to be unleashed to share that information, and to address controversial matters, because it would better serve the public interest.

I also experienced a strong liberal media bias against conservatives like myself. Part of that bias was a result of the system that fed news stories to us. For years the Associated Press has been one of the leading sources, if not *the* leading source, of news for radio stations nationwide. Individual radio stations, for the most part, were not able to hire enough reporters to adequately cover the news, so they depended on the AP wire service for much of their news content. Where did the AP get its news? Newspapers supply the majority of stories used by the AP, which were then sent to affiliated radio and television partners over the now-antiquated teletype machine. We then read those news reports, almost verbatim, into our microphones. The news reporters—journalists—claimed objectivity, but nothing is ever totally objective.

Every news story you hear, read, or watch is filtered through the reporters' views and experiences. Those reporters may strive for objectivity, but it isn't possible to achieve. One of the biggest complaints I dealt with on an ongoing basis was story bias. News writers were trained in journalism schools by liberal professors, and that bias bleeds through the system and out through your radio speakers every day, providing yet another reason to preserve free talk radio as a balancing factor.

Conservative political commentary on talk radio *is* the balance . . . one of the few places where you can hear an alternative point of view to the information that is passed through the system to mainstream news outlets nationwide. Our medium must be defended against the powerful Democrats who want to control the content of your radio programs. Without conservative talk radio, you would have one less advocate speaking out to defend your political, economic, and civil liberties.

Between 1965 and the present there have been more Republicans in the White House than Democrats. If reporters had their way, there would have been only Democrats in the White House.

A Media Research Center (MRC) survey titled "Special Report—The Liberal Media Exposed"[2] shows that the vast majority of journalists interviewed have voted for the Democrat presidential candidate since 1965. The MRC is headquartered in Alexandria, Virginia, and issues reports on the political state of the news media. The MRC Mission statement reads as follows:

"The mission of the Media Research Center is to bring balance and responsibility to the news media. Leaders of America's conservative movement have long believed that within the national news media a strident liberal bias existed that influenced the public's understanding of critical issues. On October 1, 1987, a group of young determined conservatives set out to not only prove—through sound scientific research—that liberal bias in the media does exist and undermines traditional American values, but also to neutralize its impact on the American political scene. What they launched that fall is the now acclaimed Media Research Center."

Former CBS reporter Bernard Goldberg is quoted as saying, "The Media Research Center folks don't give the media hell; they just tell the truth and the media thinks it's hell." The MRC report claims that most White House reporters show a strong liberal bias.

The Center for Media and Public Affairs commissioned a poll in 1996 showing that even the left sees liberal bias in the mainstream media. The report states, in part: "These findings challenge the argument of some journalists that bias is purely in the eye of the beholder. Although conservatives are three times more likely to see liberal rather than conservative bias, moderates and liberals alike see liberal bias in the media twice as often as they see conservative bias."[3]

Here are the key findings of the survey:

- "Majorities of all major groups in the population, including 70 percent of self-described liberals, now see a 'fair amount' or 'great deal' of bias in the news. In general, perceptions of bias rise along with levels of education and political participation."
- "Those who see a liberal tilt outnumber those who detect a conservative bias by more than a two to one margin. Forty-three percent describe the news media's perspective on politics as liberal, compared to 33 percent who see it as middle of the road, and 19 percent who find it to be conservative."
- "Even self-described liberals agree: 41 percent see the media as liberal, compared to only 22 percent who find the news to be conservative."

These reports are lauded by conservatives and scorned by liberals who have their own centers to disseminate "the truth" about conservative media. Media Matters is one of those organizations, and it is universally scorned by conservative political commentators. But the MRC and CMPA reports seem to confirm what conservatives have felt for decades, and it affirms their need for a voice. It speaks to the telephone calls I would get as a programmer at the very liberal KING 1090 in Seattle twenty years ago, when not one day went by without a conservative listener calling to beg me to put "just one conservative show" on the radio station.

When the Fairness Doctrine was repealed in 1987, that door was opened. Conservatives finally got their wish. At last they felt they had a voice to fight back against the liberal bias in the way news is disseminated in the United States and the way journalists are trained at universities nationwide. If the Fairness Doctrine is ever reimplemented, perhaps it should also apply to our colleges and universities. An equal balance between conservative and liberal professors who guide and educate our youth might seem fair.

Al Peterson, who writes his daily newsletter to the news, talk, and sports radio industry, points out, "If journalism schools could become places where people really were taught good ethical standards and a sense of fairness and unbiased balance, they'd be OK—but I don't see that to be the case based on the product they generally produce."[4]

Peterson sees a need for standards in journalism: "In today's world almost anyone with a keyboard and an Internet connection can become a 'journalist' and that's not all good either."

> *In America the president reigns for four years,*
> *and journalism governs for ever and ever.*
> —OSCAR WILDE, AUTHOR

STRAIGHT AHEAD: Constitution Day. Do you know the date?

CHAPTER 17

Constitution Day

A Celebration of Personal Freedom

September 17, 1787. Very few people know or remember the significance of the date. On that day long ago, a majority of our Founding Fathers placed their signatures on a document that would change the course of political history. The Constitution of the United States of America—only four handwritten pages long—provides the guidelines for the greatest form of government in the history of mankind.

The first and arguably the most important amendment to our Constitution was added later because Americans demanded assurance that their basic freedoms would be protected. The Bill of Rights—the first ten amendments to the Constitution—was ratified on December 15, 1791, to protect American citizens from abuse of power by the federal government. The First Amendment, in just forty-five words written by James Madison and his collaborators, guarantees us freedom of speech, freedom of the press, freedom of religion, the right to peaceably assemble, and the right to petition the government. Without these freedoms we could not be an open society.

Unfortunately, we take our freedoms for granted, and we pay little homage to those visionaries who made them possible. The Constitution of the United States of America must not be taken for granted, or else we stand to lose gradually the rights that distinguish our quality of life from that of most other people on the planet. The changes in today's political climate should send a shiver of fear through every American who cherishes the right to express himself openly without fear of reprisal.

One organization that does not take our Constitution lightly is the First Amendment Center,[1] which works to preserve the freedoms guaranteed by that first item in our Bill of Rights. The center has offices at Vanderbilt University in Nashville, Tennessee, and in Washington, D.C., and it is also associated with the Newseum in Washington, D.C., which is a must-visit for anyone touring our nation's capital.

Gene Policinski, vice president and executive director of the First Amendment Center, has noted that "the founders knew government as an often-restrictive authority or even repressive tyrant when it came to free expression, not as a benevolent protector or neutral arbiter—and certainly not as the free-speech equivalent of a favorite uncle. That hard-won, Colonial-era knowledge seems to have been lost to many in this latest generation of Americans, who would turn over to government officials what ought to be the task of every free individual—considering and measuring ideas that challenge, provoke, excite, or even incite."[2]

Each year, just before the anniversary of the signing of the U.S. Constitution, the First Amendment Center conducts a survey on the state of the First Amendment. In its 2008 survey were some findings that should be of concern to those who champion freedom of expression. In a news release, the center stated, "Sizeable numbers of Americans are unable to name their basic freedoms but would accept government limits on some of them."

Here are the results of the center's survey of 1,005 respondents, conducted by telephone between July 23 and August 3, 2008:

- 39 percent would extend to subscription cable and satellite television the government's current authority to regulate content on over-the-air broadcast television.
- 66 percent say the government should be able to require television broadcasters to offer an equal allotment of time to conservative and liberal broadcasters; 62 percent would apply that same requirement to newspapers, which never have had content regulated by the government.
- 31 percent would not permit musicians to sing songs with lyrics that others might find offensive.

The fact that 62 percent of those surveyed would choose to apply government controls to newspapers would mystify the brave patriots who signed the Constitution.[3]

Brian Buchanan, managing editor of First Amendment Center Online, writes, "Without the First Amendment, religious minorities could be persecuted, the government might well establish a national religion, protesters could be silenced, the press could not criticize government, and citizens could not mobilize for social change."

Contrary to the freedoms supposedly guaranteed by our Constitution, Senate Majority Whip Richard Durbin—

another Democrat from Illinois and a close ally of Barack Obama—said he favors restoring the Fairness Doctrine. He shares the viewpoint of other party elders who feel that balanced programming leads to better informed decisions at the ballot box. At first blush, this viewpoint sounds very positive. But why can't a citizen choose to access several different sources of information rather than having government mandate that each and every individual program must state all points of view?

A growing number of Americans fear that the overwhelmingly left-leaning results of the 2008 election have set the stage for a full-scale attack on broadcasters . . . especially on conservative talk radio. In NTS MediaOnline, the daily newsletter for talk stations nationwide, Al Peterson interviewed one of the newest syndicated talk sensations, who says he has a thick file on the Fairness Doctrine. His name is Todd Schnitt and he is quoted as saying, "I think it's scary and clearly an attempt to suppress free speech. I would imagine if it is reinstated, it will ultimately end up being challenged in the Supreme Court." Schnitt also told Peterson, "Senate Leader Harry Reid and House Speaker Nancy Pelosi have both said they want it. I think they really want to get back at talk radio. It's personal for them."[4]

Dave Elswick is a close friend and radio colleague headquartered in Little Rock, Arkansas. He programs news/talk station KARN AM/FM, a market ratings leader, and he hosts a conservative talk show in the afternoon. Elswick is a freedom fighter. He believes passionately in the rights guaranteed by our Constitution, which he has studied thoroughly. Elswick has a clear understanding of what is at stake in this fight. "The Fairness Doctrine perhaps played a part in radio at one time when there were just a handful of stations nationwide. Now there are thousands, all offering different programming and points of view while allowing listeners to chime in as well. On top of this, there is the Internet, where a huge amount of information and opinion is heard every day. Couple all that with TV, newspapers, and magazines, and the average American has more options open to him/her for information and opinion than at any time in this nation's history."[5]

Elswick feels that Democrats have a personal vendetta against conservative talk radio. "The Democrats, and some Republicans, just have heartburn because talk radio has been a burr under their saddle; a thorn in their side. We are the pamphleteers of the Revolutionary times alive and working today. We are the voices that have the audacity to challenge their view. I believe if they try to reimpose the Fairness Doctrine, the s**t storm they unleash upon themselves will make the immigration battle of 2007 look like Rebecca at Sunnybrook Farm. Long live the freedom of speech."

As Elswick notes, there are thousands of sources for information today that didn't exist when the Fairness Doctrine became a regulation controlling content of radio and television programs in 1949. With Obama in the White House, there is new leadership and Democrat control of the Federal Communications Commission that leans toward diversity in programming and media ownership. Matt Lloyd keeps an eye on the issue for Congressman Mike Pence of Indiana and says, "Since the appointments to the FCC are done at the direction of the President, and a majority of the commissioners can be members of the majority party, that indicates the FCC will be more likely to cater to the desires of the liberal left wing of the Democratic Party, which could be dangerous for those of us worried about the re-imposition of the Fairness Doctrine. One can only imagine that in a world where the content of our radio airwaves is controlled, it would not be a far stretch to begin to limit freedoms in other media outlets."[6]

Such an affront would surely result in a strong voice of opposition from the graves of those great American patriots who signed the U.S. Constitution.

> *The U.S. Constitution doesn't guarantee happiness,*
> *only the pursuit of it. You have to catch up with it yourself.*
> —BENJAMIN FRANKLIN

STRAIGHT AHEAD: Legislation both for and against the Fairness Doctrine.

CHAPTER 18

Congress Weighs In

Legislation For and Against Censorship

In recent years, Democrats have been complaining about the conservative monopoly on talk radio, and they would like to restore media content constraints. For decades conservatives have suffered under a dominance of pro-liberal media bias, but they haven't advocated constraints on those liberal messages. As noted in an earlier chapter, the repeal of the Fairness Doctrine resulted in an explosion of the number of talk radio stations nationwide. The pent-up demand for conservative views in the national dialogue mushroomed with repeal of the doctrine, and free expression by radio broadcasters flourished. But the end may be near.

One of the liberals who would like to suppress conservative political commentary on the radio is New York Democrat Congressman Maurice Hinchey, who sponsored the Media Ownership Reform Act. So far, the legislation has gotten nowhere, but—with the national vote for "change"—there are renewed calls for "balanced" radio programming. If you value conservative talk radio, now is the time to speak up.

When Hinchey's bill first came to light, he insisted his legislation would insure that different points of view would be heard. He asserted that listeners were prevented from getting the "right" information to make better decisions. He was upset that Democrats weren't fully in control in Washington. Since Democrats have picked up a substantial number of seats in the House and Senate, as well as winning the White House in the last election, talk radio fans have no reason to trust Hinchey. His intent is to kill conservative talk radio as we know it. Hinchey wants to restore program balance and other restrictions against conservative voices on the radio.

At a press conference in June, 2003, Hinchey stated the following: "The FCC has abandoned its responsibility to protect the public interest. Starting with the Reagan Administration's elimination of the Fairness Doctrine and culminating with the establishment this week of the Powell [Michael Powell, former chairman of the FCC] rules, big media corporations and their allies have succeeded in gradually pushing aside the public interest in favor of big profits. There is clearly a great deal of support for reversing the decision made by Chairman Powell and his two Republican colleagues."[1]

In this news conference over five years ago, Hinchey signaled the change Democrats have been seeking, calling it a "vital" step: "To fully restore the right of the public to have a say in the information and entertainment it has access to, we need to undo all the previous damage that's been done over the last several years. Congress has recognized that the airwaves belong to the public and that those who use them have a responsibility to serve the public interest. The process began in earnest during the Presidency of Ronald Reagan when his handpicked FCC chairman successfully fought to eliminate the Fairness Doctrine, which required that a broadcaster give equal time to opposing points of view."

Hinchey railed about the fact that a handful of radio companies own a majority of America's stations, and he concludes, "The public airwaves belong to the public, not the media elites." This is a strong message to broadcasters, especially conservative broadcasters, who fear censorship.

Congressman Mike Pence understands what is at stake in this fight. As a former broadcaster, Pence introduced legislation to ban the Fairness Doctrine. But at this writing and for nearly two years, House Speaker Nancy Pelosi of California has refused to allow his bill from reaching the floor for a vote, because many Democrats favor restoring restrictions on conservative broadcasters. If and when they act, it will be in favor of censorship of conservative views.

Frustrated by Democrats blocking his efforts, Pence issued this public statement: "I introduced the Broadcaster Freedom Act, which would permanently ban the 'Fairness Doctrine' from ever coming back. And so far, not one single House Democrat has signed our petition for an up-or-down vote on broadcast freedom . . . and now we know why. Asked yesterday if she supported reviving the Fairness Doctrine, Speaker Pelosi replied 'yes.' She told a meeting at the Christian Science Monitor that the legislation wouldn't receive a vote because 'the interest in my caucus is the reverse.'"[2]

Pence also stated: "I say to Speaker Pelosi with respect: Defending freedom is the paramount interest of every Member of the American Congress. I urge my Democrat colleagues to take a stand for freedom. Oppose the Democrat leadership's plan to censor the airwaves of American talk radio and American Christian radio."

Pence's frustration was shared by the co-sponsor of the Broadcaster Freedom Act, Congressman Greg Walden—and Oregon's lone Republican in Washington DC—who suggested restoration of the Fairness Doctrine or similar efforts to reregulate the airwaves to force balanced programming on stations was a Democrat Party plank in their platform.

A review of the recent history of the Democratic platform seems to validate that concern. The Democrats' 2000 platform called for a return of the Fairness Doctrine. The 2004 Democrat nominee, John Kerry, clearly wanted to reinstate the Fairness Doctrine. By 2008, powerful Democrats were planning a feeding frenzy on conservative talk radio, but the language was changed to accomplish the same goals by promoting a slightly different version of the Democrat mission: "We will encourage diversity in the ownership of broadcast media, promote the development of new media outlets for expression of diverse viewpoints, and clarify the public interest obligations of broadcasters who occupy the nation's spectrum." To conservatives, these are code words for introduction of what is essentially a new Fairness Doctrine. It's a backdoor approach to censoring conservative talk radio.[3]

Finally, on February 26, 2009, the Senate took action and voted to ban the Fairness Doctrine, but only because Democrats forced another amendment to accomplish the stated goal of their platform to put a noose around conservative talk radio's neck. Senate Democrats were willing to vote out the Fairness Doctrine for a new one that accomplishes the same goals. It was introduced by Senator Richard Durbin from the president's home state of Illinois. The language sounds very similar to the party's platform: "To encourage and promote diversity in communication media ownership and to ensure that the public airwaves are used in the public interest."[4]

Senator Jim DeMint (R-S.C.) said of the amendment, "Senator Durbin's amendment exposed Democrat intentions to impose radio censorship through the back door, using vague regulations dealing with media ownership." DeMint also said, "All eyes are now on the FCC. If they attempt to shut down free speech indirectly, we will fight to stop them."[5]

Writing for Newsbusters, an arm of the Media Research Center, the conservative watchdog of liberal media, Communications Director Seton Motley wrote, "Liberal censors are now traveling alternative routes to reach their original destination—silencing political speech on the airwaves." Motley writes that the Obama FCC would be able to interpret this vague language any way they want, and certainly not in favor of conservatives. "And the worst part of the Durbin amendment is the possibility that President Barack Obama's FCC may now be empowered to prematurely pull the broadcast licenses of radio stations they deem as failing to meet these new "Fairness" Doctrine–esque guidelines."[6]

House Speaker Pelosi, who favors the Fairness Doctrine, was asked if she supports the Durbin Amendment. "Certainly, I support Mr. Durbin in most things," she said, then added, "Diversity in media ownership is very, very, important." Congressman Pence responded: "It's clear to me that Democrats, having failed in their frontal assault on talk radio in America through the Fairness Doctrine, are now shifting strategy to a form of regulation that is essentially the Fairness Doctrine by stealth. It should come as little surprise that Speaker Pelosi, who openly supports returning the Fairness Doctrine to the airwaves of America, would support a new version of it."[7]

What is clear is that Democrats have finally taken action on their plan and have come forward with their stated intentions that spell disaster for conservative talk radio and for free speech in the marketplace of America. The *new* Fairness Doctrine has been exposed. The emperor is wearing new clothes.

> *How is it possible to present an issue without also discussing its pros, cons, promoters, and detractors? We do that every day anyway. My fear is that if the Fairness Doctrine is resurrected in a new and improved version, we couldn't spend five minutes talking about how bad Hitler was without allowing five minutes for someone who holds the opposite opinion. Come to think of it, we already do that, too.*
> —CHRIS WALTON, KBOI, BOISE

STRAIGHT AHEAD: A totalitarian media?

CHAPTER 19

The Digital Explosion

How the Internet Makes the Fairness Doctrine Obsolete

There is an obvious misunderstanding among liberals of the role that talk radio plays in American media.

Talk radio—specifically, conservative political commentary—works because it has an audience. It's the law of supply and demand. Americans don't have to listen, but they do.

Since the repeal of the Fairness Doctrine by the FCC the far left rails that conservative talk radio is too dominant, and they feel government should legislate more balance on America's airwaves. Some even suggest that conservative political commentary resembles what one would hear in a totalitarian regime where government closely controls radio content. This is a gross misunderstanding and a blatant attack on conservatives. Just travel to some of those non-democratic countries and listen to their programs. You certainly won't hear ordinary citizens on the radio criticizing their leaders. Talk radio is unique in the world, and its brand of free expression must be preserved. It is worth fighting for, and the fight is on.

Even in America—although we are guaranteed the right

by the First Amendment—there was little criticism of government heard on the radio prior to the repeal of the Fairness Doctrine. Americans didn't have a collective voice.

But there is no scarcity now of opinion and dialogue in the media. In fact, Americans can choose from well over 13,000 radio stations, including hundreds of left-leaning National Public Radio stations. We have a choice of more than 1,400 newspapers, more than a dozen daily network television news and talk shows, at least ten separate twenty-four hour cable news public affairs channels, countless magazines, and the Internet. The Internet in particular has changed the face of communication and dissemination of information on our planet. By itself, it renders the Fairness Doctrine argument moot by offering thousands of liberal and conservative sources of information at the click of a mouse.

And soon Americans will have even more audio sources than ever before! Mike Edwards, who programs talk radio station WTMA in Charleston, South Carolina, points out that consumer choices for information are about to explode . . . that Internet access will be infinite because of Wi-Fi technology, which will provide users with wireless, high-speed Internet connections over radio waves almost everywhere they go. Mike says, "National Wi-Fi means users will have an infinite number of listening choices in their cars and on cell phones. So we need to make sure that our website and over the air [radio] brands are their favorites so they'll keep surfing back to our local site when that times comes."[1]

Brian Westbrook is a tech expert for Newsradio 750 KXL in Portland, Oregon. He is a frequent contributor to television and radio programs covering technology, Web trends, and consumer electronics. Brian adds, "The availability of Wi-Fi has expanded beyond coffee shops, businesses, and residential homes to previously disconnected transportation options such as trains, automobiles, even airplanes. The Web-enabled car is possible now, and will only become more practical in the coming months."[2]

As vice president and managing editor for *Talkers*, Kevin Casey keeps close tabs on how the Internet is changing media consumption by Americans. He and others like him agree that "over the last fifteen years the Internet has become a legitimate and ubiquitous medium that is threatening the dominance traditional news and information outlets have enjoyed for the better part of the past fifty years."[3]

Casey continues, "Not only has the Internet become the 'cool' medium, its ability to function without archaic government-mandated regulations makes it more relevant in the less stodgy culture of contemporary America." And, Casey points out a specific impact will be felt on talk radio: "The Internet threatens to become the choice of younger Americans when it comes to all forms of communication—video, audio, and print—as it becomes easier to obtain outside the home or office and most especially in automobiles. Spoken-word communication via the Internet will develop into a beast quite different than what we think of as 'talk radio' in 2009. Operating in a universe without rules and catering to a youth-centered culture, it will break the mold that we think of as talk radio and open doors to untold varieties of subjects, interests, and disciplines."

We've already seen an array of choice in our cars. Not only can we access our favorite talk station on the AM or FM band, but we have satellite radio, which is providing us with hundreds of alternatives for information, news, and music. Edwards concurs: "The Net has and will continue to significantly shape the media landscape. Newspapers are either going out of business *or* they've changed their delivery platform from paper to website; many have already hired videographers and webmasters instead of beat reporters. Television is able to offer double their local news content with exclusive video streaming on their sites of stories that might not normally make it on the six o'clock news."

The six o'clock news itself is becoming more irrelevant thanks to the rapidly expanding choices for information. According to the nonpartisan Pew Research Center's Internet & American Life Project in Washington, D.C., growing numbers of Americans are using the Internet to search for political commentary today. In its June 15, 2008, report "The Internet and 2008 Election,"[4] researchers stated that the percentage of Americans using the Internet for politics has hit record levels. The Pew study found that "a record-breaking 46% of Americans have used the Internet, email or cell phone text messaging to get news about the campaign, share their views, and mobilize others." The researchers also noted that "40% of all Americans (Internet users and non-users alike) have gotten news and information about this year's campaign via the Internet." Furthermore, "A significant number of voters are also using the Internet to gain access to campaign events and primary documents. Some 39% of online Americans have used the Internet to access 'unfiltered' campaign materials, which includes video of candidate debates, speeches, and announcements, as well as position papers and speech transcripts." Pew Internet Project Research Specialist Aaron Smith, who helped write the report, stated "Many voters are now using the Internet to move past traditional media gatekeepers to gain their own view of the candidates and the campaign. This shows the appetite of engaged citizens to move beyond the sound-bite culture and make their own assessments of the meaning of political developments."

The survey was conducted between April 8 and May 11, 2008, and found that younger voters were more active on the Internet and that "Democrats and Obama supporters had taken the lead in their use of online tools for political engagement":

- 74% of wired Obama supporters have gotten political news and information online, compared with 57% of online Clinton supporters.
- In a head-to-head matchup with Internet users who support Republican McCain, Obama's backers are more likely to get political news and information online (65% vs. 56%).

The survey also found Obama supporters "outpaced both Clinton and McCain supporters in their usage of online video, social networking sites and other online campaign activities."

The Internet explosion makes the argument for a return of content regulations pointless. It also eliminates many of the financial constraints that were a barrier for those wanting to enter the information age. As Kevin Casey notes, "Licenses, printing presses, satellite uplinks, video studios, etc.—long the capital expenditures that made it too costly for most—are gone or at the least greatly diminished with the Internet."

With this technology just upon us, one has to wonder about the true motivations of those who advocate controlling the content of radio and television programming and, specifically, conservative talk radio. The issue must be personal. It *is* personal. The left simply wants to shut up their opposition.

Liberals don't care that they have countless media choices, most of which are dominated by their own political belief system. Nothing would please them more than censoring conservative speech and traditional values in America.

Dan Mason is another strong voice for conservative talk radio. He programs KKOH Radio in Reno, Nevada. Dan argues, "Even if radio was a completely biased source of information (which it is not), the number of alternatives available on the Internet would completely negate any of these bogus concerns. It is this reason the reemergence of discussion about the Fairness Doctrine is so absurd. There is no logical reasoning whereby one can argue that all viewpoints are not being fairly disseminated to the public. No, the only reason any politician would favor a return to the Fairness Doctrine would be for purely self-oriented interests, such as assuring an easy path to reelection by controlling the message of your opposition."[5]

With increased access to the Internet and wireless connections to audio sources in cars, Mason has a warning for radio owners and managers: "What this means for radio is increased competition. The quality of our product as broadcasters must absolutely pass a higher scrutiny than ever before. If we don't offer a product that is compelling and can compete with the large number of other sources that exist, we will certainly disappear into oblivion ourselves."

The Internet also became a vehicle for political persuasion in 2008. The number of political websites and information sources played a significant role in influencing American sentiment during the election. Since the Internet has become the "in" medium for younger users, it has opened up the political process to them so they could participate in a "cool" way. Democrats were especially aware of the Internet's potential to influence public opinion. They won the Internet advantage, and they swept the 2008 election.

In the early 1990s, few Americans were online. Today, most Americans are. The Internet has fast-tracked our ability to work and play. It has fast-tracked our nation's productivity. It has fast-tracked information access, making the debate about a Fairness Doctrine an archaic argument at best. Brian Westbrook says technologies have sped up the spread of information: "With such ready access to Internet-based information, the Fairness Doctrine is obsolete."

Soon when you get into your car you will be able to tune in to media that gives you complete access to the product of free speech—unedited, frank, maybe off-color, unfiltered, but free. You will have access to everything from advice on personal relationships to outdoor wilderness survival. You'll be able to hear commentary from every left-wing group and every right-wing group. Not only will you be able to hear conservative personalities such as Rush Limbaugh and Sean Hannity, you'll also be able to access previously unknown counter-culture audio stations offering any and every point of view conceivable to mankind. Still, many members of Congress are committed to balancing conservative talk radio with a modern Fairness Doctrine dressed in new clothes.

> *Suppose you were an idiot. Suppose you were a member of Congress. But then I repeat myself.*
> —MARK TWAIN, AUTHOR

STRAIGHT AHEAD: An argument for breakdown of media ownership and more diversity on the radio.

CHAPTER 20

Fair & Balanced

Should It Be Legislated?

Stephanie Miller is a well-known syndicated host who is working hard to create a niche for progressive talk shows, and she is truly one of the pioneers of progressive talk radio. She's smart, she works hard, and she's extremely witty. Stephanie is well-liked and respected by her conservative colleagues, including me. I have seen her at many broadcasting events and conventions and have heard her speak about fairness and diversity in radio.

Diversity will be a key buzzword as the new administration assumes control of the FCC, and what liberal groups want is more diverse ownership of radio and other media companies. In July 2007, Miller told Fox News, "I don't want the Fairness Doctrine. What I am interested in is fairness. Why is it there are 90 percent conservative stations and 10 percent progressive?"[1] The main reason is that conservative talk radio has a twenty-year head start and dominant ratings.

While progressive commentators ask why there are so many conservative talk radio stations and so few progressive talk stations, they have an ally that has published a report addressing that question. Their group suggests that a "right-wing conspiracy" keeps liberals off the radio. The left-leaning Center for American Progress, based in Washington, D.C., concludes that the dominance of conservative viewpoints on talk radio is the result of problems in the regulatory system. Along with Free Press, a media watchdog group, the group issued a report on June 21, 2007, titled "The Structural Imbalance of Political Talk Radio,"[2] which immediately caught the attention of conservative radio and big-media companies.

The report contends that a lack of "public interest" requirements from broadcasters—along with a decade of relaxed ownership regulations and massive consolidation of radio stations by a few large companies—has led to the imbalance between conservative and liberal talk radio. The report is accurate in stating that the vast majority of Americans listen to the radio each week, and that talk radio reaches approximately 50 million of those listeners each week. The report is also correct in saying that conservative talk dominates the talk radio format.

The CAP/Free Press report states, "Our analysis in the spring of 2007 of the 257 news/talk stations owned by the top five commercial station owners reveals that 91 percent of the total weekday talk radio programming is conservative, and 9 percent is progressive." The report also states, "The disparities between conservative and progressive programming reflect the absence of localism in American radio markets. This shortfall results from consolidation of ownership in radio stations and the corresponding dominance of syndicated programming operating in economies of scale that do not match the local needs of all communities."

Groups like Center for American Progress and Free Press want to break up large media companies. They hope that more diverse radio ownership will result in less conservative programming and more liberal programs. Many radio programmers don't think that's the case, because even stations owned by minorities, women, and other special interest groups face the reality of returning profit to owners and investors, and they need ratings to do that. They need the top-rated shows which are the conservative shows syndicated by the big-media companies. Even small companies broadcast Limbaugh, Hannity, Levin, Savage, and others because they are highly rated. But, while big-media companies have done well by syndicating conservative talk hosts nationwide, there is one thing they can do better—improve their local newsrooms.

In the view of many, radio consolidation has not been good for your station's ability to report local news. Many media consolidators overpaid when purchasing competing stations, resulting in considerable debt. As publicly held companies, they have an obligation to report profit to Wall Street. Some are fighting for their very financial existence, and the first place to cut expenses is in the local newsroom. Based on the experiences of many radio broadcasters working for large and small owners, smaller owners tend to be more involved in their local communities and are generally willing to invest more into news resources that serve local public interests because they don't have to answer to investors on Wall Street. Years ago, with smaller owners, many radio stations had news departments staffed with several reporters. Today only a few radio stations in each market invest in news—the most basic way to serve in the public interest. But more on that in a bit . . .

The CAP/Free Press report also suggests three ways to restore "more responsive and balanced radio programming" that liberal members of Congress are embracing more openly:

- Restore local and national caps on the ownership of commercial radio stations.
- Ensure greater local accountability over radio licensing. (This would include shortening license renewals from eight to three years.)
- Require commercial owners who fail to abide by enforceable public interest obligations to pay a fee to support public broadcasting.

There's no way commercial broadcasters should have to subsidize public broadcasters. That's robbery. And with the declining value of big-media companies whose stock has plummeted by billions of dollars in the last two years, the notion of "redistributing the wealth" is a pipe dream under any circumstance. Public broadcasting already has a permanent bailout—your tax dollars.

Conservative broadcasters say that the CAP/Free Press report is nothing more than a left-wing attempt to force liberal talk shows onto commercial radio stations. The report also tries to refute arguments that progressive talk shows are poorly rated by presenting evidence that there is a market for liberal talk radio. "It is difficult to argue that the existing audience for talk radio is only interested in hearing one side of public debates, given the diversity of the existing and potential audience."

The fact is that liberal radio network Air America is struggling to win high ratings. Ed Schultz—who is not associated with Air America—is a highly rated progressive talk show host in America and is considered to be the poster boy of liberal talk. But so far Air America programming has not resonated with a majority of listeners.

As a radio programmer, I have tried Air America shows on various stations but they didn't work. It isn't that we are biased against liberal or progressive talk. Ask any radio programmers in the country, and they will tell you that they will air whatever programming produces ratings . . . because the programmer's job is all about ratings, which drive revenue, which dictates the survival of the station. I've often told the program directors I've supervised that I would play polka music backward on the radio if it resulted in high ratings. High ratings equals job security for a radio programmer, and polka music played backward—or even forward—won't produce them.

Michael Harrison is critical of the CAP report,[3] saying, "It proves only that conservative talk radio is dominated by conservatives, a skewed view that takes it out of context with the bigger picture of radio which offers the American listener far more variety." He says the writers of the report "picked more than two hundred stations owned by certain companies and created the impression that's all of talk radio, and that all talk is dominated by conservatives. Where's National Public Radio in the report? Millions and millions of people—some of the biggest audiences in the country—are listening to NPR. It certainly is not conservative, but it certainly is talk."

Harrison also asked, "Where are the urban hosts who almost universally support the Democrats? Where are all those left-leaning shock jocks on FM morning shows? That's talk radio, too."

The vast majority of broadcasters—liberal/progressive or conservative—do not favor regulations to balance radio programming. They want to earn their way rather than legislate their way into the marketplace of ideas. And they want to create that balance through their individual talents and ideas. But there is an open debate about whether or not requiring ownership diversity and more local programs would result in more balance in radio programming. Those issues will be a hot focus of the FCC under President Obama.

Look for liberal representatives in Congress to seize on this report and others like it to further their case for restoring more "balance" to conservative talk radio. Look for a revised Fairness Doctrine—or its equivalent—as part of a broad package to reform radio broadcasting and media ownership in general. Any plan to regulate speech is censorship.

The first Amendment was designed to protect offensive speech, because nobody ever tries to ban the other kind.
—MIKE GODWIN, AUTHOR AND INTERNET LAW SPECIALIST

STRAIGHT AHEAD: Obama's back door.

CHAPTER 21

Grassroots Intimidation

Backdoor Tactics

While on the campaign trail, and again as president, as noted earlier, Barack Obama said he had no interest in restoring the Fairness Doctrine . . . but lately there have been far too many voices shouting support for the regulation. Without question, it's a national issue. Radio broadcasters are rightly concerned that a new Fairness Doctrine could be returned without the approval of our elected representation in Congress.

With a Democrat in the White House, the FCC returns to liberal control with a 3–2 Democrat majority capable of restoring equal-time controls at will. It is apparent that our new president plans to interject his background of grassroots activism into the politics of the new FCC.

The Center for American Progress (CAP), a group critical of conservative talk radio, is also aware that the Fairness Doctrine could be restored without congressional approval. The head of CAP is none other than John Podesta, who served as head of President Obama's transition team.

In its critical report about conservative talk radio, "The

Structural Imbalance of Political Talk Radio,"[1] CAP authors stated, "First, from a regulatory perspective, the Fairness Doctrine was never formally repealed. The FCC did announce in 1987 that it would no longer enforce certain regulations under the umbrella of the Fairness Doctrine, and in 1989 a circuit court upheld the FCC decision." CAP also stated that it does not favor a return of the Fairness Doctrine, and most conservatives following this heated issue know why. There are other "backdoor" ways to achieve the same results, which we will detail coming up. But, again, the Fairness Doctrine is still on the books as a regulation, and Democrats could easily choose to enforce it.

With Democrats occupying a majority of seats on the FCC, the overriding question is this: Will the Obama administration stand by the stated goal not to restore the Fairness Doctrine, or will it cave to the pressures of high-powered Democrat leaders in the House and Senate who wish to restore regulations? If the FCC attempts to reestablish enforcement of this censorship doctrine, it would immediately be challenged in the courts. Restraining orders would be sought so that radio operators could continue with normal operations while the courts, and perhaps the Supreme Court, deliberated.

When the FCC rescinded the regulation in 1987, it stated, "We believe that the role of the electronic press in our society is the same as that of the printed press. Both are sources of information and viewpoint. Accordingly, the reasons for proscribing government intrusion into the editorial discretion of print journalists provide the same basis for proscribing such interference into the editorial discretion of broadcast journalists."[2]

When the Fairness Doctrine was lifted by the Reagan administration, it didn't take long before we figured out what this meant for talk radio and for our ratings. Rush Limbaugh came out of the gate a free man, and his show began lighting up the dial with freewheeling conservative political and ideological dialogue that was also very entertaining. Within a few years after the repeal of the regulation, Limbaugh became a national phenomenon. Because of his huge ratings, stations put his show on the air in ever-increasing numbers. Talk radio had been unleashed.

Being controversial is a plus in talk radio. Polarity works in a free marketplace of ideas where people can choose to listen or not. Everyone has an on/off button on their radio. If the Obama administration chooses to enforce new fairness regulations, it will be a quick strike. Not only will there be court challenges based on the constitutionality of these rules, but it will create new headaches over how the regulations would be enforced.

Consider this statement from talk show host Michael Savage on the Talk Radio Network, following defeat in 2007 of the controversial Immigration Bill, which would have given amnesty to thousands of illegal immigrants: "We have more power than the U.S. Senate and they know it and they're fuming. The liberal bent in the mainstream media more than compensates for conservative dominance of AM talk radio. We're going to have government snitches listening to shows. And, what are they going to do, push a button and then wheel someone into the studio and give their viewpoint?"[3]

Savage's view is echoed by those who value their First Amendment rights. If the Obama administration chooses to silence its opposition, the First Amendment will be tested. This most important amendment to our Constitution was crafted for one purpose—to prevent government from imposing laws that stifle free expression. An assault on this most basic right by reenforcing the Fairness Doctrine would surely be found unconstitutional, wouldn't it?

But there is another way to accomplish the liberal goal of putting a muzzle on conservative talk radio. "Community organizer" was a relatively unfamiliar job title until recently. Then, during the presidential campaign, we repeatedly heard about Barack Obama's experience as a community organizer. We heard it in the debates . . . we saw and heard about it in his campaign ads.

The concept of the community organizer may come to make life miserable for radio broadcasters. Here's how. The new liberal administration knows the challenges that lie ahead in the courts if it attempts to reimpose the regulations of the Fairness Doctrine. The courts would probably find the doctrine unconstitutional . . . or at least we hope they would. So the left is developing a more sinister, backdoor approach to give conservative talk radio operators heartburn and possibly even drive them out of business: intimidation.

Most of us can easily grasp the concept of the Fairness Doctrine and what it does. But "localism," like community organizer, may be a fairly new term for us, and it has been creeping into the fairness discussion more and more. Localism is a concept whereby the FCC, with Democrat control, would again enforce the Federal Communications Act of 1934, which required broadcasters to seek the input of community organizations in programming their stations. Liberals have known about this concept for years and have already begun waging a war of words to build their case.

In an Obama administration, this concept translates into

"community content-advisory boards." It potentially puts these advisory groups in the program director's chair at radio stations all across the country. Such boards would decide what you could hear—and what you couldn't hear—on your radio. For fear of losing their station's license, station managers would be relegated to the role of executing advisory board strategies. It's not a new concept. Back when the Fairness Doctrine was enforced, stations were required to solicit community input from a number of local organizations, and they had to keep a written record on public file. Some stations still do this voluntarily.

The record can be of great value to a broadcaster at license renewal time. If a listener contests the license allocation to the broadcaster, this record can be a major factor in whether or not renewal is granted by the FCC. I kept these ascertainment records for years at KXL Radio in Portland, Oregon, as the station's news director and later operations manager.

Renewed focus on localism by the Obama administration raises community activism to a whole new level. We have seen and documented how the Obama campaign intimidated radio stations for airing opinions contrary to their viewpoint.

Obama's long association with the United Church of Christ could also have an impact on how the FCC regulates radio stations. This church has a long history of political and social activism and even instructs community groups on how to insert themselves into the process of license renewal for their local radio stations.

And liberals are asserting that conservative broadcasters aren't living up to their promise of serving in the public interest by providing balanced programming. When a broadcast license is granted by the FCC, the broadcaster promises to present issues of concern to its local communities. Many expect the Obama administration to put broadcasters—particularly conservative ones—under the microscope on the issue of localism and public service.

Congressman John Boehner of Ohio, Republican leader in the House of Representatives, is alarmed about the localism angle being pushed by liberal Democrats. On June 11, 2008, Boehner wrote a letter to the Honorable Kevin Martin, then chairman of the Federal Communications Commission:

> Under the rubric of "broadcast localism" it is clear that the Commission is proposing no less than a sweeping takeover by Washington bureaucrats of the broadcast media. The proposals and recommendations for Commission action contained in the [Notice of Proposed Rulemaking] amount to stealth enactment of the Fairness Doctrine, a policy designed to squelch the free speech and free expression of specifically targeted audiences.
>
> Forcing licenses to recreate so called "advisory boards" of a by-gone era will encumber broadcast media with onerous bureaucratic burdens not faced by cable, satellite or Internet. The report's assertion these boards would help stations "determine the needs and interests of their communities" or promote "localism and diversity" borders on fantasy. The recreation of pre-1980s advisory boards will place broadcast media squarely on a path toward rationed speech.
>
> Two other proposed rules completely disregard a generation of technological and media advancement . . . [and] suggest the Commission has apparently decided to regulate broadcast media based on the needs of 1934

(the year FCC was created) instead of the proven realities of 2008.

Licensees and stations should serve the needs of local citizens. But adding more restrictions and Washington mandates is retrograde considering the constant technological evolution of the media market. I urge the Commission to rescind these proposed rules.[4]

Thank you, Congressman Boehner, for speaking so eloquently for what we believe!

Conservative radio broadcasters have lined up to fight localism efforts. Some think the concept of advisory boards would provide radical groups with such potential for intimidation that, with the threat of license revocation, the situation would become intolerable. They see forced political correctness, forced program "balance," and new and burdensome reporting requirements. Some even suggest that activist groups would essentially be the police for government regulators. The localism issue remains open for debate and will be a common theme of liberals in the new Administration.

> *Free speech must be just that—free from government influence, interference and censorship.*
> —DAVID REHR, PRESIDENT,
> NATIONAL ASSOCIATION OF BROADCASTERS

STRAIGHT AHEAD: Debunking the myth of the need for balance.

CHAPTER 22
The Myth

The Need for Balance in Broadcasting

As my colleague and friend Dave Elswick at KARN Radio in Little Rock reminds me, perhaps there was a valid reason to have the Fairness Doctrine fifty or sixty years ago when there were far fewer radio stations than today, and when choices of options for obtaining information weren't so plentiful. Constitutionalists argue the hard line, and Elswick makes a strong point. As we have discussed, the need for the return of a new doctrine seems moot in 2009 with the explosion in number of media sources.

In the early days of radio broadcasting, only a few thousand radio signals existed nationwide—and only a few fledgling television stations and networks. Life moved at a leisurely pace. That is not the case today. Now, thanks to new technologies and unprecedented access to information, the average worker can get the amount of work done in one day that it took him a week to finish twenty years ago. It's simply impossible to keep up with the thousands of Internet resources being developed daily.

The argument by liberal backers of the Fairness Doctrine about a scarcity of diverse viewpoints is pure myth. According to the Culture and Media Institute (CMI)—a division of the Media Research Center in Washington, D.C., and a watchdog on liberal media—conservative dominance of talk radio does not distort the national debate about public policy issues. Here are direct highlights of the extensive report—"Unmasking the Myths Behind the Fairness Doctrine"—issued on June 10, 2008:[1]

- Americans have never enjoyed so many professional sources of news and opinion. Americans can choose from a dozen or more daily network television news shows, 10 separate 24/7 cable news and public affairs channels, 1,400 daily newspapers, and more than 2,200 [according to the report] radio stations airing news/talk.
- The Internet has exponentially increased the availability of news sources. Thanks to the Internet, Americans are no longer limited to local media. Any St. Louis resident with a modem can read the *Sacramento Bee* and listen to political talk radio stations in Washington, D.C. The World Wide Web has pushed the number of daily news sources available well into the thousands for anybody with Internet access, and 70 percent or more of Americans are online.
- Only 7 percent of American adults consider radio to be their main source for news and information. Fifty-five percent rely primarily on television news, a ratio of nearly 8 to 1. The Newspaper Association of America says 57 percent of American adults read a newspaper every day.

This report confirms what many of us in radio have known for years. Radio is a very small piece of the overall information and opinion pie. Yet it provides the listener with a powerful collective voice that resonates in Washington, D.C., and raises the ire of influential liberals such as Senators Dianne Feinstein and Harry Reid, along with a growing list of other elected representatives in Congress. The CMI study says that liberals, contrary to their feelings, are not being shut out of the American public policy debate. Six of the top twenty-five commercial talk radio hosts in 2008 were liberal, and NPR, widely considered to lean to the left, has more than eight hundred stations, with a total reach of 14 million listeners.

The CMI special report concludes that the Fairness Doctrine would curtail rather than increase discussion about public policy issues:

- When the Fairness Doctrine was in effect, talk radio avoided controversial topics. Most stations programmed only general talk and advice.
- Politicians repeatedly have used the Fairness Doctrine to chill speech. John F. Kennedy and Lyndon Johnson both used the Fairness Doctrine to stifle criticism, suppress the speech of political adversaries, and force radio stations to provide free time.

The final line of the CMI Executive Summary warns that "as liberals propose and agitate for a resumption of the Fairness Doctrine, history may repeat itself."

Liberal pundits were quick to claim that conservative talk radio has become irrelevant since the Democrat win in the general election of 2008. But these pundits don't keep the right scorecard—the ratings report. The Fall 2008 ratings for conservative talk radio were as strong as ever, and the ratings report is the only scorecard that matters for radio.

Veteran radio talk show host Lars Larson talked about what radio was like before the Fairness Doctrine was revoked by the Reagan administration. "When I worked at KXL 750 in Portland in the early 1980s, I remember we did some talk radio but it was tepid. The difference between then and now is stark. And the general public, no matter what their political belief, wins because it gets the chance to hear both sides of every issue."[2]

Larson talked about a special show he does each Friday. "Every week for the past twelve years on my Northwest show and for the past five years on my Westwood One show, I have done seven hours of 'First Amendment Friday' to remind people of their rights of free speech. Regular callers come in on the main phone lines, while two other lines are set aside for 'naysayers' who go straight to the head of the waiting line with their comments if they disagree with me. To paraphrase, I don't need no stinkin' Fairness Doctrine. I have created my own free from government intrusion or control."

Michael Harrison at *Talkers* concurs. Harrison hosted a show on a Los Angeles radio station in the years prior to revocation of the Fairness Doctrine and states that he avoided opinion and controversy. "I would never say that liberals were good and conservatives were bad, or vice versa. We would talk about, 'Hey all politicians are bad' or 'It's a shame that more people don't vote.' It was more of a superficial approach to politics."[3]

My friend Kipper McGee—a veteran major market radio programmer—echoes similar thoughts. "The marketplace of ideas is more free-flowing than ever before. I believe our Washington guardians will be very hard-pressed to make a compelling case for the Fairness Doctrine in its 'Ward & June' 1950s era incarnation. Back then a market had three or four television stations, and five or six viable radio stations, along with two or three newspapers (at least one of which was frequently co-owned with an AM/FM/TV combo). In that media landscape, it was reasonable to make a strong case for the prospect of monopolistic practices. This could be true in many areas, of which editorial content was just one."[4]

When the FCC voted in 1987 to rescind the Fairness Doctrine, it noted that many broadcasters were avoiding issues that might generate complaints. The commission concluded the doctrine had a "chilling" effect on addressing controversial topics that are now commonplace on talk radio.

Anyone who listens to talk radio hears opposing callers. You hear them on Rush Limbaugh and all the conservative radio shows nationwide. There is more diversity of opinion in American radio and other media—more than ever before in our history, and that will only continue to increase in the years to come. As veteran radio programmer Dan Mason observed from his station, KKOH in Reno, "Add to this explosion of information the fact that you can access it from the palm of your hand! As little as ten years ago most of this was unheard-of. It is for this reason the reemergence of discussion about the Fairness Doctrine is so absurd."[5]

In late 2008, the Media Research Center's Free Speech Alliance launched an online petition drive against what they now call the "Censorship Doctrine." The online petition[6] states: "As Americans, we cannot sit idly by while this gag order on conservative speech is resuscitated. The time to act

is now—so when the time comes, we are mobilized and prepared to defend our Free Speech Rights." They have a goal
of signing 500,000 citizens to "forever end the threat of the
Fairness Doctrine and other attacks on Free Speech." Half
a million e-signatures is a great goal, but tens of millions of
Americans should sign it. And, we need to fight all backdoor
moves to suppress conservative talk.

Evil to some is always good to others.

—JANE AUSTEN, NOVELIST

STRAIGHT AHEAD: Hometown radio.

CHAPTER 23

Hometown Radio

Local vs. Big Media

The media landscape has changed so radically over the years that it resembles little of what it was when the Fairness Doctrine was implemented in 1949. The good news is that we have free speech on the radio, and the government can't dictate what viewpoints we express. No form of the Fairness Doctrine or other means of regulating broadcast content should ever be restored. The bad news is that we no longer address as many of the local issues and needs in our communities, because we have almost no one in the newsroom.

Media consolidation has been a good thing in that it allows the best conservative talk show personalities to be syndicated and heard on a national scale. (Liberals think that's bad, of course.) Local companies are happy to broadcast these programs because in many cases they can't find highly talented personalities in their communities and it's more cost effective for them to air these highly rated syndicated programs.

But as they exist today, local radio stations have little news-gathering presence in their communities when compared to radio newsrooms in the past. It is common criticism by radio news reporters who want their product quality to match that of their stations' talk shows.

For years the commitment to local news on radio has been shrinking. There are no street reporters or beat reporters except at the largest radio stations in America that produce an all-news format, and those stations are few in number. The sense of obligation to truly serve the community of license with local news has diminished significantly in recent years.

In times of economic downturn, many jobs are eliminated. Some of the first employment cuts in the broadcast industry were in the nation's radio newsrooms, and the listener has been the victim. Some news/talk stations have only one news reporter on staff, which is a travesty considering what radio stations should be doing to serve in the public interest.

Local radio newsrooms rarely delve into local problems such as why our schools have low achievement scores, why police aren't responding effectively to crime and drugs in our neighborhoods, or why there aren't better safety standards at our local airports. In-depth or special reports have gone by the wayside. There are few radio features and no documentaries being produced. Gone are the days of fierce competition between newsrooms to be the first on the air with "breaking news" . . . because there is none being reported. When newsworthy events take place in our communities, many radio stations don't even know about them because they don't have news reporters on staff. Smaller radio stations often try to build relationships with television or newspaper partners and "share" news resources, resulting in the same news being broadcast by different media sources when the public deserves to get their information from a wider variety of sources.

This is not to say that stations don't serve in the community interest. Local radio still responds to community needs by raising countless millions of dollars for charities. It calls out to citizens to support blood drives and donations of food, water, and clothing during times of natural disasters. And conservative talk radio is one of the leaders in these endeavors. When radio talk show hosts send an urgent call for response, they get it . . . and listeners are more than willing to dig deep into their pockets or lend a helping hand. Radio's response after 9/11 and Hurricane Katrina clearly served the public interest and helped millions of victims. The company I worked for at the time of Katrina sent huge truckloads of emergency supplies — and millions of dollars in aid — to victims in New Orleans and Baton Rouge. It was a massive relief effort that only a medium like radio could spearhead, and conservative talk radio led that effort. But the current economic climate has resulted in massive staff reductions at many stations, and you as listener will suffer.

According to many, part of the problem is big media. The majority of radio stations in America are owned by only a handful of radio operators. Because some of these radio operators also own networks, many feel this has resulted in a preponderance of syndicated shows being broadcast, sometimes to the exclusion of local programming. Let's explore the potential effect of having more and smaller owners.

Shannon Sweatte is a longtime radio station manager, now retired, who worked in Seattle most of his career. He worked for legendary owners Danny Kaye, Lester M. Smith, and Gene Autry in what were considered the golden days of radio. I also worked for Shannon at KVI in Seattle. He says media consolidation has been bad for the public: "No. Bigger isn't better.

We used to have a lot of good local radio, a lot of creativeness and a lot of great things happened. It's become a 'cookie-cutter' industry now. I hear the same voice, the same program, the same one-liners all across the United States. We've lost the localness of radio. Once in a while I find local radio that is an absolute delight to listen to, but not often."[1]

Sweatte offered his forthright opinion when asked about deregulation, which allowed media companies to consolidate and grow larger. "Deregulation is probably the worst thing that happened to broadcasting. The Communications Act of 1934 was so well written. In exchange for a license, we served the community. We had to promise to run so many hours of news, so many public service announcements and public affairs programming, and we were all involved in the community helping business do well, raising money for charities. That's all gone. Managers right now don't get involved in the community. They can't. They have to worry about getting their stock prices up. I couldn't do it anymore."

The Bush administration FCC chairman Kevin Martin talked about localism and big-media radio operators in January 2009. In an interview with KGO Radio in San Francisco, Martin stated, "Broadcasters' unique asset is the fact that they're providing local news and information to people, and I do think it's important to try to make sure that radio doesn't lose its local feel."[2]

Jerry Del Colliano, who writes a well-read radio blog for *Inside Music Media*, concurs on the localism argument for radio. Early in January 2009, Jerry wrote the following advice for radio professionals: "Play *local* music—lots of it. Do *local* news. Yes, people love news. We all get it on our BlackBerries, iPhones, laptops or whatever. Become involved with the community. Once radio began laying off of what it thinks is corny productions in local markets, they cut the tie between the listeners and their stations. It's so transparent—radio stopped being radio when its leaders got rich in consolidation."[3]

It's ironic that President Bill Clinton signed the Telecommunications Act of 1996, which allowed a surge of media consolidation. Now Democrats want to reverse this course. They view consolidation as a mistake, considering the shape of the radio industry today. Large radio companies with suitcases full of money—with their investors salivating over the prospect of huge profits based on surging advertising revenue and great cash flow—bought stations like they were crack cocaine. A radio company that owned a few stations suddenly owned hundreds—even thousands—of stations. Because they paid exorbitant prices for these stations, they had to find ways of saving money; and employees who served the public interest were usually the first to be cut. As one longtime radio reporter told me, "When we gave up our newsrooms, we gave up the heart and soul of local radio."

One well-documented example occurred in Minot, North Dakota, in the early-morning hours of January 18, 2002.[4] A Canadian Pacific train derailed four miles from the city center. Tanker cars carrying anhydrous ammonia ruptured, and a cloud of poisonous gas quickly spread to residential areas. It was reported to be the largest such spill in U.S. history. Emergency response to the disaster was, in and of itself, a disaster. It was so early in the morning, and there was no one staffing the radio stations. There were no early warnings. Temperatures were subfreezing, and an inversion prevented the noxious cloud from dissipating. The calls to 911 made it clear that radio listeners weren't getting information about the disaster.

One caller said he had the radio on but hadn't heard any news of what had happened or information about what to do.

Clear Channel Communications, the nation's largest radio company, owns six of those Minot stations. They blamed the absence of a broadcast warning on a glitch with the Emergency Alert System and on law enforcement officials who didn't know how to operate it. Still, the stations lacked local news personnel needed to respond to such situations.

Radio newsrooms are in shambles because of media consolidation—with owners paying too much for stations then cutting back on local staffing and programming to maintain profit margins required by Wall Street. It's debatable whether smaller owners would have invested in more personnel to adequately staff these stations, but the anti-consolidation crowd thinks there is a better chance of this happening with more diversity in radio ownership. The one person who died in Minot that morning, and the hundreds who sought emergency medical treatment, would probably agree.

One of the news reporters who was downsized in the early broadcast personnel cuts is Guy Rathbun, who now serves as program director of KCBX, an NPR affiliate in Santa Barbara, California. Rathbun is a strong advocate of restoring diversity in ownership and returning localism to radio. On November 5, 2008, he interviewed Craig Aaron,[5] communications director for Free Press, a media watchdog group with liberal ties that often is critical of big media and conservative talk radio.

Aaron shared the following with Rathbun: "The intent of the Fairness Doctrine was good. It required local television and radio stations using the public airwaves to cover issues of local importance and to have a balance of viewpoints. Sounds like a good idea. The problem with the Fairness Doctrine is that it was very difficult to enforce, so there were a lot of complaints but not a lot of action. It became a tool of one side against the other. So, I don't support re-instating the Fairness Doctrine not because I don't support the goals, but because I think it's the wrong way to go about it."

While Aaron said he supports the intent of the Fairness Doctrine, he gave more specifics about why he does not favor its return. "The one thing that government is not good at, and shouldn't be in the business of, is regulating speech. Not only do I think it is the wrong way to do it, but if you're looking for greater diversity on the airwaves, if you want more voices besides Rush Limbaugh when you drive across the country, the best way to achieve that diversity across the political spectrum and also including smaller stations and new voices is through ownership regulations . . . is through rolling back media consolidation."

The communications director of Free Press also favors development of community radio and low-power FM radio frequencies and "making sure the Internet is a place where we can have free speech."

Many radio professionals, and members of Congress on both sides of the aisle, want to return localism to radio. But the Democrat version of the plan poses the threat of once again censoring conservative political commentary. The liberals' agenda would accomplish their true goal—to restore the regulations of the Fairness Doctrine, cripple conservative talk radio, and force more liberal programming onto the nation's radio stations by having the stations come under the scrutiny of programming advisory boards. Many feel these boards would simply serve as "kangaroo courts" if a radio station dismissed their input. Radio executives also fear that extremists would infiltrate these boards, forcing stations to adopt their radical viewpoints. Conservatives need to be aware of the danger of these proposals — and it is real.

Let's assume that the Obama administration is successful in breaking up big-media consolidators and opening media ownership to more diverse groups. The few owners of radio would become the many. Liberal groups are hoping that such a move will result in greater diversity in types of programs and less of the cookie-cutter radio imposed on communities by the consolidators.

The danger with the localism argument is government quotas requiring a certain amount of programming be local. If that happens, it's another form of censorship of syndicated conservative talk. Let the free market dictate what radio owners program. There should be no forced exodus of highly rated show hosts like Rush Limbaugh, Sean Hannity, Mark Levin, Michael Savage, Laura Ingraham, or Lars Larson by requiring stations to produce local programs in their place. While radio can improve its local news reporting, any requirements for programming quotas to supplant conservative talk personalities is a backdoor attempt to hush Rush and others. It should be voluntary.

But beware of proposals for advisory boards. This is what I think will happen. The new liberal administration will *attempt* to:

- accomplish the intent of the Fairness Doctrine by stopping more media consolidation and looking at ways to create more diverse ownership and localism.
- control content of radio programs by forcing stations to accept the input of community advisory boards to challenge station programming and licensing.

Reestablishing the actual Fairness Doctrine is too obvious an assault on free speech, so the goals of the left could be met by coming through the back door . . . by mandating localism and diversity of radio ownership. While many think it is time to restore more local content back into radio, the way liberals are proposing to do that is a problem. Appointing activist groups that can thwart a station's licensing renewal process through intimidation is censorship in disguise, and it would threaten to stifle free expression on conservative talk radio in the same manner as the Fairness Doctrine.

As for breaking up big media, Democrats may not have to worry—it may be a moot point. Many media companies may only survive the current economic downturn if they divest— reaffirming that American capitalism works and corrects itself, as intended, without regulation. If government stays out of the way, freedom reigns. Here's how former FCC chairman Kevin Martin put it during his KGO Radio interview:[6] "I think that you are seeing some cracks in [radio consolidation] now as some of the biggest radio conglomerates are starting to try to sell off some of those radio stations they acquired."

As for the newsrooms at our radio stations across the nation, I would encourage all media owners large and small to try to avoid cuts that impact news and programming. Good newsrooms support good talk shows, and our talk personalities deserve that backing. More important, so do listeners. That's a tough goal in hard economic times. As a programmer I know that strong newsrooms help address the need for localism and negate liberal arguments for content regulation. I hope the industry can voluntarily respond in that manner. Government should not regulate content.

I have the radio on and haven't heard anything.

CALLER TO 911 EMERGENCY SERVICES
IN MINOT, SOUTH DAKOTA

STRAIGHT AHEAD: Censorship on Armed Forces Radio?

CHAPTER 24

"Good Morning, Vietnam!"

Free Speech on Armed Forces Radio

For those of us observing the fight for free speech on radio, a major battle in this war unfolded in 2004 when liberals launched a full frontal assault on Armed Forces Radio, the link through which our troops have daily connection with news and information from back home. Armed Forces Radio provides vital emotional support for those brave men and women who protect and defend us. Ironically, at the center of this fight was one of the staunchest supporters of our troops and their efforts overseas. Here's what happened.

In late May 2004, Media Matters, the leftist organization with a self-professed agenda of "correcting conservative media misinformation" and headed by David Brock, sent a letter to then defense secretary Donald Rumsfeld asking that the Pentagon remove Rush Limbaugh's program from the Armed Forces Radio & Television Services. At the center of the argument was Limbaugh's comments on the Pentagon's prison for terrorists, Abu Ghraib, where a major controversy developed over the well-publicized hazing of prisoners that was later denounced by President Bush.

In his letter, Brock wrote, "It is abhorrent that the American taxpayer is paying to broadcast what is in effect pro-torture propaganda to American troops."[1] What he conveniently didn't say is that American Armed Forces Radio also broadcasts the programs of liberal-leaning NPR. Brock went as far as to say that Rush's show should be taken off the air to "protect" American troops from his "reckless and dangerous messages." Brock also stated that Limbaugh "continually uses prejudiced rhetoric that divides rather than unites Americans." The liberal attack dogs swept into action after Brock's letter to Rumsfeld became well publicized.

At the time Brock sent the letter, not only was NPR fully heard on Armed Forces Radio, but its left-leaning commentaries were heard as well as commentary from liberal talk host Jim Hightower, who was a major disappointment to me in commercial syndication. Dan Rather was also a contributor. Throughout the history of Armed Forces Radio, the intent has been to provide the troops with a potpourri of what they would hear at home. So, why censor Limbaugh? Why censor one of the strongest voices to defend our troops against the liberal left? The assault continued online with petitions calling for Congress and Armed Forces Radio to eliminate Rush Limbaugh from its programming lineup.

The battle would continue when a U.S. senator who had been a pilot in the United States Navy joined the chorus condemning Rush's commentary. At the same time Media Matters was petitioning for the removal of Limbaugh from Armed Forces Radio, Democratic Senator Tom Harkin from Iowa was pushing Congress to force the military's radio service to include more liberals. Harkin blasted Limbaugh in the *Congressional Record*, and he was successful in introducing a resolution that was passed unanimously by the Senate. It urged Defense Secretary Rumsfeld and Armed Forces Radio to ensure more political balance in programming. Noting that he felt $47 million dollars for Armed Forces Radio & Television Services (AFRTS) was justified, Harkin stated, "It came to my attention that the programming on AFRTS has what I consider to be a political bias in its social and political commentary." The radio broadcast of AFRTS consists of several channels. Many of them are music channels, and some are dedicated to NPR and to news, talk, and sports programming. Harkin continued, "Public criticism of Armed Forces Radio content has focused on the fact that Rush Limbaugh's commentary is carried daily on the talk radio service. I generally do not agree with Rush Limbaugh's commentaries. But I do not object to the fact that they are run on a daily basis on this service. Some people do object. However, what I do take issue with is the fact that there is no commentary on the service that would even begin to balance the extreme right-wing views that Rush Limbaugh routinely expresses on the program."

Harkin then referenced the controversial Abu Ghraib treatment of prisoners: "Critics have specifically cited Rush Limbaugh's use of his show to condone and trivialize the abuse of Iraqi prisoners by U.S. guards at the Abu Ghraib prison in Iraq. As many of my colleagues know, and as has been pointed out previously here on the Senate floor, Mr. Limbaugh reportedly likened the abuse of Iraqi prisoners by U.S. guards at Abu Ghraib to a fraternity initiation. He called some of the abusive tactics a 'brilliant maneuver.' I think the critics are right. Limbaugh's remarks—and there are many more offensive remarks by Mr. Limbaugh on this topic than I have mentioned here—are repugnant. They do damage to the American image when they are heard around the world."[2]

Back at EIB headquarters, Limbaugh was quick to respond.

"And I just read this guy's [Senator Tom Harkin] statement, and he's lying through his teeth about what was said on this program about the prison abuse scandal. He's lying about what I said. He's taking it all out of context. He's regurgitating the out-of-text quotes taken by this so-called analyst website, which is nothing more than an appendage of the Democrat Party."

Even though Harkin stated he did not want Limbaugh to be taken off of the AFR channel, Limbaugh wasn't buying it. "Now this is censorship. This is the United States government. This is a United States senator amending the Defense Appropriations Bill with the intent being to get this program . . . only one hour of which is carried on Armed Forces Radio . . . stripped from the network."[3]

By October 2005, plans were being made to balance Armed Forces Radio programming, based on Senate action on Harkin's resolution. Now-retired commander Wesley Clark, the four-star general who headed up Europe's NATO command, was leading the charge. In a widely publicized statement, Clark said, "It was just eleven years ago when seventy Republican members of Congress, led by then Congressman Bob Dornan (R-CA), demanded that President Clinton's Secretary of Defense Les Aspin broadcast Rush Limbaugh's radio and television programs to the military. Well if Armed Services Radio is good enough for Rush Limbaugh, it's certainly good enough for Ed Schultz." After one logistical hiccup, Armed Forces Radio added liberal/progressive Ed Schultz to its programming lineup on December 5, 2005.

Schultz thanked Clark for his efforts on his behalf on his radio show on November 7, 2005, and Clark responded: "I'm just so proud of you and so pleased that you're going to be on there so our soldiers can get both sides of the news. It's just wrong for Armed Forces Radio to have gotten away with presenting only one side of the news."[4]

Rush was quick to point out that he is the balance to the vast amount of NPR programming carried by Armed Forces Radio. AFR is broadcast to nearly 1 million troops, stationed in more than a thousand outlets in more than 175 foreign countries and U.S. territories.

Later a radio research firm recommended dumping talk programming on Armed Forces Radio in favor of more music that would appeal to young troops. The research report found that Limbaugh had the most popular appeal among troops, and well-known talk radio blogger Brian Maloney—known as the "Radio Equalizer"—asked, "With this kind of data, how could anyone determine that nearly all political talk radio should be eliminated from the two proposed primary worldwide broadcast stations? Why not remove the unpopular liberal shows and keep the rest?"[5]

Ed Schultz told me that his program is still heard on AFR. I think many conservatives would not object to liberal programming on AFR, but the attempt to silence Rush—one of the most popular programs among troops—was yet another assault on conservative talk radio and free speech.

My son-in-law, now a proud officer in the United States Army, served in Iraq for thirteen months. He is an avid Limbaugh fan, and at that time Rush was a link that helped him know we were all concerned about him and valued him for risking his life on behalf of all Americans who love liberty. He told me he was "sickened" when he heard of efforts to censor Rush on AFR. "Our country is based on democracy and the free speech of the American people. As an American, I am a free man and choose to listen to Rush Limbaugh. As an American soldier, speaking for many American soldiers, we need a person like Rush who will supply a conduit for all of America, a person who continues to believe in the ideals on which our great country was founded."[6]

My son-in-law was in Baghdad shortly after the Abu Ghraib prison controversy. It was a lonely experience. Soldiers had each other's company, an occasional phone call back home, and maybe an hour of Rush Limbaugh's show when there was time to listen. Like many soldiers, he questioned the actions of members of Congress who were critical of the war effort.

He spent much of his time providing convoy security throughout Iraq as a gunner and combat lifesaver, as well as providing checkpoint security for nationals working at Camp Victory and other installations throughout Iraq. He has said, "There were TVs in the chow hall when we had the ability to sit down and have a hot meal. I remember while watching CNN, Congressman John Murtha [D-Pa.] was telling reporters that what we were doing in Iraq was unjust and that we soldiers were failing at our mission. I heard this hours after watching a fellow soldier bleed out due to wounds caused by an IED [Improvised Explosive Device] while his driver, in the meantime, cried for his mother from a gut wound. They gave their lives for this country. Every single politician asked us to win a war and this is the price that soldiers have been asked to pay. We would, however, like support from the same men and women who send us into harm's way."

At the end of one of his many convoys, this soldier decided not to go into the chow hall to eat. Instead, he chose to eat an MRE [meal, ready to eat] outside his hootch. He specifically recalls listening to Limbaugh. "The *Rush Limbaugh Show* was broadcasting at the time. It was fascinating to me to hear him speak with such reverence for the armed forces. After so many hours of hearing our representatives chastise their own military, my colleagues and I were refreshed to hear someone support America and those of us fighting. He relayed over his broadcast what soldiers on the ground were experiencing, something that we soldiers knew to be true; we were winning the war."

Rush Limbaugh and other conservatives knew America was winning the war, but mainstream media was only reporting the negative side to help set the stage for a Democrat win in 2008. Without Limbaugh, morale for this soldier would have been much lower. Without Limbaugh and other conservative talk show hosts, the other side of the story would never have been told.

Fast-forward to October 2007, when liberals launched yet another attempt to take Rush Limbaugh off Armed Forces Radio. This renewed assault on Limbaugh centered on his "phony soldiers" reference, and Media Matters was there once again—along with General Wesley Clark and Democrat Senate Majority Leader Harry Reid—to add fuel to the fire. Reid had called on Limbaugh's boss to reprimand him. Instead, Clear Channel and Premiere Radio Network executives defended Rush, citing free speech rights.

At every opportunity—whenever there was a political controversy—Media Matters was there to attack the right of conservative talkers to freedom of expression. The goal is to have them removed from the air, because the group doesn't like what these conservative political commentators have to say. It's un-American. America is about defending freedom of expression even if we don't like what is being said. It's shocking and repugnant to those of us who value what the First Amendment represents.

When I began writing this important chapter I titled it "Good Morning, Vietnam!" It could just as well have been titled "Good Morning, Iraq!" But, because I am a lifelong radio junkie, one of the movies that impacted my views on censorship in radio was the movie *Good Morning, Vietnam!* starring Robin Williams. The movie is based on the real-life experiences of Adrian Cronauer, who served as a radio specialist in the Vietnam War and coined the famous phrase that became the title of the movie he helped develop. As fate would have it, I was put in touch with Adrian by David Limbaugh, Rush's brother.

Adrian Cronauer served as Special Assistant to the Director of Defense, Prisoners of War and Missing in Action Office. After he left radio, he became an attorney and today has plans to work as a country lawyer. Adrian fights for freedom of speech and has written many papers on the Fairness Doctrine. In one of his papers, Cronauer summarizes what to expect.[7] "Considering the long history of the Fairness Doctrine and the determined attempts by some congressmen to resurrect it, it is reasonable to assume we have not seen the last of it. Some speculate congressional pressure may prompt the FCC to reinstate the doctrine as a regulatory policy, while others suggest the current initiatives to rebuild our communications infrastructure may provide an opportunity for Fairness Doctrine backers to surreptitiously do what they have so far been unable to do openly." Cronauer is right on the mark.

Adrian also writes, "The necessarily subjective judgments imposed on the industry throughout the years [of the Fairness Doctrine] led to a Kafkaesque situation in which broadcasters were never sure what was expected of them nor what they could be punished for."

What Cronauer is referencing is what my radio colleagues and I know to be true. Under the Fairness Doctrine, we were operating in a wilderness of gray—not knowing from one minute to the next if some individual or group who didn't like what we said would turn us in to the FCC. Ladies and gentlemen, that puts a chill on free speech.

Cronauer also summarizes the true mission of AFR. In his words, it is intended to give a taste of "stateside" to our troops stationed thousands of miles from home fighting for our freedoms. Since his tour of duty, Adrian has addressed numerous veteran groups and is often told by former soldiers how he helped them get through their Vietnam experience. Frequently the dates of their tours of duty don't match up . . . but, no matter. Even if they didn't actually hear Adrian Cronauer on the radio in Vietnam, they were comforted by the fact that AFR gave them a taste of "stateside" and the knowledge that the folks back home cared about them. To patriots like Rush, Adrian, and my son-in-law, thanks for the good fight. And to Armed Forces Radio, thanks for keeping the conservative voice alive for our troops.

We are not afraid to entrust the American people with unpleasant facts, foreign ideas, alien philosophies, and competitive values. For a nation that is afraid to let its people judge the truth and falsehood in an open market is a nation that is afraid of its people.
—PRESIDENT JOHN F. KENNEDY

STRAIGHT AHEAD: The Speech Police.

CHAPTER 25

The Speech Police

Liberal Activist Groups Force Fairness

This is the United States of America, the land of the free. But a sinister movement has been developing for years. They are the Speech Police, and they have become intimidating and even vicious. They not only want to tell you what you should say, they also want to tell you what you should think. And if you don't obey, there are consequences. America is in a fight for freedom of speech on the radio; America is in a fight for its long-held freedoms, period. This fight is intensifying under the newly elected, liberal administration.

Although there have been sharp differences of opinion throughout our nation's history, the venom we see today found deep roots early in the Reagan administration when the president railed against big government and government controls over American lives. That wasn't in the best interest of those whose livelihoods depended on government checks, and arguments grew bitter. What were once respectable debates among family members, close friends, and co-workers became arguments—even fights—heated to the point of bitterness and divisiveness.

Then we observed the birth of conservative talk radio and Rush Limbaugh in 1988. Radio has never been the same since. Prior to repeal of the Fairness Doctrine, there was very little political talk on the radio, and rarely was it opinionated commentary. Radio station owners worried that, should a host get out of line with too much opinion or the wrong opinion, they would have to seek out an opposing viewpoint in order to protect their broadcast licenses. We avoided controversy like the plague, and our owners didn't want to invest time and money to defend us for what we said "wrong."

There was also debate over what was considered to be fair and who should define what was fair. For most of us who worked in radio prior to the repeal of the Fairness Doctrine, it was quite obvious that this regulation inhibited freedom of expression—and freedom to question—over the airwaves. In my own broadcast experience, these are some examples:

- No on-air host could endorse a political candidate, even in presidential races. That was unheard of prior to the repeal of the Fairness Doctrine.
- We could not speak in favor of a measure allowing citizens to pump their own gas at service stations in our state.
- We could not advocate for any candidate in a key political race without providing equal airtime to all other candidates.
- We could not speak out against a measure dramatically raising gasoline taxes.
- We couldn't advocate against a ridiculously expensive light-rail public transit system.

- We couldn't speak up about any issue without getting a request for airtime for a "balanced" perspective.

Ross Mitchell is the longtime morning host on KKOH, Reno, and you also hear him as the announcer on *Coast-to-Coast* with George Noory. Ross worked under the Fairness Doctrine for years and had this to say about it: "In my situation the Fairness Doctrine was many times nothing more than default censorship and had a very chilling effect on the dissemination of information. Often, in the interest of 'fairness' on the airwaves, I would opt not to explore a significant issue or topic as I was not sure I would ultimately be able to comply with the constraints of the Fairness Doctrine. This certainly did not 'serve the public interest' as broadcasters are also mandated to do, which I found to be an ironic dichotomy at best! It has been my experience over the last forty years that fairness on the airwaves is much more likely to be achieved when it is not statutorily mandated."[1]

We lived in an era of repression of free speech, and radio talk shows were boring. We subjected you, the listener, to nonstop advice shows on personal relationships, financial planning, gardening tips, do-it-yourself home repairs. These were all worthy topics, to be sure. But there was nothing of substance about the issues critical to real life in America . . . no political commentary to educate voters about the issues on the ballot. Radio programs weren't fully serving the public interest. When the doctrine was finally repealed, it's as if a black cloud was lifted. Thousands of us conservative broadcasters were able to take a critical look at America, much the same as our newspaper editorial brethren had always been free to do. The muzzle came off, and when it did, things started to happen.

Our commentary blocked the prospects for success of the fatally flawed national health-care system proposed by Hillary Clinton. We called "foul play" on pork barrel legislation that wasted countless millions of our hard-earned taxpayer dollars for the sole purpose of currying favor with voters at reelection time. The tide turned against the Democrat-controlled House and Senate, and the heat they took in the early nineties was like nothing they had ever encountered before. Conservative political commentators became reviled, and there were attempts on the part of Congress to restore the Fairness Doctrine to muzzle the opposing voices.

Liberals didn't like the input they were receiving, and they wanted to take away our rights to question, challenge, and criticize. All of a sudden, phone lines in legislative offices were flooded with calls. E-mails from listeners began flooding the Internet, and, for the first time in recent U.S. history, elected representatives were actually hearing from their constituents . . . really hearing from them! But they didn't like what they were hearing.

Then came the Republican Revolution[2], and conservative talk radio was largely given credit for helping usher Republicans back into control in Washington, D.C. Our left-wing opponents didn't like that, either, and tried to muzzle us yet again. George W. Bush, they said, was elected by a Republican Supreme Court. There were more calls for the Fairness Doctrine. Liberals were incensed. Then, in 2004, even more voters turned out across the nation and reelected George Bush. Liberals couldn't believe it. They should be eternally grateful that "W." kept our homeland safe from additional terrorist attacks, but they will never fully admit it.

There were more calls for the Fairness Doctrine to shut

up conservative talk radio. The left began plotting their attack strategy. In the spring of 2004, a group was organized for the sole purpose of fighting conservative misinformation. Media Matters for America was organized, just ahead of the 2004 presidential election, to fight conservatism. The group's tactics are well publicized and considered by conservatives to be mostly smear hits.

The new group stated its mission: "Media Matters for America is a web-based, not-for-profit progressive research and information center dedicated to comprehensively monitoring, analyzing, and correcting conservative misinformation in the U.S. media."[3]

What Media Matters considers misinformation is their interpretation and their right. Correcting what they consider to be misinformation is where the group's venom and despicable tactics stand out. Media Matters also states that the group "has the means to systematically monitor a cross section of print, broadcast, cable, radio, and Internet media outlets for conservative misinformation—news or commentary that is not accurate, reliable, or credible and that forwards the conservative agenda—every day, in real time."

Here are their tactics:

Using their website as a principal vehicle for disseminating research and information, Media Matters posts rapid-response items as well as longer research and analytic reports documenting what they think is conservative misinformation. They often post audio bites of conservative talk show hosts. Then they blast out information by e-mail to their database of followers, providing them with information to take direct action against members of the media. With Media Matters, the gloves are off. They have an open agenda of fighting conservative talk radio, and many of us think their agenda is to shut down the format. Media Matters has an action center and in it they describe how they will give members the means to hold media accountable: "Media Matters works daily to notify activists, journalists, pundits, and the general public about instances of misinformation, providing them with the resources to rebut false claims and to take direct action against offending media institutions."

In fighting Talk Radio Network's Michael Savage, they instructed their followers to seek out stations that aired *The Savage Nation* and gave them tools to tell local station managers what they thought of those stations that broadcast the program they labeled as "hate" or "racist." The attacks often came in the form of intimidating e-mails or angry phone calls—even from those who had not heard the program or the statements in question. Of course, it is their interpretation.

Stations with which this author has worked were the recipient of many of those angry communications from Media Matters followers, and they were intimidating. They threaten advertiser boycotts and, on occasion, have even contacted advertisers. They want radio stations that broadcast conservative talk programming to drop those shows that offend them—particularly Michael Savage's show.

But there isn't a conservative host who hasn't come under the Media Matters microscope. They went after Sinclair Broadcasting for plans to broadcast a controversial documentary about then Democrat presidential candidate John Kerry, and they targeted Sinclair advertisers. If they didn't like the content of a program, they did everything they could to stop it from airing. There have been many assaults on conservative media over the years, but Media Matters leads the left-wing attack dogs.

Don Imus suffered the consequences over his inappropriate remark about the Rutgers University women's basketball team. No surprise to conservatives, MSNBC pulled the television rights to broadcast Imus's show. CBS also buckled under pressure from Media Matters and others, and fired Imus. Don Imus had apologized and acknowledged his off-color attempt at humor as stupid. He even appeared on Al Sharpton's radio show and faced his enemies. But that wasn't good enough for Media Matters and their followers. They smelled blood, and they went for the jugular. Imus paid the price, but he's back where he should be—on the airwaves in New York on WABC, enjoying his free speech rights once again.

Emboldened by their victory, Media Matters redoubled their efforts to oust other conservative hosts such as Rush Limbaugh and Michael Savage, and they are not afraid to use whatever tactics will further their cause. Off the air, they've been called many names. On the air, they've been called "liars" who take statements out of context and twist them to their desired outcome.

Having watchdogs—someone to monitor everything every conservative talk host says on every broadcast every day—opened up the opportunity for Media Matters to attack Rush Limbaugh. When Limbaugh made his comments that military personnel at Abu Ghraib prison were "blowing off steam" in their handling of prisoners, Media Matters seized on Rush's language and put its attack machine into high gear. Conservatives fully understood Rush's comments. We were at war with Iraq, and look at how our captured soldiers—and even civilian reporters—were being treated. They were being decapitated while video cameras recorded the atrocities! The United States was attacking an evil dictator who wanted to see the United States—and his own dissenting citizens—

destroyed. But that wasn't important to groups like Media Matters.

Media Matters saw an opportunity because of the unpopularity of the war and a politically correct mind-set at home. While it did not succeed in getting Limbaugh thrown off AFR, the left continued its pursuit to take back the White House by trashing conservative talk show hosts in any manner they could. Media Matters doesn't want to correct conservative hosts—it wants to destroy them. It has been charged with distortion by Limbaugh, Savage, Dobbs, and others.

Media Matters is headed by David Brock,[4] a controversial journalist who considered himself conservative until he was shunned by fellow conservatives and found open arms in the liberal camp. He graduated conservative from an extremely liberal school—the University of California, Berkeley. He is smart and manipulative. After graduating, Brock began what appeared to be a great career as an investigative reporter. In 1986, he joined the weekly conservative newsmagazine *Insight on the News* and also spent some time with the conservative Heritage Foundation in Washington, D.C. In 1992, Brock wrote a story for the *American Spectator* that was acutely critical of Anita Hill—who made accusations of improprieties against Supreme Court nominee Clarence Thomas. He called her "a bit nutty and a bit slutty." The following year he published a book titled *The Real Anita Hill* expanding on her claims of sexual harassment by Clarence Thomas. The book was a hit.

Later, at the *Spectator*, Brock wrote stories about President Bill Clinton's sexual improprieties, which led to the well-publicized "Troopergate" scandal. Then he was commissioned by Simon & Schuster to write a book on Hillary Clinton. The book wasn't what conservatives expected. Brock said he couldn't dig up much dirt on Hillary. In July 1997, he told *Esquire* magazine that much of what he said in his best-known *American Spectator* articles was false. *American Spectator* declined to renew his contract. Later, in *Esquire*, he apologized to Bill Clinton for his contributions to the Troopergate scandal.

In his 2002 memoir, *Blinded by the Right: The Conscience of an Ex-Conservative*, Brock apologized to Clinton and to Anita Hill. In his 2004 book, *The Republican Noise Machine*, he wrote of alleged efforts to raise the profile of conservative opinions in the press through false accusation of liberal media bias. From this background came Media Matters for America, the left-wing nonprofit attack machine whose stated goal is to "correct conservative misinformation." To conservatives, Brock is a left-wing hit man who distorts, lies, and manipulates conservative talk show statements by taking them out of context for the purpose of destroying the medium. Media Matters has become conservatives' archenemy. Its leader, David Brock, wants to restore the Fairness Doctrine or its equivalent.[5]

That's dishonest and it's unethical.

—GLENN BECK, RADIO AND TV HOST, AUTHOR

STRAIGHT AHEAD: Talk show hosts fight back.

CHAPTER 26

The Left-Wing Smear Machine

Conservative Talk Fights Back

When the left lost the presidential election in 2000, they were angry. They felt they had been robbed by the Supreme Court, and that Al Gore rightfully deserved the job. When liberals lost again in 2004, they were incensed. They hated George W. Bush. They formed a relentless attack machine to promote liberal candidates with the goal of winning the White House in 2008. And they did.

When John Kerry lost the presidential bid in 2004, several things were set in motion to begin countering what liberals thought was the conservative juggernaut of talk radio. They were dismayed at their own lack of success when ratings fell flat for liberal radio network Air America. They were dismayed that Al Franken wasn't the radio poster boy for the left as Rush Limbaugh was for the right. Franken was horrible on the radio. He didn't understand that there has to be something between the ears to do a three-hour talk show. I later watched him embarass himself before a group of talk radio executives in New York. Even before he finished speaking, almost every-one had left the room.

Failing at radio, the left decided to promote their cause another way. They formed Media Matters with the intention of electing Hillary Clinton as our next president. The group has been relentless in attacking conservatives ever since. Hillary admitted ties to Media Matters when she told a liberal gathering on August 4, 2007, that she helped form the left-wing smear machine, talking about "institutions that I helped to start and support like Media Matters and [the] Center for American Progress."[1] When David Brock founded Media Matters in 2004, he was quoted as saying, "The right wing in this country has dominated the debate over liberal bias. By dominating that debate, my belief is they've moved the media itself to the right and therefore they've moved American politics to the right."[2]

Rush Limbaugh successfully defended his phony soldier comment and made Senate Democrats look like fools. When he sold Senator "Dingy Harry" Reid's letter on eBay, then donated the proceeds to charity, Media Matters turned up their attacks. But Rush got an assist from conservative talk show host Glenn Beck, who ripped Media Matters on his television show.

Beck stated the organization wasn't telling the whole truth about Limbaugh's statements: ". . . the hit squad Media Matters has twisted [Rush's] words to make it seem like he called all soldiers who disagreed with him 'phony soldiers.' The *whole* truth of his statement was that he was specifically referring to one soldier who had lied about his military service. Of course, Media Matters didn't have a word to say when Congressman John Murtha accused American Marines of being guilty of murdering innocent Iraqi civilians—servicemen who actually turned out to be innocent heroes."[3]

Beck also noted the intimidation practices of Media Matters: "That's the game of 'gotcha.' This is the game that has been brought to perfection by the socialist ultraleft that have been playing with Rush Limbaugh and anybody else they disagree with . . . that they're trying to destroy. That's dishonest and it's unethical."

Media Matters has been at war with most of the conservative hosts in America, including Rush Limbaugh, Bill O'Reilly, and Lou Dobbs. On his highly rated talk show, O'Reilly has called David Brock a "hatchet man." On October 2, 2007, on *The Factor*, O'Reilly said of Brock, "This guy has emerged as the biggest villain, in my opinion, in the country. He'll do anything. He'll say anything—doesn't matter if it's true—for money. And, the money is coming from the left."[4]

When Media Matters went after Dobbs, he countered on his television show. They had accused Dobbs of passing along "myths" about immigration prior to the defeat of the highly controversial Immigration Bill in June 2007. Dobbs was masterful in his defense and told his guest, Paul Waldman of Media Matters, "Your report is a scurrilous attack, and you pretend it has some scholarly basis. It is an absolute pitiful joke."[5]

One of Media Matters's prime targets is the nationally syndicated talk show host Michael Savage. The organization began monitoring Savage in 2004, and they put him under the microscope on a daily basis. Savage is the author of two bestselling books and is one of the most highly rated talk show hosts in America. Media Matters isolates many Savage statements they don't like and then, in typical fashion, e-mails their database urging listeners to confront the radio stations that carry his show.

Followers and contributors to Media Matters—many of

whom haven't even listened to Savage or his show—respond like faithful sheep. They have isolated several statements made by Savage on the Iraq War, on our treatment of Iraqi war prisoners, on interrogation tactics of terrorists and war prisoners, on radical Islam, and other controversial topics, suggesting that they are "hate" speech that shouldn't be on the nation's airwaves. The attack is relentless. They simply don't like what Savage has to say, and they would take his rights of free speech away. While some detest Michael Savage, many Americans love him and the bluntness of his commentary. Media Matters's relentless attacks led Savage to issue these words to a Seattle caller on April 13, 2007, about David Brock, the conservative-turned-liberal leader of Media Matters. Here's the transcript:

Savage: Seattle, Washington [caller], you're up on *The Savage
          Nation*. Topic, please . . .

Caller: Hello, sir, how are you doing? Yes, I was looking on
          NewsMax.com today, and there was a story about George
          Soros's group taking responsibility for the Imus hit, and that
          they assigned monitors to his show, and . . .

Savage: Right. They're people who attack me. It's run by a
          homosexual activist who hates anybody in the media
          who does not kowtow to homosexual . . . the homosexual
          agenda. It's called "Media Matters." The man who runs
          it is, in my opinion, a straight-out maniac. He would
          belong much more happily in the ex–Soviet Union. But
          we found out today on NewsMax that Media Matters is not
          an independent watchdog agency. In fact, it's funded by
          George Soros. I thought that something that did come out
          in the laundry in this whole affair that's very interesting.

They've held themselves up as somehow above the fray, only looking for fairmindedness in the media. It turns out that they are, in fact, funded by one of the most vile anti-American creatures in the world, George Soros. I saw that as well . . .

Caller: Yeah, it just disturbed me because, you know, only . . . how can in America . . . can these people be allowed to operate like that, you know?

Savage: Well, George Soros should be stripped of his citizenship. George Soros is a totally dangerous individual. He tried to buy the last election. Remember he spent thirty million dollars of his own money to defeat George Bush? I mean, this is crazy. This guy doesn't miss an opportunity to attack this country. And here he was, a Hungarian Jewish refugee to this country.[6]

Media Matters denies it has received funds from George Soros, the billionaire who spent millions to fund left-wing groups to attack President Bush and conservative media. But Soros doesn't hold back in expressing his disdain for President Bush, and he told Fox's Neal Cavuto in October 2006, "I really became engaged in domestic politics in 2004 . . . because I felt the single most important thing I could do to make the world a better place is to help get President Bush out of the White House."[7] No surprise that David Brock of Media Matters has also supported the return of the Fairness Doctrine.

Sometimes free speech isn't pretty, but this is America, where free speech still exists. Michael Savage is heard by 8.5 million Americans on approximately 350 stations nationwide. He hits hard and minces no words on what he considers an erosion of American values. Free speech is a very fragile thing in America, but it must be defended no matter how vile someone thinks it is. Michael Savage was the recipient of the *Talkers* magazine Freedom of Speech Award in 2007. He fights the good fight for free speech.

Media Matters monitors everything conservatives in the media say, then it browbeats them for saying it. They have taken statements out of context in hopes of making a point for their side. They try to generate paranoia. They are America's thought and speech police. Their goal is to program the minds of all conservatives so that, when their words are spoken, they are what Media Matters want to hear. To conservative talk hosts, Media Matters is a huge, unbridled smear machine that enjoys the same freedom of speech it is trying to take away from them.

> *You [reporters] should have printed
> what he meant, not what he said.*
> —EARL BUSH, PRESS AIDE TO
> MAYOR RICHARD J. DALEY OF CHICAGO

STRAIGHT AHEAD: Free speech in Canada, eh? The implications for America.

CHAPTER 27

Is America Next?

Canadian Free Speech Squelched

I have shocking news to share about the free speech rights of our neighbors to the North. Could this same kind of censorship eventually become the law of the land in the United States of America?

Canadian-born Mark Steyn is considered by many to be one of North America's leading journalists and writers. He is the author of the bestselling book *America Alone*, in which he suggests that Islam is reproducing faster than its Western counterparts, potentially leading to the downfall of the West. The book focuses on the War on Terror and, as the title indicates, expresses the view that America is basically "in it alone." Steyn has also written articles for *Maclean's* magazine, and one of them, "The Future Belongs to Islam," grabbed the attention of the Canadian Islamic Congress (CIC). The CIC complaint accused the *Maclean's* articles of being "flagrantly Islamophobic" and claimed the magazine "subjects Canadian Muslims to hatred and contempt."[1]

Canada is a country with human rights commissions. As

is the case when civilizations progress or regress, political correctness became the order of the day. The commissions began to investigate alleged "hate speech," much as neo-Nazis were often the target of investigation in the United States. Speech against individuals or groups who were quick to charge racism, sexism, or homophobia was eventually investigated, as well. If you write in Canada, you write at your own risk.

Hate speech is defined by the ear of the listener, and the CIC was successful in getting the British Columbia Human Rights Tribunal, and then the national Canadian Human Rights Commission, to hear its complaint. But after much publicity and much criticism that free speech was being trampled in Canada, the national commission rightly dismissed the case. *Maclean's* then issued this statement:

> Maclean's *magazine is pleased that the Canadian Human Rights Commission has dismissed the complaint brought against it by the Canadian Islamic Congress. The decision is in keeping with our long-standing position that the article in question, "The Future Belongs to Islam," an excerpt from Mark Steyn's best-selling book* America Alone, *was a worthy piece of commentary on important geopolitical issues, entirely within the bounds of normal journalistic practice.*
>
> *Though gratified by the decision,* Maclean's *continues to assert that no human rights commission, whether at the federal or provincial level, has the mandate or the expertise to monitor, inquire into, or assess the editorial decisions of the nation's media. And we continue to have grave concerns about a system of complaint and adjudication that allows a media outlet to be pursued in mul-*

*tiple jurisdictions on the same complaint, brought by the
same complainants, subjecting it to costs of hundreds of
thousands of dollars, to say nothing of the inconvenience.
We enthusiastically support those parliamentarians who
are calling for legislative review of the commissions with
regard to speech issues.*[2]

While the case against Steyn and *Maclean's* was being
heard by the various Canadian tribunals, Mark delivered a
lecture at Hillsdale College in Michigan while in residence as
a Eugene C. Pulliam Visiting Fellow in Journalism. He talked
about his accuser, and his comments were carried by the
school's publication, *Imprimis*. The school emphasizes that
opinions expressed in *Imprimis* are not necessarily the views of
Hillsdale College. Steyn's comments are reprinted by permission from *Imprimis*:

"Because I discussed these facts in print, my publisher is
now being sued before three Canadian human rights commissions. The plaintiff in my case is Dr. Mohamed Elmasry,
a man who announced on Canadian TV that he approves of
the murder of all Israeli civilians over the age of 18. He is thus
an objective supporter of terrorism. I don't begrudge him the
right to his opinions, but I wish he felt the same about mine.
Far from that, posing as a leader of the anti-hate movement in
Canada, he is using the squeamishness of the politically correct society to squash freedom."[3]

The CIC would issue a release following Elmasry's inflammatory comments, stating he was trying to express the view of
Palestinians and not his personal opinion. Elmasry was quoted
in the statement as regretting that his comments were misunderstood, but his critics were skeptical, at best.

There are other chilling accounts of assaults on free speech in Canada by the human rights tribunals:

- A Calgary bishop was brought before the Alberta Human Rights Tribunal for a letter he wrote to Catholics about homosexuals. Eventually, he was forced to apologize and told never to write disparagingly about gays again. The action by the Alberta tribunal specifically disallowed the defendant to publish "discriminatory" letters in newspapers, by e-mail, on the radio, in public speeches, or on the Internet in the future. He was fined $7,000 dollars.[4]
- A pamphlet was distributed that outlined health hazards associated with gay sex. The Saskatchewan Human Rights Tribunal ruled the author in violation of their rules against publishing anything that would promote hatred on the basis of sexual orientation. The writer was fined $17,500.[5]

If you are a conservative talk radio fan, you probably know of Michael Savage. It's a good thing he doesn't broadcast a show in Canada. If he did, he'd be behind bars for his strong words against Islamic radicals.

Mark Steyn's words pale in comparison to Savage's:

The Islamists smell weakness in the West and are attacking us on several fronts at once: one, through outright war; two, through immigration; three, through their propaganda disseminated through the liberal media; and four, through the liberal courts. Only a devastating military blow against the hearts of Islamic terror coupled with an outright ban on Muslim immigration, laws mak-

*ing the dissemination of enemy propaganda illegal, and
the uncoupling of the liberal ACLU can save the United
States. I would also make the construction of mosques illegal in America and the speaking of English only in the
streets of the United States the law.*[6]

This is just one example of many statements Michael Savage has made against radical Islam . . . and many Americans
agree with him and would defend his right to say it. Taken in
the context of Islamic beheadings, torture, rape, car bombs,
and other human atrocities, millions of Americans feel the
same way. Imagine if Savage lived in Canada. The speech
police would be on his doorstep the minute he uttered those
statements. In fact, they have been. The Canadians have
the CIC and here in the United States we have CAIR—the
"Council on American-Islamic Relations," a controversial Islamic civil rights group. CAIR went after Savage in much the
same manner as what Steyn faced in Canada, targeting many
of Savage's national advertisers. Undaunted, Savage continues
to exercise his free speech rights.

Media Matters for America is, of course, another form of
speech police, and they dog Savage and every conservative
talk show host in America. If Canada has a kangaroo court in
the Canadian Human Rights Commissions, then so does the
United States. It is Media Matters for America. And imagine if
we had human rights tribunals here. Oh, wait . . . we do!

Many states have human rights commissions to monitor
citizen complaints about such things as "hate speech." In
New Mexico, a Christian husband and wife who own a pho-
tography studio in Albuquerque were approached by a lesbian
couple to photograph their "commitment ceremony." Because

of their beliefs about marriage based on biblical teachings, the photographers declined. One of the lesbians filed a complaint with the New Mexico Human Rights Commission, claiming the photographers discriminated against her because of her sexual orientation. The New Mexico commission found the Christian couple guilty of discrimination under state anti-discrimination laws, and they were fined approximately six thousand dollars. The ruling was stunning in its blatant disregard for religious liberty and First Amendment freedoms. There are so many examples of muzzling free speech in our country that one has to wonder if this is really still America.[7]

The Canadian term "human rights tribunal" conjures up a chilling image. *Tribunal* is simply a legal term meaning that a judge or a designated group is authorized to investigate the offense and to decide the fate of someone found guilty of that offense. But it gives us pause as we contemplate the fate of American conservative talk radio with the possible return of speech regulations and the establishment of community advisory boards that could turn into tribunals for broadcast license holders. The potential for loss of our First Amendment freedoms is staggering. How much power do we potentially give to community advisory boards in the Federal Communications Commission's licensing process for radio stations? As Republican Congressman John Boehner of Ohio put it in his letter to then FCC chairman Kevin Martin, "The re-creation of pre-1980s advisory boards will place broadcast media squarely on a path toward rationed speech."

Are these advisory boards the precursors of tribunals? We only have to look to our northern neighbors to feel the Arctic freeze descend on free speech in the United States, where there already is a chill in the air. If the speech police hate what you say, they can convict you of hate crimes. Where offensive speech is prohibited, tyranny will follow. Creating protected classes of people free from criticism is the first step . . . and from there the foundation of a free people crumbles.

> *I may not agree with what you say, but I will*
> *defend to the death your right to say it.*
> —VOLTAIRE, AUTHOR

STRAIGHT AHEAD: "They are speech terrorists." The CEO of a major talk network speaks up.

CHAPTER 28

The Speech Terrorists

Conservative Talk vs. Radical Islam

Most of us are not even aware that there is a stealth form of censorship taking place in this country that some think may be sponsored, in part, by enemies outside our borders.

The Council on American-Islamic Relations (CAIR) was formed in 1994. With headquarters in Washington, D.C., the group operates as a nonprofit organization and calls itself the largest Islamic civil rights group in America.[1] Although CAIR says it has consistently condemned terrorism, some have publicly accused the organization of having connections to terrorist groups.[2] Since September 11, 2001, the organization has compiled a lengthy document expressing its condemnation of acts of terror. But conservative political commentators—who enjoy free speech rights in America—have challenged violent acts by radical Islamists using words that CAIR then labeled as hate speech.

In certain cases, CAIR has been successful in muzzling the conservative talk radio voice. The best-known example is that of Michael Graham, who was a talk show personality in Washington, D.C., at conservative talk station WMAL. Graham stated on the air that Islamist religious leaders in the United States seemed reluctant to criticize extremists who spread terror. CAIR contacted its subscribers, encouraging them to request that WMAL reprimand Graham for his anti-Islam statement. Graham was suspended and ultimately fired by WMAL. Later Graham was quoted as saying, "What CAIR does is try to portray all criticism of all Muslims everywhere as bigotry."[3]

Over the years there have been other battles between CAIR and various politicians and conservative talk show hosts. Along with the War on Terror, the war of words has reached a fever pitch in America. Dr. Laura Schlessinger was challenged for advising one of her callers against allowing her daughter to attend a school field trip to a local mosque unless that mosque was known not to harbor terrorists.[4] Broadcasting icon Paul Harvey was challenged for remarks deemed critical of the Muslim religion and of terrorism worldwide.[5] With more than thirty outreach offices in the United States and Canada, CAIR has made conservative talk radio one of its targets.

Michael Savage and his criticism of radical Islam is where the battle for freedom of expression has reached epic proportions. Frustrated over continuing reports of violence and terrorism, Savage exploded. In his October 29, 2007, broadcast he verbalized the populist feelings of many Americans when he said that Muslims needed to prove their claim that Islam is a religion of peace. Giving vent to his frustrations, Savage said, "I'm not gonna put my wife in a hijab. And I'm not gonna put my daughter in a burqa. And I'm not getting on my all-fours and braying to Mecca. And you could drop dead if you don't like it. You can shove it up your pipe. I don't wanna hear any more about Islam. I don't wanna hear one more word about

Islam. Take your religion and shove it up your behind. I'm sick of you."[6]

Savage continued, "I have never lived through a brain-washing like I have lived through for the last five years . . . wherever you look on the earth there's a bomb going off or a car going up in flames, and it's Muslims screaming for the blood of Christians or Jews or anyone they hate, and every day we're told the opposite here . . . everything we know to be true we're told 'oh don't believe what your mind tells you, believe what the diversity trainers tell you, believe what the government tells you, it's a religion of peace.' Well, why don't they prove it's a religion of peace?" The high ratings of Michael Savage's program would suggest that millions of Americans agree with these and other views he freely expresses.

CAIR was quick to respond and called upon listeners to boycott *The Savage Nation*. Their prepared statement said, "A prominent national Islamic civil rights and advocacy group today called on radio listeners of all faiths to contact companies that advertise on Michael Savage's nationally-syndicated radio program to express their concerns about the host's recent anti-Muslim tirade."[7] CAIR posted Savage's remarks on its website and further stated, "Michael Savage obviously cares little about the safety or civil rights of American Muslims, but the stations that carry his hate-filled rants do care about listeners' attitudes toward advertisers who pay to air commercials during the program."[8] Said CAIR communications coordinator Amina Rubin, "Americans of all faiths should take a few minutes to contact any local station that broadcasts Savage's inflammatory tirades to say they will not buy the goods or services of his advertisers."

Talk Radio Network (TRN) syndicates *The Savage Nation*, and I have placed the show on many stations across the country in the past. Mark Masters is CEO of TRN and one of my close friends in the radio business. He told me, "CAIR threw the kitchen sink at us with the goal of getting Savage fired, but we weren't intimidated. His audience supports him and so do his sponsors who have renewed. They tried to intimidate us, but we didn't take notice."[9] About Savage, Masters says, "He's just a guy with an opinion venting his heartfelt feelings to his audience, and they support him. In fact, he's had many Muslim callers thank him for speaking out against radicals." Mark Masters describes Savage as a "populist" voice in America and said he supports Savage's free speech rights as an American.

I asked Masters if he thinks organizations like CAIR and Media Matters for America are speech terrorists. His immediate and emphatic reply was "Yes!" Masters also stated, "These groups would like to have a Fairness Doctrine because that would shut down free speech. But the more speech we have in America, the richer the marketplace of ideas. Talk radio provides pressure valve relief, and it's one of the most valuable services we can provide. Groups like Media Matters often take statements out of context and weaponize their followers to contact advertisers. But I support free speech—even the free speech that groups like CAIR enjoy—and I will fight for our collective rights to have it in America." Mark Masters understands this precious freedom, and his many syndicated hosts exercise it daily. Opposing the free expression of opinion is one thing; shutting it down is censorship.

On December 3, 2007, Cliff Kincaid, writing for Accuracy in Media, an organization promoting balance and accuracy in media, interviewed Bill Warner of the Center for the Study of Political Islam. Warner had this warning; "In the United States we're getting Sharia law by the inch. Islam cannot be criticized. It is a sin against Allah. What Savage has done is a grievous sin against Allah, Mohammed, and Islam. They are not making this up. CAIR has no choice here. As a real Muslim, they must condemn anyone who criticizes Islam."[10] Sharia law is viewed as anti–human rights by most Western nations. It restricts the rights of women and gays, among other things.

Kincaid himself writes, "Whether you like Savage or not, he must not be forced off the air as the result of a special interest political pressure campaign. Beyond that, however, the public must be educated about how CAIR's campaign against Savage is part of the effort to force Sharia law on the world."

Since the attacks on the World Trade Center and the Pentagon on September 11, 2001, the U.S. view on global terrorism has changed radically. Along with the presidential election, the economy, and immigration reform, terrorism is one of the hottest topics discussed on talk radio today. It has also been center stage in Washington, D.C. Two years after the attack that killed more than three thousand of our citizens, the Senate Judiciary Subcommittee on Terrorism, Technology, and Homeland Security held a hearing called "Terrorism: Two Years After 9/11, Connecting the Dots."[11] Senator Charles Schumer discussed the role that top officials in the Saudi government play in spreading militant views in the United States.

These were Senator Schumer's comments before the subcommittee as stated in a press release on September 10, 2003:

> *Before I start my statement . . . I want to make one point crystal clear: Mainstream Islam is a peaceful religion that deserves the respect of all Americans. It has a proud*

history and many of the people who follow its beliefs here in the United States are hardworking, patriotic citizens. Wahhabism is known throughout the Muslim world for its puritanical and severe approach to the teachings of the Muslim prophet Mohammed. It preaches violence against non-believers or infidels and serves as the religious basis for Osama Bin Laden and al Qaeda. Experts agree that Saudi Arabia is the epicenter of Wahhabist belief and its extreme teachings. Unfortunately, there is mounting evidence that Saudi sponsored groups are trying to hijack mainstream Islam here in the United States—in mosques, in schools, and even in prisons and the military—and replace it with Wahhabism. As we will hear today, in the 1960's and 1970's the Saudi royal family made a deal with the devil, offering to sponsor the teaching of Wahhabist clerics in exchange for their support of the Royal Family's rule. Wahhabist teachings include examples of Allah cursing Jews and Christians and turning some of them into apes and pigs; and warnings that Muslims must consider non-Muslims or infidels their enemy.[12]

Senator Schumer went on to state that Saudi influence is having a profound impact on Muslim communities in the United States. "While all this is terribly alarming—and no doubt contributed to the events of 9/11—the most disturbing news is that Wahhabism—backed by truckloads of Saudi oil money—is now making inroads here in the United States. Saudi Arabia boasts of directly supporting over 18 mosques and schools across the country, including Islamic Centers in Washington and New York." The senator listed various recipients of Saudi money. "And that's not all. Grassroots political organizations that claim to act as the official voice of the American Muslim community here in Washington are also major recipients of Saudi money. The Council on American Islamic Relations—perhaps the most famous of these groups—reportedly received financial support from Saudi-funded organizations to build its $3.5 million headquarters here in Washington."

Several paragraphs later the senator stated, "To make matters worse, prominent members of the Council's current leadership—people who were invited to the hearings today but declined to testify—also have intimate connections with Hamas—a group that receives substantial funding from Saudi Arabia and subscribes to Wahhabist teachings. I wish they had taken us up on our invitation so they could explain themselves."

Since this Senate hearing on 9/11, CAIR has come under repeated scrutiny that causes conservative talk show commentators to question the organization's true motives. For instance, the group has opposed the Patriot Act's expanding the powers of the FBI and other government intelligence-gathering organizations to monitor the activities of suspected terrorists inside and outside our borders.[13] The group has also inserted itself into "diversity training" measures now undertaken by the Transportation Security Administration at our nation's airports.[14]

CAIR's Communications Director, Ibrahim Hooper, left no question about his hope for Islam in America when he made this statement to the *Minneapolis Star Tribune* on April 4, 1993, before CAIR was founded: "I wouldn't want to create the impression that I wouldn't like the government of the

United States to be Islamic sometime in the future. But I'm not going to do anything violent to promote that. I'm going to do it through education."[15]

Years after this statement to the *Star Tribune*, Salem Radio Network's Michael Medved, based in Seattle, talked to Hooper and confirmed Hooper's stated intent for Islam in America. Medved told me he was able to pin Hooper down and confirm that his long-term goal is to see an Islamic United States, which would bring our nation under Shariah Law—law that would curtail our personal freedoms and make criticism of Islam a crime. Free speech would cease to exist. Talk radio would be in grave jeopardy.

Medved says he was polite and courteous to Hooper during the interview and has invited him to return as a guest, but as of this writing Hooper has not returned to the Medved show.[16]

More recently, in April 2008, Republican Congresswoman Sue Myrick of North Carolina released what she calls her "Wake Up America" agenda. The ten-point agenda called for the Internal Revenue Service to investigate the nonprofit status of the Council on American-Islamic Relations. Section 501(c)(3) of the IRS code defining nonprofit status restricts "lobbying on behalf of a foreign government."

Taylor Stanford, press secretary in Representative Myrick's office, was kind enough to act as go-between in obtaining answers to my questions. I wondered if groups like CAIR would demand equal airtime, and if that could threaten our nation's security. Congresswoman Myrick responded, "CAIR can—and constantly does—use our freedoms against us. Claiming balanced time in our media would be no different. It absolutely does threaten us in our battle against global terrorism."

Myrick is a supporter of the Broadcaster Freedom Act. She is opposed to any reinstatement of the Fairness Doctrine, feeling that it is not the job of the government to censor political voices. She issued this rather dire warning: "Radical Islamists are using any and all resources from within our government system to undermine us. But we must be aware that it's not just the potential use of the Fairness Doctrine. We must also be concerned with what they are doing with regard to Sharia Finance within our banking systems. In our current economic situation, American bankers are buying into Sharia Finance because they so desperately need the money—and they have no clue as to what the consequences are in accepting that money. It means being Sharia compliant, or under the control of Sharia Law, which violates human rights and oppresses women, homosexuals and non-Muslims." [17]

When such public statements are made by our elected leaders, conservative talk show hosts are listening. There are approximately 1,200 mosques in the United States, and since 9/11 the volume of the arguments from both sides has gotten louder as the War on Terror continues. You can bet that Michael Savage won't "get on all fours braying to Mecca." Conservative talk radio fears that attempts to restore censorship regulations requiring equal time for all viewpoints on our nation's airwaves would not only be an unconstitutional assault on free speech but also undermine our country's efforts to fight global terrorism, because radicals—with the intent of destroying our basic rights and freedoms—could petition for broadcast time.

As a point of interest, Senator Schumer and his wife were married at the top of the World Trade Center's North Tower almost twenty-one years to the day before 9/11 . . . yet he supports the Fairness Doctrine that would give radicals a voice in American media.

We must encourage the majority of peaceful Muslims to

speak out against their radical brothers. To secure their own freedom—and to preserve ours—they must stand with us against terrorism. When *America Alone* author Mark Steyn was charged with hate speech by the Canadian Islamic Congress, those of us who fight for free speech rights were horrified that such a thing could happen. As we saw earlier, at the time the charges were being heard by the various human rights tribunals in Canada, Steyn made an appearance at Hillsdale College in Michigan, where he spoke at length about the challenge to his freedom of expression. Following are some of his comments, again reprinted with permission from *Imprimis*, a publication of Hillsdale College:

"As the famous saying goes, the price of liberty is eternal vigilance. What the Canadian Islamic Congress and similar groups in the West are trying to do is criminalize vigilance. They want to use the legal system to circumscribe debate on one of the great questions of the age: the relationship between Islam and the West and the increasing Islamization of much of the Western world, in what the United Nations itself calls the fastest population transformation in history."[18]

Hispanic groups have also begun targeting conservative talk radio. Citing FBI statistics showing hate crimes have increased on Hispanics, the National Hispanic Media Coalition is calling on the FCC to probe hate speech and conservative talk radio. Alex Nogales, President and CEO of the NHMC told a news conference on January 28, 2009, "We are very respectful of the first amendment and free speech, but the hateful rhetoric, particularly against the immigrant minority communities, espoused by irresponsible TV and radio talk show hosts on American airwaves needs to be addressed and today we will present a three-prong strategy to do so."[19]

The NHMC specifically looked at language in three

programs—the highly rated John and Ken show on KFI, Los Angeles, the Michael Savage show, and the Lou Dobbs show. All have been critical of illegal immigration. Using the UCLA/Chicano Studies Research Center, the group claims to have quantified hate speech on commercial talk radio. Their report states, "We identified four types of speech that through negative statements, create a climate of hate and prejudice."[20] They state that they isolated 334 instances of hate speech in eighty minutes of radio programming.

Groups like the NHMC want to redefine what is and what is not acceptable to say on the air. Conservative hosts feel that when they speak out against illegal immigration and its drain on the U.S. economy, they are automatically branded as racists promoting hate speech. I have seen it first hand at many of the stations where I supervised programming. When a host spoke out against illegal immigration, he was labeled a racist. The reality is clear—conservative talk radio and conservative values are under siege in America—from forces inside and outside our borders. The intent is to quash free speech by convincing everyone it's hate speech. Speech is only free on their terms. The story will continue to unfold. . . . Stay tuned.

Not all Muslims may be terrorists,
but all terrorists are Muslims. . . .

—ANN COULTER, AUTHOR AND POLITICAL ANALYST
SEPTEMBER 28, 2001

STRAIGHT AHEAD: "God damn America!" A church dedicated to change on the airwaves.

CHAPTER 29

The Obama Doctrine

The United Church of Fairness

On April 13, 2003, the Reverend Jeremiah Wright issued his now-famous words condemning the United States of America. But that statement wouldn't come home to roost until March 2008, when his inflammatory rhetoric would catch up to the Democratic presidential campaign and the ultimately victorious Barack Obama. Wright's statement that blacks should not sing " 'God Bless America,' but 'God Damn America' " caused a furor across the nation . . . and especially with conservative talk radio hosts and their listeners.

Reverend Wright served as President Obama's pastor for twenty years—although Obama would later conveniently deny remembering any inflammatory sermons—and both the reverend and the most famous member of his congregation would be forced to leave the Trinity United Church of Christ because of the damage to Obama's campaign.

Reverend Wright performed the marriage of Barack Obama and his wife Michelle, he baptized their two daughters, and one of his sermons was the inspiration for Obama's 2006 memoir, *The Audacity of Hope.* The controversial pastor's sermons further divided our nation over color and tainted Obama's image . . . but only after conservative talk radio brought the comments to the attention of the general public.

For months afterward, dozens of talk radio hosts kept reminding listeners of the worst of Wright's wrath while mainstream media carefully ignored what seemed like one of the most sensational stories of the campaign. Imagine if John McCain's pastor of twenty years had preached hatred of the United States of America. Imagine if he had put forward the theory that the U.S. government created and spread the AIDS virus to exterminate a particular race of people. Would the *New York Times*, NPR, and Katie Couric have ignored the story?

Located on Chicago's South Side, Trinity UCC[1] is the largest congregation of the United Church of Christ, claiming approximately ten thousand members. The church advertises itself as "Unashamedly Black and Unapologetically Christian with roots in the Black religious experience."

The United Church of Christ was founded in 1957 and claims 1.2 million members nationwide. It has historically come down on the liberal side of most social issues. It was the first church to ordain an African-American pastor, the first to ordain a woman, and the first to ordain an openly gay man. The UCC supports same-gender marriages. Its Cathedral of Hope in Dallas is the largest church in the United States with a primary outreach to gays, bisexuals, and transgender people. The United Church of Christ is all about community organizing, and they have the media—and very likely conservative talk radio—in their sights.

The UCC Office of Communications was formed in 1959.

It was founded by Dr. Everett C. Parker, a media reformer who set out to reform television stations in the South that "were doing a poor job of covering the civil rights movement." The church website includes a video of Parker's work in this regard. These efforts resulted in the revocation of a television broadcast license in Jackson, Mississippi, and challenges to many other media outlets. The UCC website states, "The case continues today to protect citizen rights in the field of media advocacy."

The United Church of Christ has also issued statements on media consolidation and has a "Media Empowerment Project."[2] The mission includes:

- monitoring and making the mainstream media accountable around their framing of issues.
- participating in making media that truly represents themselves and their lives.
- ensuring ways to distribute untold stories and histories that create connections, unity, and inspiration to demand a just world.

The Media Empowerment Project began in 2004, and, along with a number of well-publicized liberal watchdog groups, worked to help put a Democrat in the White House in 2008. The project is "grounded in the belief that a powerful social movement is possible today and that media and communications are central to building it. MEP is seeding locally-driven, innovative strategies in diverse communities to demand and build media justice."

The UCC Office of Communications has organized a series of seven brochures targeting faith-based groups, immigration groups, labor activists, parents, independent artists, community organizers, and environmental advocates to "help educate the public about the role media plays in shaping current social justice issues." It asks, "Are the views of your group and the issues concerning your organizing efforts covered fairly—if at all—in the media?"

The Reverend John H. Thomas, the UCC's general minister and president, said in an online statement that the denomination's only organization interest in Obama's candidacy was for the media to accurately portray Obama's faith: "Our church's rich historical legacy is interwoven with the history of this nation, and the heritage of the United Church of Christ makes it clear that faith is to be expressed actively in public life on behalf of the community and the world. While it is not appropriate for the church to advocate for any one candidate in electoral politics, I am proud that Sen. Obama is an active UCC member and speaks to many of the values that our church holds dear."[3]

The United Church of Christ has issued statements on media consolidation and even an online petition to "tell the FCC not to allow media companies to grow larger." It has a big-media resource page that states, "Media concentration affects us all negatively. We don't hear about the issues—from the school board to the mayor to other issues. We cannot vote intelligently in our local elections. UCC fights to ensure that large media companies remain accountable, comply with current laws, and cover local issues."[4]

The church has been active in media issues such as restoring localism and fighting consolidation. Another page on the UCC website states, "The airwaves over which media broadcast actually are owned by us, the public. Our needs, interests and cultures are supposed to be reflected in broadcast programming. Around the country, communities are organizing to hold TV and radio stations accountable. Together, our voices are louder and stronger than our fragmented, individual voices. Join this growing movement to reclaim our right to speak and be heard on our airwaves."

On the surface, the church's mission and words about reclaiming the airwaves don't seem outrageous—the airwaves do belong to the public, and many think big-media owners are not serving local communities as well as smaller operators. But are there concerns for conservative talk radio? The church's use of language such as "reclaim our right" and "monitoring and making the mainstream media accountable" causes concern for conservative talk show hosts. Whose viewpoint are they going to monitor and reclaim? Limbaugh's? Hannity's? Savage's? Or Levin's?

To say that the United Church of Christ is politically active is an understatement. This author has a good friend who attended UCC seminary for a year but found the denomination's agenda to be too political for his tastes. He spoke to me on the condition of anonymity:

This was the early eighties, and the movement towards political correctness was clearly the order of the day. Perhaps most distressing was the move to support specific political causes, which had little if any theological foundation. Feeding and caring for the poor seemed viable and reasonable to me. Developing suburban youth programs and elder care were not only scripturally supported, but seemed a very appropriate focus for a congregation serving its community. However, some pet projects did not fit that mold. As an example, while pushing for gay rights and gay unions seems within the rights of any individual (within the church or not), for the church to develop, advocate, and give preferential treatment to a "Gay Caucus" seemed a bit extreme—especially as it was difficult to find any scriptural support on this topic.[5]

Disillusioned, this student left the seminary after a year and returned to broadcasting, intent on utilizing the stations to "serve in the public interest" and do as much good as possible for each respective community. He has done just that.

In June 2008, Barack Obama's spokesman Michael Ortiz stated that Obama "considers [the Fairness Doctrine] debate to be a distraction from the conversation we should be having about opening up the airwaves and modern communications to as many diverse viewpoints as possible." This sounds very similar to what the United Church of Christ states about the media.

The Obama administration is much too smart to try to force the *old* Fairness Doctrine back on broadcasters. It would provide conservative talk radio with nonstop show prep material, that would in turn result in a flood of protest that would make Senator Trent Lott's widely publicized statement that "talk radio is running America" seem like an understatement. Such a move would wind up in the courts, where it would most likely be ruled unconstitutional. The damage they could do to conservative talk radio during that time, however, would be significant.

The new administration is more likely to attack conservative talk radio with a *new* Fairness Doctrine—based on the activism of organizations like the United Church of Christ and community interest groups—to push localism through the FCC and into the media.

In October 2007, Obama sent a letter to then FCC chairman Kevin Martin stating, "The Commission has failed to further the goals of diversity in the media and promote localism."[6] Left-leaning activist groups such as the Center for American Progress concluded that there is an "absence of localism in American radio markets" and are urging greater accountability of radio licensing. Feeling Democrat pressure, the FCC proposed the creation of "permanent station advisory boards comprised of local officials and other community leaders to periodically advise stations of local needs and issues to ensure content diversity on the air."

And what advisory organization succeeded in revoking a station's license in Mississippi? It was the United Church of Christ, parent organization of Trinity UCC in Chicago, which was, until May 2008, President Barack Obama's church.

For advocates of the antiquated Fairness Doctrine, localism is the new way of forcing balanced radio programming. Radio advisory panels would have the right to challenge station programming and the right to force their liberal views on conservative talk radio using the intimidation factor of losing a broadcast license if they didn't comply. And the United Church of Christ knows how to revoke a broadcast license. The community activist was well trained in the UCC. The battle is heating up, and with Democrat dominance in Washington, D.C., from the White House to the FCC, dark clouds are forming over conservative talk radio. Oregon Republican Congressman Greg Walden advises us, "I'd be watching for an 'all of the above' strategy to come at corporate media."[7]

FCC allies of localism are lining up. On December 13,

2007, the FCC's Kevin Martin filed a brief before the Senate Committee on Commerce, Science and Transportation stating,[8] "In order to ensure that the American people have the benefit of a competitive and diverse media marketplace, we need to create more opportunities for different, new and independent voices to be heard." Martin also stated in his brief, "Establishing and maintaining a system of local broadcasting that is responsive to the unique interests and needs of individual communities is an extremely important goal for the commission. The rules that I propose are intended to promote localism by providing viewers and listeners greater access to locally responsive programming including, but not limited to, local news and other civic affairs programming."

Among Martin's specific proposals are "permanent advisory boards in each community (including representatives of underserved community segments) with which to consult periodically on community needs and issues." This should send a shiver through every conservative political commentator.

An editorial on November 12, 2008, by the online service *The Examiner*,[9] sounded an urgent warning about advisory boards: "If this proposed regulation is adopted, political activists with ideological agendas on advisory boards will be able to dictate content by producing allies to complain that their interests are not being considered."

In a brief filed with the FCC, the Minority Media and Telecommunications Council[10] stated it wanted advisory boards to be independent of advertisers: "In other words, it would not do for broadcasters to meet with the business leaders whose companies advertise on their stations." Such a move would be of grave concern to conservative radio broadcasters because they derive much of their advertising revenue from businesses with conservative values. To exclude them from advisory boards would not only deprive them of a voice in the community, but also result in an erosion of advertising revenue and eventually kill conservative talk radio. This shocking suggestion would muzzle the voices of the community's business leaders—who provide jobs and drive the economy—and give a loud voice to fringe activist groups. What is "fair-and-balanced" about that?

It is the goal of those promoting localism to develop a more transparent and meaningful process for license renewal that could be based on more detailed information and documentation about a station's actual performance. Programming would be under intense scrutiny. As nationally syndicated talk host Lars Larson puts it, "No station general manager wants this kind of headache and the cost it would take to fight it."[11] The message is clear. Conservative talk radio would be under assault. In the past, most complaints to the FCC by activist groups were thrown out . . . but there were thousands of complaints during the Fairness Doctrine era that cost stations ridiculous amounts of time and money to fight, taking their focus and resources away from serving their communities. For that reason, talk radio didn't exist then as it does now. The localism fight is the new Fairness Doctrine, and is a sinister, stealth way of stopping conservative talk radio in its tracks.

The Office of Communications of the United Church of Christ set the stage for media activism when it successfully petitioned the FCC to revoke the license of WLBT TV in Jackson, Mississippi, for racist practices during the civil rights era. This historic ruling established that the airwaves are public. The church's activism has spread far and wide since that decision forty years ago.

Today, media activism is a cornerstone of the UCC Office of Communications mission. Here is an interesting example of how church and state may no longer be all that far separated: From 2004–2006, a former FCC commissioner, Gloria Tristani, joined the Office of Communications of the UCC to manage its Washington, D.C., office. She had served on the FCC from 1997 to 2001, and prior to that she had worked for New Mexico Democrat Senator Jeff Bingaman, a staunch advocate of the Fairness Doctrine. It might seem that the UCC's definition of mission no longer means spreading the story of Jesus Christ in some faraway land.

> *My personal view is that government should be*
> *reluctant to regulate content for anybody.*
> —MICHAEL POWELL, FORMER CHAIRMAN,
> FEDERAL COMMUNICATIONS COMMISSION

STRAIGHT AHEAD: The "Fairness" Communications Commission.

CHAPTER 30

The "Fairness" Communications Commission

How the FCC Will Censor

The Federal Communications Commission is composed of five members, who are appointed to five-year terms by the president. Obama has appointed former FCC staffer and media exec Julius Genachowski as chairman, which will give the Democrats the 3–2 majority needed to establish left-leaning regulations that include many of their pet projects such as programming balance, localism, and diversity in media ownership. Josh Silver of Free Press has stated, "Under Julius Genachowski's leadership, the FCC's compass would point toward the public interest."[1] These are code words for controversial localism and ownership diversity initiatives that have conservative talk radio rightfully worried.

The FCC regulates over-the-air broadcasters—traditional radio and television stations in America. Specific vulgar language, nudity, and other programming deemed inappropriate are not permitted on these public channels. Cable television channels and satellite radio do not come under the same rules as traditional broadcasters and are not subject to the same content constraints, because they do not utilize the public airwaves. While basic cable self-regulates, you can subscribe to premium channels that contain profane language and nudity that is not permitted on traditional radio and television stations. If one wants to hear unfiltered free speech, Howard Stern can be heard on Sirius satellite radio, unfettered by FCC content regulations. There are those who would like to regulate content on cable and satellite radio, too, but the likelihood of that ever occurring is remote.

Because big-media companies have consolidated the majority of radio and television stations in America, certain government policies have come under more scrutiny from citizens concerned about media concentration. Since Bill Clinton signed the Telecommunications Act of 1996, permitting deregulation of media ownership, consolidation has occurred at a rapid rate. Several companies now each own hundreds of radio stations, and citizen groups have become increasingly concerned about the public interest being respected by large media license holders who answer to stockholders on Wall Street rather than to listeners and viewers on Main Street. The implications for conservative talk radio are staggering.

There is agitation by many groups who are hoping the Obama administration will make radio and television more accountable to their interests. Media Matters, Free Press, the Center for American Progress, the Media and Democracy Coalition, the United Church of Christ, and many others speak of breaking up media consolidation and returning localism and diversity of ownership to American communities. They have the power in Washington, D.C., to begin the process.

What does this mean?

- Rather than having a few big radio conglomerates, these coalitions want many companies to own the nation's radio and television stations.
- These activist groups believe diversity in ownership would result in more competition and improved programming to better meet local needs.
- They believe the breakup of big media would give them a stronger voice and increased access to the airwaves to be better heard in their communities.
- Liberals also believe this would result in more progressive talk and less conservative political commentary on the radio.

The diversification movement is also supported by some members of the current FCC. In April 2004, FCC Commissioners Michael Copps and Jonathan Adelstein helped launch the Public Interest, Public Airwaves Coalition (PIPAC) and urged the FCC to hold the nation's commercial broadcasters to a more accountable standard of public service. PIPAC was a coalition of many other public activist organizations.

At a meeting of the National Association of Broadcasters in Las Vegas in the spring of 2004, Copps told reporters, "What we get from our media, Big Media in particular, is less of America."[2] Copps was also critical of his own agency's record of defining guidelines for public interest for broadcasters. Later, he would say he was unaware of any attempt to bring back the Fairness Doctrine. However, he uses code words that signal other ways of restoring a type of regulation. On many occasions, he's stated a desire to give all sides an opportunity to talk and be heard on radio today. He has also made statements that if there were less consolidation in media we would have more diversity in viewpoints and perspectives heard on the American airwaves. On December 3, 2008, he stated in an interview on Milwaukee radio station WKLH, "I still think we have to be working toward making sure that controversial issues are brought up on radio and television and that all sides are given an opportunity to talk."[3]

More recently, Copps, who was named acting Chairman of the FCC, has amplified his statements. In an interview with CNSNews.com, he reiterated that he does not support bringing back the old Fairness Doctrine, but he again signaled his intent for a new Fairness Doctrine. "What I've always said, and this is always obviously up to the discretion of the Congress, not the FCC, whether we do or we don't, to me we have to find a way to make radio reflect the public interest." The effort to make radio reflect the public interest could include new licensing requirements, according to Copps. "I think we have a tremendous opportunity going forward to reinvigorate our media to ensure that the public airwaves truly deliver the kind of news and information that we need to sustain our democratic dialogue and to reflect the great diversity of our country." Copps also told CNSNews.com that it's appropriate for government to regulate media content. "If markets cannot produce what society really cares about, like a media that reflects the true diversity and spirit of our country, then government has a legitimate role to play."[4]

Clearly, Copps is hearing the Democrat marching orders to infuse public interest accountability back into the broadcast licensing system. But, there is no refuting that all sides are being heard—the liberal left have their talk shows hosts on radio and television, the Internet, and in print. Conservative talk radio is the minority balance, but Copps and other liberals refuse to admit it.

When George W. Bush was reelected to a second term in the White House, the public outcry for more broadcast accountability picked up steam as Democrats vowed to take back the White House in 2008. On October 31, 2007, FCC commissioner Adelstein opened the final hearing of the Localism Task Force by stating, "We need to implement concrete steps to enhance localism. It means we need to put more rules in place that improve the accountability of analog and digital media outlets to the communities to which they are licensed."[5]

Adelstein also addressed the oft-repeated call for more minority ownership: "We also need to complete action on improving the number of women and people of color who own broadcast media outlets." He cited Chicago, where minorities are the majority "yet they own just five percent of the broadcast stations. Today's media landscape does not reflect the diversity of America. We must carefully weigh whether media ownership that does not reflect the communities to whom they are licensed are truly delivering the local service that reflects the diversity of issues facing the community—including those of concern to women and people of color."

Adelstein says that Americans are not getting the information they need to make informed decisions: "It is also clear from our hearings that local issues that the electorate needs to know about are not being covered in a way that prepares voters to make educated decisions. The problem we hear is that 'breaking news' is being replaced by 'breaking gossip.' In community after community we hear from citizens that serious coverage of local and state government has diminished. There is a virtual blackout of coverage of state and local elections and while news operations say they have to slash resources, some are offering up to one million dollars for an interview with Paris Hilton."

The FCC has many issues before it that will be amplified by the Obama administration, with the encouragement of left-leaning activist groups whose anger boiled over when they lost the previous two presidential elections. They will be pushing the new administration hard to break down large media conglomerates and clarify public interest obligations for radio broadcasters. These will include a strong possibility of more aggressive and possibly permanent advisory boards and changes in the license renewal process, making it more difficult, which most broadcasters will oppose.

These issues must be addressed before the FCC tackles the bigger issue of media consolidation, according to Adelstein: "The public comments we received at hearings across the country were overwhelmingly negative on how consolidation has detracted from the responsiveness of media outlets to local concerns. The public is not interested in further consolidation. Americans distrust big media whether including those on the right, the left, and virtually everybody in between. Distrust of big media, like distrust of big government, is rooted in the American spirit."

With the political changes in Washington, D.C., media change is also in the wind. The changing of the guard has conservatives worried that an assault on our treasured conservative talk radio format is well under way. Code words such as "localism," "public service obligations," "permanent advisory boards" for programming content—all raise major concerns about the preservation of First Amendment rights for broadcasters. It is a strong and powerful agenda . . . a desire for the left to control the right.

> *The Fairness Doctrine has no place in our First Amendment regime. It puts the head of the camel inside the tent and enables administration after administration to toy with TV or radio.*
> —WILLIAM O. DOUGLAS, SUPREME COURT JUSTICE, 1973

STRAIGHT AHEAD: "They may as well return the old Fairness Doctrine."

CHAPTER 31

Radio Fights Back

Radio Managers Take a Stand

CEO of Greater Media, Inc., Peter Smyth, writes a monthly Web letter to employees and anyone who wishes to read it online. In his December 1, 2008, commentary, Smyth wrote about the Fairness Doctrine: "If Congress is truly concerned about viewpoint variety and balance, it should focus on supporting emerging technologies such as HD radio and Wi-Fi technologies, and whatever the next generation of telecommunications might be. A robust and competitive communications marketplace is a far superior tool for promoting balance and diversity of viewpoints than a vague and arbitrary government regulation that is constitutionally suspect out of the gate."[1]

New media technologies have an impact in this argument, and as Paul Giammarco, program director at Providence, Rhode Island's "Station of Record," WPRO, puts it, "When you get right down to it, the information that the Internet provides in many ways mirrors radio's spoken word format. For generations millions have turned to radio for late-breaking news, conversation, entertainment and companionship. Talk radio seems to be better poised to work in tandem with the Internet than any other medium."[2] Like many of his colleagues, Giammarco thinks the Fairness Doctrine is meaningless today: "The glut of information that is now available to talk radio hosts and producers has created an incredible advantage for the spoken word format. This advantage is leading to a better informed and prepared talk product and listener."

Mark Masters is the CEO of Oregon-based Talk Radio Network (TRN), which syndicates well-known hosts such as Michael Savage and Laura Ingraham. Masters says any attempt to bring back the *old* Fairness Doctrine to require balanced talk programming will backfire: "If they bring it back, it will just piss off fifty-seven million Americans who will make sure they lose the Senate and House in a few years." Masters says conservative talk radio is a "pressure valve" for America and that "Democrats should understand it helps release a national tension on key issues."[3]

Masters also contends that Democrats benefited from conservative talk radio in the 2008 general election: "In many ways, conservative talk radio helped elect Obama because conservative hosts weren't completely satisfied with John McCain as their candidate." This theme is echoed far and wide in the talk radio industry.

Dan Mason is a longtime radio programmer in Reno who has worked in both music and talk radio formats. I met Dan in 1995 when I was asked to scope him out as a program director candidate for my company's newly established KKOH Radio. When I flew into Reno, I grabbed a rental car, grabbed Dan, and we headed to Virginia City's Bucket of Blood saloon . . . because great talk begins at a great saloon. The radio format is just an extension of the free speech enjoyed at pubs around the nation! Mason's station has enjoyed eight years as the top-rated radio station in Reno, and he is one of the foremost authorities on talk radio today.

We talked about the Fairness Doctrine and what it would represent to his station. Dan shared his perception: "The idea of restoring the *old* Fairness Doctrine, or a *new* Fairness Doctrine, has become merely another political ideological battle that has nothing to do with actual fairness. It is a strategy liberal-minded politicians and others have adopted that has become all too familiar—if you can't win the argument on its merits, then you attempt to change the rules."[4]

Mason's success has come under fire over the years. His station has been attacked by members of left-wing Media Matters, and protestors have shown up on his station's doorstep. KKOH has been accused by the left of being racist for advocating legal immigration on the air, and Mason offers up reasons for the attack: "Conservative talk radio is being targeted because it is successful and because, so far at least, liberal talk radio is not. The only thing unfair is the notion of punishing radio stations for being successful. *Localism*, or lack of it, is a word often used to criticize radio in general. I submit that there is nothing more local than a radio station that broadcasts regular news reports and also has local talk shows where the issues of the day can be discussed. Many music stations do none of this type of programming, yet conservative viewpoints are targeted as the problem."

Mason also warns about the dangers of radio community advisory boards, which liberal groups and some members of the FCC support: "As the FCC considers the creation of local advisory boards so stations can be 'advised' on programming and other community needs, the red flags should be waving. Radio stations will become nothing more than mouthpieces for every activist under the sun. Stations will find generating ratings to be much more difficult. Revenues will shrink. Local news departments and talk shows will be cut, and the end result will be less . . . not more."

On what radio was like before the Fairness Doctrine was repealed, Dan says: "Talk radio stations that discussed issues and politics were pretty much nonexistent. There were far fewer outlets for diverse opinions, whereas today you would have to try very hard to avoid finding information about any viewpoint you choose. A return of the Fairness Doctrine implies that divergent opinions are not being heard, and that access to nonconservative voices is somehow being suppressed. This philosophy is primed to backfire in a big way."

Tom Tradup is a veteran radio programming executive who heads Salem Communications Corporation's talk division, overseeing such hosts as Mike Gallagher and Michael Medved. Tradup turns the argument from conservative talk radio back to those who are elected and feel a mandate to set the course for radio fairness: "Up front, the concept of permanent advisory boards would be better suited to having citizen oversight of the president or Congress rather than having Washington meddle in private, commercial enterprises like talk radio. We already have two permanent advisory boards called listeners and advertisers. If we aren't delivering compelling, thought-provoking programming, listeners vote with their feet and our ratings drop. When that happens, advertisers chime in by withdrawing their business."[5]

Tradup worries about a backdoor approach to invoking fairness in conservative talk radio: "I am actually less concerned about the obvious, clumsy, unconstitutional and sledgehammer-like Fairness Doctrine than I am of several other potential cancers: so-called 'localism' requirements which would drastically curtail the successful nationally syndicated talk shows in market after market. These include media ownership reform which Obama supports and clarification (code reeducation) of public interest obligations which Obama explicitly supports, along with revising the FCC licensing procedures." Tradup concluded, "Any of these [proposals] would amount to nothing less than a full, frontal assault on the free and open exchange of ideas and opinions on talk radio in America, while leaving left-leaning blogs, newspapers, TV networks, podcasts, and other media options unfettered in their liberal bias. Bottom line — if talk radio is 'all powerful' as critics such as U.S. Senators Charles Schumer (D-NY) and Jeff Bingaman (D-NM) contend in their zeal to muzzle the format, how come Barack Obama — despite strong, vocal opposition from talk radio hosts, guests and callers — ended up the 44th President of the United States?"

James Derby is a young rising star in talk and sports radio programming. He is based in Portland, Oregon, at KXL Radio, which is owned by former Microsoft mogul Paul Allen. Derby says that if any form of Fairness Doctrine is invoked, talk radio will die: "If a Fairness Doctrine — new or old — is enacted, talk radio as we know it will end and thousands of radio employees will lose their jobs. It's not an overstatement, it's reality. Just look at the history. AM radio was on life support when the Fairness Doctrine was abolished. A free market allowed a format to develop, and listeners grew into the millions. Jobs in our industry were created."[6] Derby agrees with Tom Tradup about the socialist assault on free speech: "If they're going to implement advisory boards they may just as well implement the *Old* Fairness Doctrine. Program directors are held to the standards set by listeners and ratings. Is that not the best advisory board available?"

Dan Mason echoes Derby's thoughts: "Those in favor of a Fairness Doctrine have apparently forgotten their history and the reasons it existed in the first place. Media was incredibly smaller and much different than today. There were fewer radio stations. Television was relatively new. The Internet wasn't even a figment of Al Gore's imagination."[7]

Kipper McGee, a major market radio programmer, formerly at WLS in Chicago, presents this view on radio localism and permanent advisory boards: "I think the advent of permanent advisory boards might be a far greater immediate consideration for corporate radio. With many of the top broadcast corporations involved both in the distribution of network and local programming, the inevitable conflict arises between the desire to clear network programming and the mandate to serve in the public interest the communities to which each station is licensed."[8]

McGee's point is the mantra of liberals wanting to break up big media companies and stop consolidation. Fearing fines or possible license revocation because the holder is not responsive to programming advisory boards would kill conservative political commentary and perhaps all of talk radio as we know it. But here's the irony. It's a two-way street, because conservatives can petition liberal stations for the same purpose. There is a reason why there are all-conservative stations and all-liberal stations. And there is a reason why radio programmers don't balance their lineups. Most listeners want to hear one or the other, not both at the same time.

Derby understands this well-established programming concept, which we discovered at KVI in Seattle when we helped
establish the initial all-conservative station: "It's what worked
on FM music stations from the very beginning. Rock stations
played rock music. You'd never hear a rap song on a country
station. Why? Country music fans would not listen. The station would die. Talk is no different. Sports radio stations must
talk about sports 24/7. Liberal talk stations must be liberal
24/7. Conservative stations must be conservative talk 24/7.
Find me a successful radio station that (in a market of compet-
itors of like format) offers a smorgasbord of talk? Just one?"[9]

Still, liberals would like to hear their talk show hosts on
the bigger, more successful conservative stations . . . and they
have support in the White House to make it happen. Unless involuntary advisory board proposals are left out of the
fairness equation, localism is a disaster for free speech rights
of broadcasters and all Americans. The thought and speech
police don't need to run amok in America any more than they
are—the thought of permanent advisory boards to influence
radio station programming is repugnant to the free market that
has guided America for 232 years. It sends a message to the
rest of the world that we are not free as we purport to be. The
speech police must not be allowed to take control of America's
airwaves.

Glenn Beck, one of Premiere Radio's conservative talk
show hosts, told the *Hollywood Reporter* in December 2008,
"Talk radio is the only format where the audience can immediately talk back. Instead of trying to silence their voices,
politicians should start listening to them."[10]

What the "Fairness Doctrine" ought to be called is the "Censorship Doctrine," but the liberals won't call it that because they refuse to admit out loud that that is their intent.
—Rocky D, radio host, WTMA
Charleston, South Carolina

STRAIGHT AHEAD: Losing free speech rights if you pack a gun.

CHAPTER 32

Censors in Action

Radio Hosts Silenced

Can you lose your First Amendment rights because you believe in your Second Amendment rights? Following are some examples of how our fellow conservatives have had to defend themselves against threats and intimidation from the left.

In March of 2004, conservative talk show host Lars Larson was invited to speak at Southern Oregon University's "First Amendment Forum." Forum organizer Paul Steinle—a journalism professor at SOU—learned that Larson carries a concealed weapon, and he asked Lars to adhere to the university's rule prohibiting people from bringing firearms onto the public campus. "He asked me not to bring a gun. He told me that it violated the university's rules. I told him that the university's rules were in violation of state law. The university has no authority to restrict legal concealed carry [weapons] on campus. He told me if I would not agree to leave my gun behind, then the invitation was rescinded. To me this would be the equivalent of violating any of my other civil rights." [1]

Republican leaders and gun rights organizations agreed

with Larson. Bryan Platt, Chairman of the Jackson County Republican Central Committee told the *Ashland Daily Tidings*, "The campus policy is in violation of rights and can be directly challenged. They went beyond the scope of their authority to limit him to come on campus with his weapon."[2]

Maintaining that Larson's invitation was withdrawn because he insisted upon carrying his firearm on campus, Steinle told the *Ashland Daily Tidings*, "I didn't feel I could responsibly invite someone onto campus carrying a firearm. This is a campus. There are students here."[3]

Larson has spent countless hours in handgun safety training and has submitted to a thorough background check. Concealed carriers are highly respected by law enforcement. Crimes are generally committed by those who do not obtain firearms legally. Ironically, Larson's First Amendment rights were taken away by a public institution because he maintained his Second Amendment rights.

Liberal host Thom Hartmann is one of the progressive talk radio personalities who rose from the news reporting ranks to a nationally syndicated host in America. He shared his story of personal intimidation that led to censorship on Al Peterson's NTS MediaOnline: "When I was doing news at WITL/Lansing, MI, in the early 1970's, a guy from the IRS and a state police officer dropped by to 'discuss' whether or not we would cover the mass arrest of a group of tax protesters in a nearby small town. They made it clear, without saying it, that they didn't want us to even mention the arrest. Then they wrote down my driver's license info—with much fanfare—and asked for my Social Security number and home phone number. It was totally intimidating, and I'm embarrassed to say, in retrospect, that we didn't cover the story, giving them the news blackout they wanted."[4]

Even my morning news coanchor, Jeff Grimes, and I received telephone threats when we were on the air at KXL in Portland . . . and that was during the Fairness Doctrine days when we weren't discussing anything controversial! It was unnerving to have law enforcement officials recommend that Jeff and I vary our daily schedules—and constantly change the routes we drove to and from work—so we would be more difficult targets for our radical detractors. And needless to say, there were tight security measures in place whenever we hosted high-profile personalities such as Larry King, Bruce Williams, and Sally Jessy Raphael at major station-sponsored events.

Brian Maloney is a staunch conservative who pulls no punches. Today he writes a radio industry blog that is widely read and respected. He recalls a threatening situation at my old station: "In 1998, just as I was arriving at Seattle's KVI to begin a new position as evening host, a violent demonstration took place in the building's lobby, spilling out into the streets. The reason for the OUTRAGE (!!!): KVI hosts were adamantly supporting Initiative 200, which banned certain racial preferences. It ultimately passed."[5]

The purpose of Initiative 200[6] was to prohibit the state of Washington from using race or ethnicity in deciding student admissions, employment, or contract awards. The initiative passed, and there was ample liberal coverage opposing it in the mainstream media—yet conservative talk radio was the target of attacks for exercising free speech rights to voice support. KVI talk host John Carlson was the chairman of the campaign to promote Initiative 200, and the station experienced liberal backlash with threats to advertisers. If the left doesn't like what you have to say, they will prevent you from saying it if at all possible.

Since passage of Initiative 200, there have been numerous attempts to modify the initiative to once again require colleges and universities to assign student admissions based on skin color or nationality.

There have been other high-profile visits by conservative talk personalities to stations throughout our nation that have required strong security teams because of angry threats received from peace-loving liberals. Free—conservative—speech comes with a price tag.

Another incident also involves Lars Larson and an intimidating assault against him and his station KXL. The liberal city of Portland, Oregon, espouses diversity and tolerance, which makes this story all the more ironic. For many years one of the great traditions in Portland was the lighting of the Christmas tree in Pioneer Square. It is now called the Holiday Tree, which Lars thinks is ridiculous. He said, "A city that proclaims its tolerance every single day is apparently intolerant of the religious beliefs of the majority of people in this country . . . who are Christians."

Lars continued, "For the past few years I've been mentioning the ridiculous name of the tree in the square . . . and mentioning the Jewish Menorah that is put up every year as a symbol of Hanukah and asking that someone find a way to put up a symbol of the real Reason for the Season. No one else would do it, so I offered to find a way through this talk show."

Lars obtained a permit to put up a Christmas cross in Pioneer Square, he found Portland-area Christian churches to sponsor it, and KXL Radio offered to pay for liability insurance. But as soon as word got out about the project, the threats from left-wing groups began . . . and the threats turned into promises to damage or to destroy the cross if it was erected.

Knowing that people can be hurt—or killed—during protests of this type, Larson canceled plans to put up the Christmas cross. "I won't put it up only to be destroyed or vandalized. Aimed at any group you would see this labeled a 'hate crime,' but it seems Christians are fair game."[7] Once again, the liberal hate mongers shouted the loudest and got their way. Peace on earth—goodwill to men.

Who needs a Fairness Doctrine?

P.S.—my dad, President Reagan,
killed the Fairness Doctrine.
—MICHAEL REAGAN,
RADIO HOST AND SON OF PRESIDENT RONALD REAGAN

STRAIGHT AHEAD: Michael Reagan speaks up next.

CHAPTER 33

What Would the Great Communicator Say?

Michael Reagan Speaks Out

I first met Michael Reagan early in 1992. I was planning the full conservative talk show lineup at KVI Radio in Seattle. Mike was doing some work on various stations in Southern California. Being a strong Reaganite, I called Mike at his home one evening and told him I was searching for a host to help fill out our radio programming lineup. Would he be interested? "Yes." A few days later, he flew to Seattle and we auditioned Mike for a week on KVI. He sounded great. It felt right. The Reagan name is golden with conservatives, and the response to Mike on Seattle radio was very positive. I wanted to hire him on the spot.

We discussed his employment at length, and, along with Shannon Sweatte, the station's general manager, we decided to help Mike syndicate his conservative political talk show. Reagan had been negotiating with a network based in San Diego, and we promised him that KVI would put his show on the air. Within a few weeks the deal was completed, and KVI became Michael Reagan's first network station. He continues to enjoy a national radio platform today.

When it came time for Mike to return to Los Angeles at the end of his KVI visit, my wife, Karen, and I rushed him to Seattle-Tacoma International Airport. During the drive we discussed talk radio at length, and that experience would become the foundation of a lasting friendship. Mike is the adopted son of President Ronald Reagan and his wife, Nancy. But to Mike he was "Dad" . . . and whenever he spoke of the president, it was with love, admiration, and respect. Years later, when his dad passed away, Mike and I talked about the president and the legacy he would leave to America. Later that week, Mike spoke eloquently about his father as the nation paid its final respects to the president when he was laid to rest at the Reagan Library.

When the Fairness Doctrine came up in conversation at one of our many industry meetings later on, Mike was quick to remind me that it was his father who had abolished it. The seeds of modern talk radio—mostly conservative—were sown at that moment in 1987 when the FCC voted 4–0 to rescind the Fairness Doctrine. Michael Reagan's show was heard on more than 150 stations nationwide by then, and without repeal of the doctrine by the Reagan FCC, his rise to the national radio spotlight might not have happened. Talk radio history would have been much different without President Reagan, so it is fitting I dedicate much of this chapter to Michael Reagan and his thoughts on radio's fight for fairness and free speech.

In the early part of his administration, President Reagan had appointed Mike Fowler as chairman of the Federal Communications Commission. Fowler went to work examining the

Fairness Doctrine. In 1985, the FCC issued a report conclud-
ing that the Fairness Doctrine no longer served the public
interest because it caused broadcasters to limit their coverage
of controversial issues. No radio station wanted the constant
fight from groups demanding a counter viewpoint, so radio
broadcasters avoided controversy. As Rush Limbaugh stated
earlier, you could telephone a radio station to report your lost
dog, and that was about as controversial as radio was at that
time. A congressional effort to restore the Fairness Doctrine
was vetoed by President Reagan on June 22, 1987. Mike Reagan calls the left-wing assault on conservative talk radio "in-
sidious." Reagan accurately notes that the FCC adopted the
Fairness Doctrine as a regulation—it was never a law enacted
by Congress.

"When the rule was in place, radio and TV stations could
face hefty fines if their stations aired controversial statements
on public affairs without providing 'equal time' to opposing
viewpoints,"[1] Reagan wrote on his website, *ReaganAction.com*,
on November 18, 2008, following the Obama election. When
I talked to Mike he reminded me that radio and TV broadcasters used "self-censorship" to avoid politics and thus any potential harassment or fines by the FCC.

At that time in radio history we were constantly reminded
to seek out the opposing viewpoint, even if there was no other
viewpoint. It was a ridiculous exercise in covering your butt to
make sure the station license would not be jeopardized. There
was a fear factor that certainly did nothing to support freedom
of expression.

In Michael Reagan's commentary on his website, he wrote,
"When this rule was dropped in 1987 under my father, Ronald Reagan, it led directly to the rise of conservative talk radio

that enabled average citizens to have their voices heard across America. If it weren't for the Reagan Administration abolishing the Fairness Doctrine, we would never have heard of Rush Limbaugh, Sean Hannity, Glenn Beck, Michael Savage, Martha Zoller, Neal Boortz, Janet Folger, or the hundreds of other conservative talk radio hosts that dot the land and expose the lies and misdeeds of the left."

Reagan accurately notes that when stations were required to provide equal time, it did nothing to promote dialogue on the airwaves. In fact it inhibited public debate of controversial issues. "What station manager in his right mind would air a [profitable] conservative talk radio show for two or three hours every day if it meant he had to also air liberal shows as well — shows that have consistently lost money whenever they've been tried?"[2]

Veteran radio executive and general manager Milt McConnell at KKOB, Albuquerque, agrees with Reagan's assessment: "There would have to be both listener and advertiser attrition as a result of what no doubt would be a huge shift in content management. Part of the benefit to advertisers in news/talk is the active listeners who are engaged. Talk radio has one of the best ratios of advertising to format ratings out of all the formats that are on the air. There is no question that advertisers would not return to the same degree with a watered down version of what is available today."[3]

How hard is it for liberal stations to sell advertising? In Portland, Oregon, radio sellers tell me that while the liberal station has respectable ratings — often top ten ratings in key demographics — the station is generating only a very small amount of revenue, when compared to conservative stations like KXL. There are reasons, but in general terms many small-business owners share the same conservative values they like to hear on the radio, and they advertise where the largest audience is found—conservative talk radio.

Mike Reagan also notes the root of liberal left-wing rage against conservative talk radio: "Ever since the birth of conservative talk radio and the Internet ended the liberals' total monopoly over the news, the left has been simmering with rage—over the loss of their absolute control over what Americans are allowed to see and hear, and their inability to do anything about it. Time and time again, liberal attempts to sell the nation their shoddy goods have been frustrated when talk radio hosts have taken to the airwaves and warned their millions of listeners that they were about to be taken to the cleaners."[4]

In his website commentary, Reagan notes the power of conservative talk radio and the impact it has left on an angered Congress: "It was not until last year's [June 2007] fatally flawed immigration reform Amnesty bill—that seemed destined for passage—was derailed by an army of angry voters recruited by talk radio hosts and conservative internet websites, that the left understood both the incredible power of the new media, and their utter helplessness in the face of it."[5] Michael Reagan accurately notes that the threat is real. Neither Congress nor the president has to take action. The FCC can bring back the regulation of the Fairness Doctrine without congressional or presidential approval. And the FCC will have a 3–2 Democrat edge in the Obama administration. If the FCC does not reinstate the old doctrine, other means of regulation are available that would result in the demise of conservative talk radio.

"Really, what they're trying to do shows just how desperate the liberals have become," says Reagan. "Without the new media to keep an eye on them, their failure to accomplish their stated goals since winning control of Congress would have been covered up by the subservient mainstream media. Those of us in talk radio and the Internet are the left's worst nightmare—our monitoring of their activities had been shining the light of truth on their attempts to deceive the nation, so now they're trying to do whatever it takes to kill us off." McConnell adds, "It would have our founding fathers rolling in their graves to know that the government might have a hand in sequestering free speech. The thought of there not being a public watchdog on the actions of government and the mass distribution of information is a sobering thought."[6]

I caught up with Mike Reagan on November 29, 2008, and asked him what the president would think if he knew what was occurring more than two decades after he had his FCC rescind a regulation that impeded rather than enhanced free speech: "The president would have one word: 'Veto.' In the twenty years since my father vetoed an attempt by Congress to restore the Fairness Doctrine, nothing has changed. He would have one word for today's attempt to restore it . . . 'Veto.' "[7]

President Ronald Reagan was a champion of deregulation and free-market practices. His rich background in film, radio, and television obviously influenced his philosophy on what role radio and television should play in America. Reagan's days as a radio announcer at legendary WHO Radio in Des Moines, Iowa, are well documented. My parents-in-law met in Des Moines when they worked during college at Bishop's Cafeteria, housed in the same building as the radio station. They often served "Dutch" his lunch, and they remember him fondly to this day. Years later, they would finally meet Michael Reagan when he made an appearance in their hometown of

Yakima, Washington, and they enjoyed sharing their stories of knowing Dutch as a young man.

Americans who cherish freedom of speech also remember President Reagan fondly—the president who thought the FCC's role was the regulation of the broadcast spectrum but not regulation of what is heard on that spectrum. His lesson and legacy is to not fear the marketplace; rather, let it work the way it was meant to work—freely. Free speech can only exist in a free marketplace of ideas. To muzzle conservative talk radio by "regulating" liberals onto the airwaves is placing government in the programming content chair—the supreme chair of free speech. President Reagan would not allow that to happen, and America is better for his wise view of how the media—all media—should operate in the United States. Fans of conservative talk radio owe a debt of gratitude to President Ronald Reagan.

Much credit has been given to Rush Limbaugh for being the "father" of conservative talk radio. I myself have been given credit for establishing arguably the first all-conservative talk station in America. But the true father of conservative talk radio is President Ronald Reagan. Michael Reagan is accurate in his perspective on his father's role in fighting for free speech in the media: "Had my father not gotten rid of the Fairness Doctrine, Rush Limbaugh would not have existed. It opened the door, and Rush Limbaugh was the first one to run through it."[8]

President Ronald Reagan broke down two walls during his administration—first the Berlin Wall and then the Fairness Doctrine. Michael said, "In one case he freed people from communism. In the other, he freed the American people to truly have a choice in conservative talk radio."[9]

*You can accomplish much if you don't
care who gets the credit.*

—PRESIDENT RONALD REAGAN

STRAIGHT AHEAD: A grave danger to America.

CHAPTER 34

Censorship

Don't Let It Happen Again!

I logged nearly 1.5 million air miles during my time as corporate head of programming for one of the nation's largest radio companies. On one of those trips I grabbed a rental car in Atlanta and was driving to Columbia and Charleston, South Carolina, for market visits. While driving, I listened to my friend Neal Boortz on WSB, Atlanta, one of America's finest radio stations. Neal is a brilliant talk show host, and I must credit his show that particular day with awakening me to the real threat and potential disaster that restoration of the Fairness Doctrine would pose for talk radio. In some ways, Boortz is responsible for the decision to write this book. On that day, he started me thinking about history repeating itself. It's been said in many different ways that unless we learn from our mistakes, we are destined to repeat them.

Is there a lesson to be learned? Can the Fairness Doctrine—or its equivalent—be used to intimidate broadcasters and curtail free expression? Is there evidence that freedom of speech was diminished when the regulation was enforced?

The answers to those questions are clearly "Yes." Anyone who cherishes their rights as Americans—guaranteed by the First Amendment—should oppose any form of a Fairness Doctrine . . . any Federal Communications Commission regulation that would meddle with content of radio and television programming across our great nation. Government simply has no right to decide what we can and cannot hear on our radio stations, because without free speech, no other freedoms matter.

Fred Friendly was one of the great pioneers in broadcast history. He began his career in radio at WEAN Radio in Providence, Rhode Island, and later used his experiences to enrich television journalism. As a producer he was teamed with the great Edward R. Murrow and helped popularize radio documentaries in a series of albums titled *I Can Hear It Now*. Friendly enjoyed a sixty-year media career before stepping down as head of CBS News in 1966.

He then began a second career as an author, lecturer, and professor at Columbia University. I never met Fred Friendly, but his book *The Good Guys, the Bad Guys, and the First Amendment*, published by Random House in 1976, is an inspiration to all who cherish free speech. The book examines the role government played at that time in the broadcast media, and it detailed abuses of free speech through government regulation and intimidation—through censorship. In his book, Friendly details how Presidents Kennedy and Nixon used the Fairness Doctrine to their advantage. Bill Ruder, assistant secretary of commerce during the Kennedy administration, spoke of the abuses saying, "Our massive strategy was to use the Fairness Doctrine to challenge and harass right-wing broadcasters and hope that the challenges would be so costly to them that they would be inhibited and decide it was too expensive to continue."[1]

Friendly was a strong advocate of allowing the free marketplace to determine the fate of free speech—not the courtrooms and not the government. His thoughts should be heeded today, because no matter what form of Fairness Doctrine may be proposed—whether restoration of the current Fairness Doctrine still on the books, or programming advisory boards and localism—the potential for abuse still exists. This is the reality facing us in 2009 with a new liberal administration. If Congress had integrity in this matter, it would avoid regulating balanced programming and other requirements that would censor conservative talk. Government must avoid regulating content on all media. Democrats who favor the Fairness Doctrine missed one of the most important lessons in school . . . the lesson about the Constitution of the United States of America and its First Amendment.

In a brief prepared for the Senate Republican Policy Committee on July 24, 2007, Republicans warned of the consequences of a return of the Fairness Doctrine. "In practice, the Fairness Doctrine was regularly used for political purposes." The brief also states, "Regardless of party, a reinstatement of the Fairness Doctrine has the potential to place bureaucrats and political appointees in a position to squelch free speech. The threat of politically motivated censorship is inconstant with America's deeply held right to free speech."[2]

In late December, a major voice in liberal radio added his voice to those who do not favor the Fairness Doctrine. Jon Sinton said, "As the founding President of Air America Radio, I believe that for the last eight years Rush Limbaugh and his ilk have been cheerleaders for everything wrong with our economic, foreign, and domestic policies. But, when it comes to the Fairness Doctrine, I couldn't agree with them more."[3]

Michael Harrison of *Talkers* wrote about the Fairness Doctrine in his December 2008 issue. All of us in conservative talk radio hope his words ring true:

The Threat of the Reinstitution of the Fairness Doctrine

I do not think it will come to pass, but even a whiff of it should be resisted regardless of political leaning, left or right, because it is clearly a First Amendment issue. It has proven in the past to stifle free speech and the unfettered discussion of controversial political issues which is why it was tossed in the first place. But more importantly, it supports the mistaken notion that conservatives dominate talk radio—or "radio" in general—and as a result some sort of deep unfairness is being hoisted on the American public's access to information and opinion. This is statistically untrue! The only kind of talk radio that conservatives dominate is conservative talk radio. It's nobody's fault that the conservative slice of the greater talk radio pie has been relatively successful and capable of generating huge mainstream media buzz along with respectable (although highly over-rated) political influence. But when stepping back and looking at "talk" or spoken word radio as a whole, one cannot discount the growth and marketplace opportunity accorded progressive political hosts—some of whom are achieving serious traction—not to mention the liberal "shock jocks" (hate the term but what the heck) who do morning shows all across the FM dial and are quick to comment on politics, often from the left. Add to that the significant presence of urban talk hosts (most of whom support Democrats), moderate independents (who hardly get outside media attention), all-news radio, sports talk radio, and all the other forms of special interest talk radio garnering huge audiences and serving the needs of the listening public. Last, but certainly not least, there's public radio—NPR and several other fine operations that range from moderate to liberal on their numerous high-quality talk shows. The Fairness Doctrine as it is presently being pitched would only serve to snuff out conservative talk radio, and that would be a travesty.[4]

The word *fairness* was used to disguise the doctrine's intent and purpose. It was a tool government used to regulate media and control content of programs broadcast over America's airwaves. From time to time, freedom of speech is put under a microscope. For all its inconsistencies and deficiencies, our right to express our thoughts, beliefs, and opinions must remain free of government control if we are to continue to be "the land of liberty."

As so many radio voices have warned in these pages, the threat of loss of our right of free expression is a threat to our American way of life. And it is a threat to the rest of the world, which still looks upon us as the beacon of freedom. Our form of talk radio doesn't exist in most other countries, because their governments won't allow media to give the people a collective voice. If we go down the unbridled path of an antiquated Fairness Doctrine—or a new version under which programming advisory boards can usurp control—we give up this great freedom.

There is no question that our values are under attack. Outside forces are using our own systems to muzzle free speech. Give these forces access to a Fairness Doctrine and it's "game over." Take a look at what is happening worldwide. While covering the Beijing Olympics, reporters were granted access only to the sports venues. Anything outside of that was tightly controlled—off-limits in many cases. There are content controls on the Internet in China. There are those who would do the same in the United States of America. It's censorship.

What if Rush Limbaugh, Sean Hannity, Mark Levin, Michael Savage, or Mark Steyn were to do a talk show in Saudi Arabia? It's an impossible notion. Yet there are radical Islamic forces using the politically correct landscape in America to embed their values in our culture and to ultimately destroy our freedoms.

Sometimes we can't see the forest for the trees. Americans become focused on the actual "war" on terror, when much of the war is nonviolent and subtle. The nonviolent war being waged in our culture is second only to the physically violent acts of terrorism that grab the headlines. To restore any form of a Fairness Doctrine not only suppresses freedom of expression, it also undermines the security of our nation, because our enemies know how to use our guaranteed liberties against us.

In remarks before the Media Institute on January 28, 2009, FCC Commissioner Robert McDowell warned against restoring any form of Fairness Doctrine. "History proves that abuses of power brought forth by the doctrine are not partisan. Both right-leaning and left-leaning broadcasters have been attacked and intimidated. With that in mind, if the doctrine is reimposed in any form, how do we know that it will not be used to silence political adversaries?"[5]

All it would take to silence free speech is a directive against a media outlet that wasn't in lockstep with an offended political party. For conservative talk radio this is a very thin line between freedom of speech and censorship. McDowell also had this warning to liberals concerned with conservative talk radio, saying they should "pause to consider the widespread popularity—and potential vulnerability—of public radio programs to doctrine complaints."

In his inaugural address, the president said those who "cling to power through corruption and deceit and the silencing of dissent know that you are on the wrong side of history."[6] While the president's remarks were directed at totalitarian leaders opposed to the West, they also hit the mark for those of us concerned about censorship at home. The wrong side of history would be to muzzle conservative talk radio.

Simply put, government has no business sitting in America's broadcast content chair. This was well understood by our Founding Fathers, but it is not understood by left-wing radicals—a minority in our country—who want to snuff out our conservative voice. We cannot allow it to happen.

Congress shall make no law respecting an establishment of religion, or prohibiting the free exercise thereof; or abridging the freedom of speech, or of the press; or the right of the people peaceably to assemble, and to petition the Government for a redress of grievances.

This is the First Amendment in the Bill of Rights . . . the First Amendment to the Constitution of the United States of America. Let no liberal tear it asunder.

Throughout this book we have used the terms "Fairness Doctrine" or "new Fairness Doctrine." Let there be no mistake. Democrats have backed away from using the term "Fairness Doctrine" for obvious reasons. They are now dropping that onerous term in hopes of outfitting their censorship tactics in new clothes.

The new Fairness Doctrine is the Durbin Amendment sponsored by Richard Durbin of Illinois. The "Durbin Doctrine," as previously noted, resembles the language contained in the 2008 Democrat platform. It also resembles the language used by President Obama. It resembles the language contained in the Center for American Progress report on localism and diversity, and it is the foundation of their "new" Fairness Doctrine.

Let there be no question that Democrats want to establish diversity in programming, and by doing so, they will push aside conservative voices. This is censorship. No matter how they deny it, it is their goal. Conservative voices—and those who love talk radio as it exists today—beware!

I'll sign off for now, but hope to be back soon. Thank you for listening and helping defend free speech.

Those who cannot remember the past
are condemned to repeat it.
—GEORGE SANTAYANA, SPANISH PHILOSOPHER

Notes

Introduction: Us vs. Them

1. http://www.nypost.com/seven/01262009/news/politics/limbaugh
   _slams_obama_152128.htm.
2. http://www.newsmax.com/insidecover/obama_rush_limbaugh/
   2009/01/25/175082.html.
3. http://eyeblast.tv/public/video.aspx?v=yduznz8zVr; http://www
   .newsmax.com/insidecover/bozell_slams_obama/2009/01/27/
   175551.html.
4. http://www.billpress.com/.
5. http://www.billpress.com/; http://newsbusters.org/blogs/seton-motley/
   2009/02/11/politico-sen-harkin-we-need-fairness-doctrine.
6. http://www.gotomario.com/; http://www.politico.com/blogs/michael
   calderone/0209/Clinton_wants_more_balance_on_the_airwaves
   .html.
7. *The Savage Nation*, February 13, 2009.

Chapter 1: Talk Radio in Jeopardy

1. Author interview of Lars Larson, KXL Radio, Portland, Ore., De-
   cember 2008; ftp.media.radcity.net/zmst/insideradio/Interviews/
   LarsonArticle02-26.pdf; http://www.wnd.com/news/article.asp?
   ARTICLE_ID=35298.
2. *The Lars Larson Show*, November 3, 2004, KXL Radio, Portland,
   Ore.

3. Author interview of Lars Larson, December 2008.
4. http://mediamatters.org/about_us/

Chapter 2: The First Amendment

1. http://www.cnn.com/2007/POLITICS/06/28/immigration.con
   gress/index.html.
2. http://www.nytimes.com/2007/06/15/washington/15immig.html
3. Fox News, June 24, 2007, http://www.foxnews.com/story/0,2933
   ,286442,00.html.
4. http://radioequalizer.blogspot.com/2007/06/rush-limbaugh-trent-
   lott-talk-radio.html.
5. Fox News, June 24, 2007, http://www.foxnews.com/story/0,2933
   ,286442,00.html.
6. http://www.politico.com/news/stories/1107/6757.html.
7. Statement of Lars Larson, KXL Radio, to author, October 2008.
8. http://www.rasmussenreports.com/public_content/politics/general
   _politics/47_favor_government_mandated_political_balance_on
   _radio_tv.

Chapter 3: The Fairness Doctrine

1. Statement of Chris Berry to author, October 2008.
2. Fox News, June 24, 2007, http://www.foxnews.com/story/0,2933
   ,286442,00.html.
3. http://law.jrank.org/pages/12638/Red-Lion-Broadcasting-Co-v
   -Federal-Communications-Commission.html.
4. http://www.usdoj.gov/osg/briefs/1989/sg890390.txt.
5. http://www.humanevents.com/article.php?id=27185.
6. http://thehill.com/leading-the-news/gop-preps-for-talk-radio
   -confrontation-2007-06-27.html.
7. http://www.rasmussenreports.com/public_content/general_politics/
   47_favor_government_mandated_political_balance_on_radio_tv.

8. Statement of Doug McIntyre, KABC Radio, to author, Los Angeles, December 2008.

Chapter 4: The Bingaman Bombshell

1. *Jim Villanucci Show*, October 22, 2008, 3–6 p.m. KKOB Radio, Albuquerque.
2. Author interview of Pat Frisch, KKOB Radio, Albuquerque, October 24, 2008.
3. Statement of Jim Villanucci, KKOB Radio, Albuquerque, to author, October 24, 2008.
4. http://republicanleader.house.gov/News/DocumentSingle.aspx? DocumentID=105070.
5. Statement of Milt McConnell, KKOB Radio, Albuquerque, to author, October 24, 2008.
6. Statement of Chris Berry to author, October 2008.
7. Statement of Sean Hannity to author, December 2008.
8. *Albuquerque Journal*, November 4, 2008.
9. Constituent email, November 2008, authorized by constituent.

Chapter 5: Hush Rush

1. *Talkers* magazine, December 2008, http://talkers.com.
2. *The Rush Limbaugh Show*, October 23, 2008.

Chapter 6: Radio Hosts Tee Off

1. http://www.ntsmediaonline.com/, October 24, 2008.
2. Statement of Mark Davis to Al Peterson, ntsmediaonline.com, October 24, 2008.
3. Statement of Ken Charles to Al Peterson, ntsmediaonline.com, October 24, 2008.
4. Statement of Andrew Deal to Al Peterson, ntsmediaonline.com, October 24, 2008.

5. Statement of Shawn Smith to Al Peterson, ntsmediaonline.com, October 24, 2008.
6. Statement of Roy Fredricks to Al Peterson, ntsmediaonline.com October 24, 2008.
7. David Mamet, "The Media Must Not Allow Government to Proscribe Free Speech," © *The Independent* (London), November 19, 2008.

Chapter 7: The Lilliputians

1. *The Mark Levin Show*, October 23, 2008.
2. Author interview with Lars Larson, *The Lars Larson Show*, Westwood One, December 2008.
3. Author interview with Doug McIntyre, KABC Radio, Los Angeles, November 2008.
4. Statement of Bill Manders, KKOH Radio, to author, Reno, November 2008.
5. *The Glenn Beck Program*, October 23, 2008.
6. *The Savage Nation*, October 23, 2008.
7. http://www.humanevents.com/article.php?id=26968#continueA, June 11, 2008.

Chapter 8: Silence

1. http://www.youtube.com/watch?v=34I3kg7BeF8.
2. Suit against KRLA, http://www.glendalenewspress.com/articles/2008/09/09/news/gnp-filing09.txt.
3. http://seattletimes.nwsource.com/html/localnews/2003683328_talkradio27m.html, April 27, 2007.
4. Author interview of John Carlson, KOMO Radio, Seattle, November 2008.

Chapter 9: Dingy Harry

1. Statements of Bill Manders & Sean Patrick, KKOH Radio, to author, Reno, November 2008.
2. http://www.politico.com/blogs/thecrypt/1007/Clear_Channel_CEO_responds_to_Reid.html.
3. *The Rush Limbaugh Show*, October 19, 2007.
4. http://seattletimes.nwsource.com/html/localnews/2003895483_webmacbeth21m.html, September 21, 2007.
5. *The Rush Limbaugh Show*, October 19, 2007.
6. Ibid.
7. http://thinkprogress.org/2007/10/01/harkin-maybe-limbaugh-was-high-on-drugs-again/.
8. http://www.opinionjournal.com/extra/?id=110005497, August 19, 2004.
9. http://www.lvrj.com/news/10545847.html, October 15, 2007.
10. http://email.newsmax.com/politics/zogby_fairness_doctrine/2008/10/27/144486.html, October 27, 2008; http://www.reuters.com/article/pressRelease/idUS210147+17-Sep-2008+PRN20080917.
11. Statement of Congressman Greg Walden to author, October 2008.
12. http://delauro.house.gov/release.cfm?id=566, May 6, 2008.
13. Rowan Scarborough, "FCC Probe Signals Democratic Attack Machine," *Human Events*, http://www.humanevents.com/article.php?id=29263. October 30, 2008.
14. Ibid.
15. Ibid.

Chapter 10: Censorship by Congress

1. Statement of Congressman Greg Walden to author, October 2008.

2. http://www.pbs.org/now/politics/slaughter.html, 12/17/2004.

3. http://www.worldnetdaily.com/news/article.asp? ARTICLE_ID= 56398, 6/27/2007.

4. Statement of Congressman Greg Walden to author, October 2008.

5. http://www.onenewsnow.com/Politics/Default.aspx?id=312136 ,11/6/2008; http://www.youtube.com/watch?v=NIhFm9Mxpxg.

6. Author interview with Lars Larson, KXL Radio, Portland, Ore., December 2008.

7. http://www.wbal.com/apps/news/templates/default.aspx?a=15204 &template=print-article.htm, 10/27/2008; http://www.tvnewsday .com/articles/2008/11/03/daily.1/.

Chapter 11: Obama Weighs In

1. http://www.aim.org/aim-column/the-obama-fairness-doctrine/; http://www.humanevents.com/article.php?id=29566, June 2008.

2. http://www.huffingtonpost.com/2008/08/28/obama-takes-aim-at -wgn-ra_n_122081.html.

3. Statement of Bob Shomper to author, October 2008.

4. Congressman Mike Pence, WBT Radio, September 3, 2008.

5. http://blogs.orlandosentinel.com/entertainment_tv_tvblog/2008/ 10/obama-campaign.html.

6. http://www.kmov.com/video/index.html?nvid=285793&shu=1; http://www.kmov.com/localnews/stories/kmov_election_092808 _truthsquad.bec69e89.html.

7. http://governor.mo.gov/cgi-bin/coranto/viewnews.cgi?id=EkkkV FulkpOzXqGMaj; http://gatewaypundit.blogspot.com/2008/09/ breaking-gov-matt-blunt-releases.html, 9/27/2008.

8. http://www.nypost.com/seven/10152008/news/politics/obama_ fires_a_robin_hood_warning_shot_133685.htm, 10/16/2008; http:// www.youtube.com/watch?v=vFC9jv9jfoA

9. http://www.foxnews.com/story/0,2933,446586,00.html, November 4, 2008.

10. http://www.youtube.com/watch?v=aCeD1RcJjAg, November 4, 2008.

11. http://www.cnn.com/2008/POLITICS/05/29/obamas.first.campaign/index.html, May 30, 2008.

12. Statement of Ed Schultz to author, December 2008.

Chapter 12: That's Entertainment!

1. Statement of Michael Harrison, *Talkers* magazine, to author, December 2008.

2. http://townhall.com/columnists/DavidLimbaugh/2007/01/19/the_unfairness_doctrine_unevening_the_playing_field,_by_law.

3. Statement of Tony Russell, WNBF, Binghamton, to author, October 2008.

4. http://www.radioink.com/listingsEntry.asp?ID=553846&PT=industryqa, 10/06/08.

5. Statement of Greg Tantum, WTNT Radio, to author, February 2009.

6. http://www.politico.com/blogs/michaelcalderone/0209/Sen_Stabenow_wants_hearings_on_radio_accountability_talks_fairness_doctrine.html?showall, February 5, 2008.

7. http://www.washingtonpost.com/wp-dyn/content/article/2009/02/06/AR2009020602511.html?referrer=emailarticle.

8. Jim Bohannon statement to Al Peterson, NTSMediaOnline, February 6, 2009.

Chapter 13: A Liberal Rejects Censorship

1. http://www.taylormarsh.com/archives_view.php?id=25085; http://seanbraisted.blogspot.com/2007/01/cohen-on-hannity-colmes.html

2. Author interview of Alan Colmes, December 2008.

3. Statement of Rocky D, WTMA, Charleston, S.C. to author, interview, December 2008.

4. *The Ed Schultz Show*, http://crushliberalism.com/2007/06/27/popular-liberal-talk-radio-host-claims-libs-cant-get-fair-shot-on-radio/.

5. Statement of Michael Harrison, *Talkers* magazine, to author, December 2008.
6. Statement of Ed Schultz to author December 2008.
7. Statement of Doug McIntyre, KABC, Los Angeles, to author, December 2008.

Chapter 14: The Gospel According to Radio

1. Statement of Chris Squires, KERI Radio, Bakersfield, Calif., to author, December 2008.
2. http://www.focuspetitions.com/155/petition.asp; http://www.citi zenlink.org/content/a000007662.cfm.
3. http://focusfamaction.edgeboss.net/download/focusfamaction/pdfs/ 10-22-08_2012letter.pdf.
4. http://www.christiannewswire.com/news/334569112.html.
5. http://www.whitehouse.gov/news/releases/2008/03/20080311-3 .html.
6. http://www.aim.org/special-report/censoring-the-conservative -media/, April 10, 2007.
7. www.leadingtheway.org/site/DocServer/NRB_Fairness_Doctrine .pdf?docID=1861, July 2007.

Chapter 15: Bias!

1. http://www.timesonline.co.uk/tol/news/world/iraq/article4276486 .ece, June 6, 2008.
2. http://www.journalism.org/node/13307, October 22, 2008.
3. http://people-press.org/report/463/media-wants-obama, October 22, 2008.
4. http://mediamatters.org/about_us/.
5. http://www.howobamagotelected.com/; http://www.johnziegler .com/editorials_details.asp?editorial=182; http://www.youtube .com/watch?v=-95wkCMeUkk.

6. http://www.cmpa.com/media_room_press_10_30_08.htm.
7. http://www.discoverthenetworks.org/individualProfile.asp?indid =1793, November 19, 2003.
8. http://newsbusters.org/static/2007/11/112607%20Laura&Brokaw .mp3.
9. http://www.howobamagotelected.com/.
10. http://www.johnziegler.com/editorials_details.asp?editorial=176, November 18, 2008.
11. Statement of Doug McIntyre, KABC Radio, Los Angeles, to author, December 2008.

Chapter 16: The Birth of Talk Radio

1. Author interview of Lars Larson, KXL Radio and Westwood One, December 2008.
2. http://www.mrc.org/biasbasics/pdf/BiasBasics.pdf.
3. http://www.mediaresearch.org/biasbasics/printer/biasbasics4.asp, November 1996.
4. Statement of Al Peterson to author, http://www.ntsmediaonline .com/, December 2008.

Chapter 17: Constitution Day

1. http://www.firstamendmentcenter.org/.
2. Statement of Gene Policinski to author, December 2008.
3. http://www.firstamendmentcenter.org/news.aspx?id=20534, July 23–August 3, 2008.
4. Todd Schnitt statement to Al Peterson, ntsmediaonline.com, November 7, 2008.
5. Statement of Dave Elswick, KARN A/F radio, Little Rock, to author, October 2008.
6. Statement of Matt Lloyd, Congressman Mike Pence's office, to author, December 2008.

Chapter 18: Congress Weighs In

1. http://www.house.gov/hinchey/issues/mora.shtml; http://www.house
   .gov/apps/list/press/ny22_hinchey/060503FCC.html; http://www
   .house.gov/hinchey/newsroom/press_2004/033004mora.html,
   March 30, 2004.

2. http://www.standardnewswire.com/news/194482934.html; http://
   mikepence.house.gov/news/DocumentSingle.aspx?DocumentID
   =93812, June 11, 2008; http://www.houseconservatives.com/blog/
   rep-pense-responds-to-pelosis-fairness-doctrine-plan/.

3. http://www.tvweek.com/news/2008/08/democratic_party_platform
   _more.php, August 14, 2008.

4. http://newsbusters.org/blogs/seton-motley/2009/02/27/essay-durbin-
   amendment-new-fairness-doctrine-kicker.

5. http://demint.senate.gov/public/index.cfm?FuseAction=Press
   Releases.Detail&PressRelease_id=b45d291a-e719-3b58-d60c-59eaf
   39afd81&Month=2&Year=2009.

6. http://www.cnsnews.com/public/content/article.aspx?RsrcID=
   44588.

7. http://newsbusters.org/blogs/seton-motley/2009/02/27/essay-durbin-
   amendment-new-fairness-doctrine-kicker.

Chapter 19: The Digital Explosion

1. Statement of Mike Edwards, WTMA, Charleston, S.C., to author, December 2008.

2. Statement of Brian Westbrook, KXL Portland, Ore., to author,
   December 2008.

3. Statement of Kevin Casey, *Talkers* magazine, to author, December 2008.

4. http://www.pewinternet.org/PPF/r/252/report_display.asp, June
   15, 2008; http://www.pewinternet.org/PPF/r/303/press_release.asp.

5. Statement of Dan Mason, KKOH, Reno, to author, December
   2008.

Chapter 20: Fair & Balanced

1. http://www.dailykos.com/story/2007/7/6/232418/7716/78/354873.
2. http://www.americanprogress.org/issues/2007/06/talk_radio.html.
3. Statement of Michael Harrison, *Talkers* magazine, to author, December 2008.

Chapter 21: Grassroots Intimidation

1. http://www.americanprogress.org/issues/2007/06/talk_radio.html.
2. http://www.heritage.org/research/regulation/wm1472.cfm#_tn ref10.
3. http://articles.latimes.com/2007/jul/23/business/fi-fairness23.
4. http://michellemalkin.com/2008/06/13/fight-the-smearsagainst-rush-and-the-right/; http://granitegrok.com/blog/2008/06/the _fairness_doctrine_by_another_means.html.

Chapter 22: The Myth

1. http://www.cultureandmediainstitute.org/specialreports/2008/Fair ness_Doctrine/FairnessDoctrine_ExecSum.htm.
2. Statement of Lars Larson, KXL, Portland, Ore., to author, November 2008.
3. Statement of Michael Harrison, *Talkers* magazine, to author, December 2008.
4. Statement of Kipper McGee to author, December 2008.
5. Statement of Dan Mason, KKOH, Reno, to author, December 2008.
6. http://www.mrcaction.org/517/petition.asp?PID=18645182.

Chapter 23: Hometown Radio

1. Author interview of Shannon Sweatte, October 2008.
2. http://sfppc.blogspot.com/2009/01/ed-baxter-questions-fcc-chair -kevin.html.

3. Statement of Jerry Del Colliano, Inside Radio, to author, January 2009.

4. http://en.wikipedia.org/wiki/Minot,_North_Dakota; http://query.nytimes.com/gst/fullpage.html?res=9C05EED61539F932A057 50C0A9659C8B63, March 31, 2003.

5. Guy Rathbun, KCBX Radio, November 5, 2008.

6. http://sfppc.blogspot.com/2009/01/ed-baxter-questions-fcc-chair -kevin.html.

Chapter 24: "Good Morning, Vietnam!"

1. http://mediamatters.org/items/200405260001, May 25, 2004.

2. http://209.85.173.132/search?q=cache:Q2q4jVbLoAMJ:media matters.org/items/200406170004+Senator+Harkin+comments +asking+fairness+on+Armed+Forces+radio&hl=en&ct=clnk& cd=1&gl=us, June 17, 2004.

3. *The Rush Limbaugh Show*, June 17, 2004.

4. *The Ed Schultz Show*, November 7, 2005, http://securingamerica .com/node/320.

5. http://radioequalizer.blogspot.com/2006/06/limbaugh-hannity -afrts.html.

6. Interview of author's son-in-law, who served in Iraq 2004–2005 and is now an officer in U.S. Army.

7. Statements of Adrian Cronauer & author interview of Adrian Cronauer, January 2009.

Chapter 25: The Speech Police

1. Statement of Ross Mitchell, KKOH Radio, Reno, to author, December 2008.

2. http://en.wikipedia.org/wiki/Republican_Revolution; http://www .usnews.com/usnews/photography/1994/bigpicture.php?image=1; http://www.politico.com/news/stories/1107/6757.html.

3. http://mediamatters.org/about_us/.
4. http://en.wikipedia.org/wiki/David_Brock; http://mediamatters.org/about_us/staff_advisors; http://www.nationalreview.com/york/york 200405281333.asp; http://newsbusters.org/blogs/noel-sheppard/2007/09/30/group-behind-smear-campaigns-against-limbaugh-o-reilly.
5. http://www.aim.org/special-report/the-liberal-plan-to-take-over-talk-radio/; http://sweetness-light.com/archive/does=media-matters-violate-its-501c3-status, October 21, 2004; http://www.fairnessdoctrine.com; http://www.frontpagemag.com/Articles/Read.aspx?GUID=C5429F9E-A632-4A4B-827F-FB88C6965612.

Chapter 26: The Left-Wing Smear Machine

1. http://newsbusters.org/blogs/noel-sheppard/2007/10/01/hillary-clinton-told-yearlykos-convention-she-helped-start-media-matt.
2. http://query.nytimes.com/gst/fullpage.html?res=9C02E0DE133 DF930A35756C0A9629C8B63, May 3, 2004.
3. *The Glenn Beck Show*, http://www.youtube.com/watch?v=M4 scaVyFTIA.
4. Bill O'Reilly, *The O'Reilly Factor*, October 2, 2007.
5. http://transcripts.cnn.com/TRANSCRIPTS/0805/22/ldt.01.html, May 22, 2008.
6. http://coloradomm.org/items/200704170012; http://mediamatters.org/items/200704170012.
7. http://www.foxnews.com/story/0,2933,218233,00.html, October 11, 2006.

Chapter 27: Is America Next?

1. http://en.wikipedia.org/wiki/Human_rights_complaints_against _Maclean's_magazine; http://www.ohrc.on.ca/en/resources/news/statement; http://www2.canada.com/theprovince/news/story.html

?id=ba1deb3e-1dda-4efb-b033-129ee4b3160d; http://pundita.blog
spot.com/2008/01/macleans-magazine-affair-reveals-deep.html.

2. http://www.newswire.ca/en/releases/archive/June2008/26/c8368
.html; http://macleans.ca/article.jsp?content=20080627_120859
_5592.

3. http://www.hillsdale.edu/news/imprimis/archive/issue.asp?year=
2008&month=08.

4. http://www.albertahumanrights.ab.ca/1249.asp,http://www.life
sitenews.com/ldn/2008/jun/08062304.html; http://cumenism
.net/archive/news/2008/07/bishop_henry_on_albertas_human
_rights_act.htm.

5. http://www.familyaction.org/Articles/issues/freedoms/speech/mo
nopoly-on-truth.htm; http://www.worldnetdaily.com/news/article
.asp?ARTICLE_ID=59217.

6. http://mediamatters.org/items/200611290005, November 27,
2006.

7. http://www.washingtontimes.com/news/2008/feb/25/artist-hit-for
-refusal-on-beliefs/; www.telladf.org/UserDocs/ElaneRuling.pdf.

Chapter 28: The Speech Terrorists

1. http://www.cair.com/; http://www.cair.com/AmericanMuslims/
AntiTerrorism.aspx.

2. http://www.foxnews.com/politics/2009/01/30/fbi-cut-ties-cair-fol
lowing-terror-financing-trial/; http://www.steveemerson.com/
4283/one-muslim-advocacy-groups-not-so-secret; http://en.wiki
pedia.org/wiki/Council_on_American-Islamic_Relations; http://
www.danielpipes.org/blog/2003/06/cairs-legal-tribulations.html;
www.investigativeproject.org/documents/misc/117.pdf; kyl.senate
.gov/legis_center/subdocs/091003_epstein.pdf; http://frwebgate
.access.gpo.gov/cgi-bin/getdoc.cgi?dbname=108_senate_hear
ings=f:93083.wais;http://frwebgate.access.gpo.gov/cgi-bin/getdoc
.cgi?dbname=108_senate_hearings&docid=f:93083.wais; http://

www.amislam.com/pundit11.htm; http://www.worldnetdaily.com
/index.php?fa=PAGE.view=87498; http://www.worldnetdaily
.com/index.php?fa=PAGE.view&pageId=87498; http://www
.americansagainsthate.org/press_releases/PR-BoxerRescinds
Award.php; http://www.steveemerson.com/2008/03/some-cair
-officials-convicted-of.

3. http://en.wikipedia.org/wiki/Michael_Graham.

4. http://www.worldnetdaily.com/news/article.asp?ARTICLE_ID=
35767, November 2003.

5. http://www.encyclopedia.com/doc/1G1-110932076.html,December
ber 2003; http://www.washingtontimes.com/news/2004/may/11/
20040511-085204-8815r/.

6. http://www.worldnetdaily.com/index.php?fa=PAGE.view&pageId
=58691; http://www.cair.com/ArticleDetails.aspx?ArticleID=236
08&&name=n&&currPage=1&&Active=1, October 29, 2007.

7. http://www.cair.com/ArticleDetails.aspx?ArticleID=23608&&name
=n&&currPage=1&&Active=1; http://www.aim.org/aim-column/
islamists-target-michael-savage/; http://sun.cair.com/ArticleDetails
.aspx?mid1=763&&ArticleID=23609&&name=n&&currPage=1;
http://radioequalizer.blogspot.com/2007/11/michael-savage-loses
-major-sponsor-cair.html.

8. http://www.cair.com/ArticleDetails.aspx?ArticleID=23608&&name
=n&&currPage=1&&Active=1.

9. Statement of Mark Masters, CEO, Talk Radio Networks, to author, December 2008.

10. http://www.aim.org/aim-column/islamists-target-michael-savage/.

11. http://frwebgate.access.gpo.gov/cgi-bin/getdoc.cgi?dbname=108
_senate_hearings&docid=f:93083.wais.

12. http://www.senate.gov/~schumer/SchumerWebsite/pressroom/
press_releases/PR02009.html; http://schumer.senate.gov/new
_website/searchresults.cfm?q=Press+Release%2C+September
+10%2C+2003%2C+Connecting+the+Dots&btnG=Search&
site=schumer&num=10&filter=0.

13. http://www.cairchicago.org/actionalterts.php?file=aa_blog1201 2005.

14. http://www.redorbit.com/news/business/781676/cair_welcomes _tsa_hajj_sensitivity_training/index.html; http://www.amren.com/ mtnews/archives/2004/12/cair_trains_fbi.php.

15. http://www.anti-cair-net.org/HooperStarTrib; http://en.wikipedia .org/wiki/Ibrahim_Hooper; http://www.danielpipes.org/2811/cair -founded-by-islamic-terrorists; http://www.nationmaster.com/ encyclopedia/Ibrahim-Hooper.

16. Author interview of Michael Medved, Salem Radio Network, January 2009.

17. Statement of Congresswoman Sue Myrick to author, January 2009.

18. http://www.hillsdale.edu/news/imprimis/archive/issue.asp?year =2008&month=08.

19. http://www.latinosagainsthatespeech.org/news/1_30_09.html.

20. http://newsroom.ucla.edu/portal/ucla/ucla-study-finds-extensive -use-79402.aspx; www.nhmc.org/documents/PB22new_re3.pdf.

Chapter 29: The Obama Doctrine

1. http://www.tucc.org.

2. http://www.ucc.org/media-justice/media-empowerment-project/.

3. http://www.wfn.org/2007/02/msg00094.html; http://www.ucc .org/news/barack-obama-candidate.html, February 9, 2007.

4. http://www.ucc.org/media-justice/media-consolidation/.

5. Statement of anonymous source to author, December 2008.

6. http://www.targetmarketnews.com/storyid10230701.htm; http:// obama.senate.gov/press/071022-obama_fcc_policy.

7. Statement of Congressman Greg Walden to author, October 2008.

8. www.ltgov.mo.gov/ruralhsi/pdf/SenateTestimony-ChmMARTIN _121307.pdf.

9. http://www.dcexaminer.com/opinion/Another_Assault_on_Free dom_of_the_Airwaves.html.

10. www.keeprushontheair.com/FCCMinorityMediaComments.PDF.
11. Author interview of Lars Larson, Westwood One, November 2008.

Chapter 30: The "Fairness" Communications Commission

1. http://www.dmwmedia.com/news/2009/01/13/reports:-venture
   -capitalist-julius-genachowski-head-fcc, January 13, 2009.
2. http://findarticles.com/p/articles/mi_hb5053/is_/ai_n18353586.
3. http://www.radioandrecords.com/RRWebSite/NewsStoryPage.aspx
   ?ContentID=EaW1DHqzsUk%3D&, Dec. 3, 2008.
4. http://cnsnews.com/public/content/article.aspx?RsrcID=43414.
5. http://www.reclaimthemedia.org/legislation_and_regulation/local
   ism_and_diversity_at_the_%3D5564, October 31, 2007.

Chapter 31: Radio Fights Back

1. http://www.greatermedia.com/corner/index.html, Dec. 1, 2008.
2. Statement of Paul Giammarco, WPRO, Providence, to author,
   December 2008.
3. Statement of Mark Masters, CEO, Talk Radio Networks, to author, November 2008.
4. Statement of Dan Mason, KKOH, Reno, to author, December
   2008.
5. Statement of Tom Tradup, Salem Radio Network, to author, December 2008.
6. Statement of James Derby, KXL, Portland, Ore, to author, December 2008.
7. Statement of Dan Mason, KKOH, Reno, to author, December
   2008.
8. Statement of Kipper McGee to author, December 2008.
9. Statement of James Derby, KXL, Portland, Ore., to author, December 2008.
10. http://www.hollywoodreporter.com/hr/content_display/news/e3i7

b1dd533ab2eae76821f31b7def9907b; http://www.portlandtribune
.com/us_world_news/story.php?story_id=TRE4AP15J.

Chapter 32: Censors in Action

1. Statement of Lars Larson, KXL, Portland, to author, December 2008.
2. http://archive.dailytidings.com/2004/0302/030204n3.shtml; http://archive.dailytidings.com/2004/0228/022804nl.shtml.
3. http://archive.dailytidings.com/2004/0228/022804nl.shtml.
4. http://www.ntsmediaonline.com, January 9, 2009.
5. Statement of Brian Maloney to author, January 2009, http://www.savewrko.com/tag/brian-maloney/.
6. http://www.adversity.net/i200.htm.
7. Author interview of Lars Larson, KXL, Portland, January 2009.

Chapter 33: What Would the Great Communicator Say?

1. http://michiganredneck.wordpress.com/2008/11/16/reagan-activists-must-stop-fairness-doctrine/.
2. Ibid.
3. Statement of Milt McConnell, KKOB, Albuquerque, to author, November 2008.
4. http://michiganredneck.wordpress.com/2008/11/16/reagan-activists-must-stop-fairness-doctrine/.
5. Ibid.
6. Statement of Milt McConnell, KKOB, Albuquerque, to author, November 2008.
7. Author interview with Michael Reagan, November 2008.
8. Ibid.
9. Ibid.

Chapter 34: Censorship

1. http://www.washingtontimes.com/news/2008/dec/16/exhuming
   -the-fairness-doctrine/, December 16, 2008.
2. http://rpc.senate.gov/public/index.cfm?FuseAction=Issues.Issue&
   Issue_ID=1735f02e-b706-4974-9e6b-b337ca2bcb24, July 24, 2007.
3. http://online.wsj.com/article/SB122990390599425181.html.
4. *Talkers* magazine, December/January 2008.
5. http://www.radioink.com/Article.asp?id=1134954&spid=24698.
6. http://jta.org/news/article/2009/01/20/1002389/obama-extends
   -hands-to-muslims-in-inauguration.